The Immigrant Heritage of America Series

Village woman reading the
author's fortune in coffee grounds
Photograph by Jean Carlisle Vavoulis

The Greek Americans

By Alice Scourby

C.W. Post Center
Long Island University

Twayne Publishers • Boston

The Greek Americans

Alice Scourby

Copyright © 1984 by G. K. Hall & Company
All Rights Reserved
Published by Twayne Publishers
A Division of G. K. Hall & Company
70 Lincoln Street
Boston, Massachusetts 02111

Book Production by Marne B. Sultz

Book Design by Barbara Anderson

Printed on permanent/durable acid-free
paper and bound in the United States of
America.

Library of Congress Cataloging in
Publication Data

Scourby, Alice.
The Greek Americans.

(The Immigrant heritage of America
series)
Bibliography: p. 178
Includes index.
1. Greek Americans.
I. Title.   II. Series.
E184.G7S36   1984   305.8'893'073
83-18566
ISBN 0-8057-8423-3

For
My parents
William and Katherine Vavoulis
My brother
Theodore
My son
Lex

Contents

About the Author
Preface
Acknowledgments

Chapter One
Background to Immigration   1

Chapter Two
The Immigrants   23

Chapter Three
The Changing Immigrant: Community Perspectives   61

Chapter Four
Ethnicity: Evolutionary Change   80

Chapter Five
The Family: Redefining Sex Roles and Relationships   121

Chapter Six
Epilogue   152

Notes and References   161
Selected Bibliography   178
Index   181

About the Author

Alice Scourby received her Ph.D. from the Graduate Faculty of the New School for Social Research. She is professor of sociology and coordinator of women's studies at C. W. Post Center of Long Island University. She is author of *Third Generation Greek Americans: A Study of Religious Attitudes* (Arno Press), coeditor of *Marriage and the Family: A Comparative Analysis of Contemporary Problems* (Random House), and *The Greek American Community in Transition* (Pella), in addition to numerous published articles. She has served as consultant to various groups including the Anti-Defamation League of B'nai B'rith. She was a major participant in a Public Broadcasting Service documentary film on *The New Immigrants: The Greeks of New York City.*

Preface

An ethnic group is defined or set off by its religious or national origin. The word itself comes from the Greek *ethnos* meaning "people or nation." The ancestry and heritage of such a group make a difference to its members and to the society in which they live, affecting finally their destiny.

Customs, language, religion, family names, social ties, prescribed food, physical appearance—all play a part in defining an ethnic group and provide the framework within which the worth of the individual is validated. The ethnic group itself and the larger society together set the boundaries within which the group is expected to think and act.

The process by which successive ethnic groups shape and are themselves shaped by the cultural values of their adopted country is the social history of an entire people. Czeslaw Milosz, who won the Nobel Prize for Literature in 1980, remarked, in awe, about his good fortune in being able to teach his own culture and language in the United States, remembering that earlier immigrants in vastly different circumstances—poor, illiterate, abused, neglected—were not accorded such a cordial reception. Despite this he felt close to them, to their pain as well as to their accomplishments and joy. To grasp the history of a people, one must move from the particular to the universal, for if one does not know the particulars, it is impossible to understand the experience and pain of others. Many have wished to deny their past, not wanting others to know how much humiliation and suffering their cultural dislocation and marginality have caused them. And yet, to ignore this experience is an obstacle not only to understanding one's own group but to understanding the suffering of others.[1]

To the extent that learning moves forward by particulars, ethnic studies are an integral part of the extraordinary record of American history. This book traces the migratory process of one group—the Greek people—during the twentieth century. Beginning with a historical prelude, it establishes the political, economic, and social conditions that gave form to the cultural heritage the Greeks brought with them to the

New World, a heritage that each new wave of immigrants and each generation interpreted anew. In this process, the group's ethnicity developed its elusive chameleon quality.

This book focuses on this change within its social milieu. Change in ethnic life cannot be viewed as an isolated phenomenon but, rather, as integrated aspects of group life modified in their expression by the social context in which the change occurs. The Greek church, the media, politics, and ethnic organizations are all part of this contextual matrix. For this reason, community studies have been selected that demonstrate both the uniformity and the diversity of the Greek experience in America.

In emphasizing the crucial aspects of social change and its consequences for group and individual behavior, the tenets of authoritarian, patriarchal, and traditional family patterns have been examined in an effort to understand the numerous permutations and combinations that the traditional division of gender roles may entail.

Alice Scourby

C. W. Post Center
Long Island University

Acknowledgments

I would like to express my appreciation to those individuals who gave so generously of themselves in relating segments of their Greek experience in America; segments that proved painfully poignant for some.

Numerous individuals have contributed to this volume during its various stages. First, I am indebted to Peter L. Berger for having encouraged me to pursue the religious dimension among Greek Americans as my Ph.D. dissertation. For the support given me during that period, I am deeply grateful.

To Gus Grammas, New York University; Thalia Cheronis Selz, Trinity College; and Jean Carlisle Vavoulis, MSW, I feel a special debt of gratitude for the immeasurable contributions they made. Acknowledgment is extended to Alexander Karanikas, University of Illinois; Charles C. Moskos, Northwestern University; and to the Rev. Alexander Karloutsos, Director of Communications of the Greek Orthodox Archdiocese of North and South America, who offered considerable assistance. My thanks to Dr. Nicholas Kladopoulos, Director of the Registry of the Greek Archdiocese, and to John P. Kaiteris, Director of the Hellenic American Neighborhood Action Committee.

I wish to acknowledge my indebtedness to the late Theodore Saloutos, Professor Emeritus of History, University of California, Los Angeles, for the many enlightening discussions I shared with him regarding the Greek experience in America.

Appreciation is extended to the library staff of C. W. Post Center of Long Island University for their inimitable skills and scholarship. They were unfailing in their courtesy and cooperation. I would also like to thank the Research Committee of C. W. Post Center for a Minor Grant awarded to me. I owe thanks to Shirley Goldstein, who typed the manuscript with painstaking care and with a creative sensitivity that went beyond her typing expertise. My sincere thanks to Caroline L. Birdsall, Senior Editor of Twayne Publishers Heritage Series, for her initial enthusiasm and support of the project and, finally to my editor, Emily McKeigue, who conscientiously guided the manuscript to publication.

sparse the earth beneath your feet
  so that you have no room to spread your roots
  and keep reaching down in depth
and broad the sky above
  so that you read the infinite on your own

Odysseus Elytis
Winner of the Nobel Prize
for Literature, 1979

Chapter One
Background to Immigration
Historical Prelude

Most of us think of Greece as one of the world's oldest civilizations and forget that it is also a very young nation that gained its independence in 1832 after four centuries of Turkish domination. Before Greece was conquered by the Ottoman Turks in 1453, it comprised the eastern half of the Roman Empire. Byzantium, as it was called, was essentially a Greek empire: its prevailing language was Greek rather than Latin, and its culture was Hellenic. It Christianized a large segment of the Slavic world, and it was here that Christianity received official recognition by the Emperor Constantine in A.D. 313.

After the fall of the Roman Empire, Byzantium thrived intellectually and commercially for a thousand years, while Western Europe was going through its Dark Ages. Byzantium was more than a mere repository of ancient Greece, it had a profound impact upon the medieval world and hence, indirectly, upon the modern Western world. It introduced the guild system and made an impact upon industrial techniques, law, diplomacy, art, music, and liturgy; clearly, it was not a period of "intellectual ossification."[1] This point should be stressed because there is a tendency to view the fall of the Roman Empire and the ensuing Dark Ages as constituting the alpha and omega of Western civilization. A historic jump is made from classical Greece to modern Greece without considering the influence of Byzantium.

In 1453, the Turks captured Constantinople (the capital of Byzantium), and within a short time, they ruled the whole Balkan peninsula. For a thousand years, the Christian Empire of Byzantium had been taken for granted as the center of the Christian world. Now, the Greeks were confined to an inferior status; they were deprived of rights, and Christianity under Islam became a second-class religion. The Greek population was heavily taxed. One of the taxes, known as the "tribute of children,"

1

was imposed as a means of recruiting men for the sultan's army; it required that in every Christian family one male in five between the ages of ten and twenty be taken away to serve.[2] Although the Western world may not have forgotten the ancient Greeks, contact with Greece at this time was practically nonexistent. During the four hundred years of Turkish rule, Greece sank to obscurity and oblivion.

The Ottoman Turks made no distinction between religious and secular law, and it was tacitly assumed that this approach to law applied to the Greeks and other non-Muslims. Each religious community was regarded by the Turks as an autonomous *millet* ("nation") under its religious leaders, supervised at the top by the patriarch of Constantinople. The millet system did not imply national identity nor national boundaries. It was simply a convenient administrative structure that worked well.[3] As a result of the millet system, the Orthodox church was endowed with considerable power. The patriarch was not only the spiritual head of the Greek Orthodox church, but also the political head of the Greek community. The millet system performed one invaluable service: it made possible the survival of the Greeks through four centuries of alien rule.[4] At the same time, it fused religion with nationalism which provided the arsenal necessary to actualize a people's dream for independence.

In the early nineteenth century, Greek dreams of independence were stimulated by the growing spirit of nationalism, the ideals of the French Revolution, the reversals experienced by the Turks in the Russo-Turkish wars, and by the world's sentiment which was in support of Greece. Philhellenes rallied to its cause, and many volunteered to join the Greek forces; the most celebrated of those volunteers was Lord Byron.[5]

The bitter struggle for independence endured for nine years (1821–29). Greece emerged as a sovereign nation in 1832, becoming a constitutional monarchy in 1862. The young nation had a population of approximately 750,000 as against three times that number living under Ottoman imperial and British colonial rule.[6] The boundaries of Greece encompassed little more than a third of its present area. At the conclusion of the struggle for liberty, the country was reborn under a profound handicap. She was given a small, comparatively unproductive territory, containing only a small minority of the world's Greek population. The state consisted of central Greece, the Peloponnese, and the Aegean Islands of the Cyclades. Its northern frontier ran from the Gulf of Volos in Thessaly on the Aegean Sea, and the fertile provinces to the north of what is now Macedonia and Thessaly remained under Ottoman control. The island of Crete and most of the Aegean Islands were excluded. To the west, the Ionian Islands were controlled by the English.[7]

As a result of this territorial allotment by the major powers (England, France, Russia), the political goal of Greece throughout the nineteenth century was to extend her frontiers to include all Greeks and those of Greek ancestry. It was the statesman Eleutherios Venizelos who nurtured what came to be called the "Megali Idea" (Great Idea): the consolidation of all Greeks as they had lived under the Byzantine Empire. Despite the strength of the Megali Idea, this territorial picture of Greece was achieved only at a great cost to its people. Some lands became part of Greece by negotiation and agreement (usually following a war), but the largest number of Greeks to reach the nation from other lands did so as a result of mass flight and population exchange. Following the devastating defeat of Greece in the Greco-Turkish War of 1919 and the burning of the city of Smyrna by the Turks in 1922, a massive exchange of population took place. Nearly 1.3 million Greeks left Turkey and some 400,000 Turks left Greece. The exchange provided Greece with linguistic and ethnic homogeneity, and had the unintended consequence of reducing its minority groups to less than 6 percent of the total population of 5,820,000.[8]

Gradually, the Greek state grew, altering its national boundaries. The territories ceded to Greece were the Ionian Islands in 1864; Thessaly, 1881; Macedonia and Epirus, 1912; Crete, 1913; the eastern Aegean Islands, 1914; Thrace, 1919; and the Dodecanese, 1948. Thus by piecemeal additions, the country about doubled its original size, and its population became more homogeneous.[9]

Given these fluctuations of Greece's national boundaries, one is compelled to ask, "What is a Greek?" In dealing with this question, the historian C. M. Woodhouse writes the following:

It is a simple, almost naive idea, which can best be put like this: the only practicable definition of a Greek is that he is somebody who thinks he is a Greek; and it is the Greek people as so defined, neither more nor less, that is the subject of history.[10]

The historical record shows that Ottoman rule had a paralyzing effect upon the Greek people and their country. The patient peasants pushing their wooden ploughs behind small, bony oxen and the women grinding their cereals between primitive millstones were as typical of 1821 as of 1453.[11] Greece had undergone no Renaissance, no Reformation, no Age of Enlightenment, although it was affected obliquely by the cultural and religious upheaval that transformed Western Europe.[12] In 1879, almost fifty years after the War of Independence, about 82 percent of the Greek population lived in rural communities. While the political leadership was consumed with regaining all its unredeemed territories, the vast majority of Greeks were trying to eke out a living in a barren and arid land of which two-thirds was mountainous. Writing in the latter part of the nineteenth century, Sir Rennell Rodd reported that the mountain slopes were nearly bare of vegetation as a result of centuries of deforestation and unchecked erosion.[13] A story that is part of the folklore of Greece reflects the plight of the country. When the world was made, God put all the earth through a sieve. He set some good soil down here, and this was one country. And He set some down there, and that was another country. And so He went on, and when He was finished, He threw all the stones over his shoulder, and that was Greece.

Historian Theodore Saloutos reports that one major economic crisis that was precipitous in causing the large wave of emigration at the turn of the century was the decline in the price of currants, Greece's chief export crop. When France had replanted its own vineyards, which had been destroyed by the vine pest, it enacted, along with Russia, a protective tariff that legislated Greek currants out of the market. This meant disaster for the Greeks who had destroyed their olive trees in order to grow a greater currant crop for export. The response of many Greeks to this depressed state was emigration.[14]

On the political front, national agitation in favor of a Cretan insurrection against the Turks led to the Greco-Turkish War of 1896–97 in which Greece was defeated. Eventually, because of pressure emanating from the major powers, Crete was made independent and incorporated into Greece in 1913.

The national priority given to the Megali Idea was sustained until 1922, after which Greece, for the first time, turned its attention to solving its internal problems.[15]

With the exception of the Venizelos government (1928–32) and the Metaxas dictatorship (1936–40), Greek political life was subject to coups d'etat, corruption, and inefficiency.[16] It was during the dictatorship of General Metaxas that the Second World War broke out and Mussolini sent the Greek government an ultimatum: surrender or be attacked. In the annals of Greek history, Independence Day and the Greeks' resistance to Fascist Italy are seared in the memory of every Greek. *Oxi* ("No") Day, as it has come to be called, occurred on October 28, 1940 when the Greeks responded with a resounding "oxi" to Mussolini's ultimatum and were drawn into destruction on an unprecedented scale. For six months later, Germany attacked Greece, and the Greek mainland was in its hands.

The country was plunged into abject misery. Less than a year after the beginning of the occupation in 1942, some 450,000 Greeks had died of starvation alone, and the industrial sector of the country had been destroyed.[17] Resistance grew and guerrilla bands controlled large rural areas. However, by late 1943, civil war had broken out between the leftist guerrilla groups, the Greek Peoples' Liberation Army, and the rightist groups, the Greek Republican National League. Both sides were guilty of atrocities and executions.

From 1946 to 1949, Greece was engaged in a destructive civil war and was on the brink of collapse. But in 1947, President Harry Truman announced the Truman Doctrine under which military, economic aid, and advisers would be sent to help the Greek government, and by 1949, the communists had suffered a severe setback. The war was marked with brutality, economic conditions were devastating, and the casualties to the country staggering.

The civil struggle, as well as the occupation of Greece, affected the traditional patterns of rural life. Not only was the traditional authority of the father questioned but women were called upon to perform tasks in the name of the nation that might not have been sanctioned by their husbands and fathers in the past. The temporary resettlement of villagers to more secure provincial towns increased their social mobility, giving the young and the women new ideas and expectations that the traditional peasant world could not satisfy.[18]

The dramatic role played by women in the resistance movement has not received sufficient attention. Their heroic sacrifices, their refusal to compromise their commitment to the cause of freedom has been described by a victim of the atrocities that took place. A journalist, Aphrodite Mavroede, has recorded the events occurring among a group of women from January 27 to July 30, 1950, on the island of Makronisos, revealing in detail the total dehumanization to which they, their children, and grandmothers were subjected.

They had sat together, listening to a blast coming from a microphone urging them to admit their mistake in resisting: "Women, the chains of rebellion are not suited for your hands! Return to your homes! Your leaders have been exterminated! Ask your country's forgiveness!"[19]

At one point, they were given three days to admit that they had been traitors to their country; if they refused to submit, torture and finally death would be their fate. Then they were whipped and their children were used as pawns; although some women repented, many did not. The means

of torture varied, driving them to the brink of insanity, yet they continued
to resist. On January 30 in the early morning, they were ordered to fall to
the ground; as the children clung to their mothers, all were told they
would be killed if they did not sign a confession. After beating them, the
soldiers took away their children, telling them that the youngsters were
Greek and, therefore, belonged to Greece. "Whoever wants her child must
become a Greek first."[20]

The beatings, withholding of water, hard physical labor and constant
relocations wreaked their havoc. On March 13, still refusing to submit,
they took a step toward affirmation; leaving their hovels at dawn, they
made their way to an outside area where foreign correspondents were
investigating the compound. Hopeful of freedom if they could reach the
ears of the correspondents, they told them of the terror that was going
on. By May 17, however, the women were still living under brutal
conditions, but their resilience, their courage, their sharing of the
experience enabled them to survive. They lived with the hope of amnesty, but the amnesty came only for the very old. The others were to be
sent to another island. The sick women lay on their cots asking to be
killed, but the commander was unmoved even as the women spat blood.
They were forced to go to a place they knew well, another island called
Trikeri where they had suffered before coming to Makronisos.[21]

After 1949, Greece sought to recover from an appalling morass. By 1952
the economy had been extensively repaired and rebuilt to equal and even
surpass its condition before the Second World War.[22] For the first time,
Greece enjoyed stability of government. In 1964 Greece gained a new
head of state, King Constantine II, who succeeded his father, King Paul.
But political tensions began to surface between the young king and Prime
Minister George Papandreou, leader of the liberal opposition, the Center
Union party.

The prime minister's son, Andreas, had left for America at the age of
twenty-one, arriving in New York in 1940. He had become an American
citizen in 1944, but in 1964, he gave it up in order to run for Parliament
from his father's home district of Patras. He won, and his father subsequently named him as his chief aide. The more liberal of his father's
party rallied to Andreas's side as he launched attacks on the palace, the
military, and the United States which he accused of interfering in Greece's
internal affairs.

This situation provided the pretext for King Constantine to overthrow the government of George Papandreou, and the ensuing political instability triggered the military coup of April 21, 1967. The two Papandreous were arrested along with thousands of other political prisoners, and the younger Papandreou was kept in solitary confinement for eight months. It was pressure emanating from his influential friends in the United States, including John Kenneth Galbraith and Arthur Schlesinger of Harvard, and Stephen Rousseas of Vassar that persuaded the military to release him.

The dictatorship was in effect from 1967 to 1974. Woodhouse writes, "Apart from thousands of detentions without trial, severe pressure was put on those who wished to restore democracy."[23] But democracy *was* restored in 1974. At that time, Greek voters rejected the reestablishment of the monarchy, and the powers bestowed upon it came to an end. Greece had become a presidential republic.

In the first postjunta election of 1974, Constantine Karamanlis, head of the New Democracy party, was elected prime minister. Karamanlis had been prime minister from 1955 to 1963 when he left for Paris in self-imposed exile, returning after the collapse of the dictatorship. He focused much of his attention now upon the effort to have Greece accepted as a full member of the European Common Market. The turning point in the political scene came in May 1980 when Karamanlis was elected president of Greece, and the leadership of his party was assumed by George Rallis. In the election that followed on October 18, 1981, Andreas Papandreou, founder and leader of the Panhellenic Socialist Movement (PASOK), scored a decisive victory over the New Democracy party which had exercised power for the past seven years.

The present premier of Greece, Andreas Papandreou, received his Ph.D. in economics from Harvard University in 1943. When he returned from the navy in 1946, he taught briefly at Harvard as a lecturer in economics, and then went to the University of Minnesota as an associate professor. In 1955 he became chairman of the economics department at the University of California, Berkeley. In 1959, urged by his father to return to Greece, he agreed, accepting an offer from Prime Minister Karamanlis that he form a center for economic research in Athens. His election to Parliament followed.

By the time Andreas Papandreou assumed office, Greece had become a member of the United Nations, the Council of Europe, the North Atlantic Treaty Organization, and in 1981, the European Economic Community. Although self-confidence is slowly being restored, the political instability and the chronic weakness of the national economy that for centuries has driven Greeks to seek economic opportunities elsewhere remains formidable.[24]

The chief economic problem for Greece is its age-old lack of natural resources. The structure of employment and national income shows Greece's great dependence upon secondary economic activities. Since the 1970s, only about 25 percent of the working population has been engaged in manufacturing and construction, and very nearly half of the gross national profit is generated in the services sector.[25] The gravest problem of the Greek economy lies in the extremely low productivity of both agriculture and industry.

The economic and political problems have resulted in several waves of emigration: one at the turn of the century, another following the holocaust of the Civil War, and yet another spawned by the liberalized immigration laws of the United States in 1965. Contributing to this exodus has been the continuing urbanization of the country coupled with a high birthrate following the Second World War. This trend produced a youthful population; about 25 percent of the people are less than fifteen years of age and 45 percent less than thirty.[26] The transition from a rural to an urban society is illustrated by the fact that approximately 82 percent of the Greek population was rural in 1879, as noted earlier, compared with 67 percent in 1920, and only about 40 percent in 1967.[27] In 1971 one out of three Greeks lived in the Greater Athens area. The failure to implement structural changes in Greek agriculture that could lead to increased productivity has resulted in the young abandoning the countryside. The majority of them were left to swell the ranks of the unskilled in the cities or to emigrate for improved conditions elsewhere.[28] The Greek Press and Information Office in a *Review of the Week* release, June 22, 1983, reported that the Prime Minister, in appraising the current situation said that "with the passage of time there are huge social problems which remain unsolved despite wishful thinking." Among the problems specifically mentioned was that of unemployment, especially among the young.

Greece has a population of 9 million and Foreign Ministry statistics show an additional 4 million abroad, nearly 3 million of them are estimated to be in the United States. Of the 800,000 Greeks counted as migrant workers, nearly a quarter returned between 1974 and 1980. Since 1974 the rate of returning emigrants has been larger than that of departure, a rare development in terms of Greek social history. This has been explained as being partly due to the slowdown in the development pace and partly to increased unemployment in the advanced Western countries as well as to the growing needs of the Greek employment market for more qualified workers. However, government officials point out that migration to the United States is much greater than statistics indicate, since many migrate from intermediate countries as students. They stay because their earnings are higher than in Greece and because their managerial and technological skills cannot be absorbed by the Greek market. To be sure, personal reasons also play an important role in the decision each individual makes.

Emigrants' remittances, once so important in their motivation to leave the country, have been superseded by shipping and tourism. As late as 1955, remittances to their families constituted the largest source of income. In 1979 such remittances totaled $1.2 billion, compared with $1.7 billion received from tourism and $1.5 billion from shipping. Economic development and expectations have risen so fast that people no longer want to do the menial and unskilled jobs they once emigrated for.[29] As a result, the experience of the recent immigrant in the United States reflects different attitudes correlated with different expectations when compared with their earlier counterparts.

In summary, the background of a people, drawn in very broad strokes, presents a picture of foreign subjugation, wars, dictatorships, enemy occupation, civil war, as well as political and economic instability. It also reflects sacrifice, tenacity, courage, pathos, and resiliency which ensure survival. Anthropologist Peter Allen notes in his paper "Postwar Urbanization in Greece: Some Positive Aspects," delivered at the Graduate Center of the City University of New York in 1982, that the rapid urban growth experienced by Greece without a heavy industrial base has nevertheless managed to avoid the rancid poverty and high rates of crime characteristic of so many developing countries. The consequences of social change have touched the lives of both urban and rural settlements, changing the very contours of the country. Allen adds that the prime motivation for emigrating stems from a desire to improve one's lot, and is not the consequence of dire economic need: a need that typified earlier immigrants.

Since premigration patterns are helpful in understanding the acculturation process of the Greeks in the United States, we turn now to the belief system that has governed the lives of the vast majority of Greek immigrants.

The Individual in Relation to Society

While to the world a person may be a Greek, to other Greeks the individual is identified in regional terms: one is a Cretan or a Spartan or a

Chioti, and so on. These regional divisions are accentuated by the topography of Greece, whose mountains divide the land into small districts. This was the same terrain that in ancient times divided Greece into independent, mutually jealous city-states.[30] Indeed, these city-states remained in a state of hostility until united by Alexander the Great in 335 B.C. In 197, the Romans conquered Greece which was, as we saw, part of the Roman Empire until A.D. 1453. (It is interesting to note that the Romans gave us the words *Greeks* and *Greece*. They called all Hellenes *Graicoi* and their country *Graecia* after an early Hellenic tribe that settled in Italy.[31] In Greece, the people refer to themselves as Hellenes and their country as Hellas.)

Despite the presence of regional variations, Greek rural life shared the same fundamental value system: the people were all members of the Greek Orthodox church; they all shared in an agricultural economy in which the role and status of each member was clearly defined. The basic unit was the family with strong patriarchal control and deeply binding extended kinship relationships. Lineal relationships were strong, and the need to defend family *philotimo* ("honor") inhered in a code strong enough to support vendetta claims of individual family members.

Individualism has been notably absent in Greek life. A Greek was born into a group whose members were interdependent. It was a dependency free of any puritanical stigma, and each member was a part of the group until he or she died. The focus was the family, not the child and certainly not the married couple. Individual interests and group interests were inseparable. There is no Greek word for *privacy*. There is no craving for aloneness; when it occurs, it is endured as a hardship.[32]

In contrast, the American cultural ideal is that of the "self-made" person, one who is not the product of parents, ancestors, or kin, and who is expected to make choices on the basis of rational—or sometimes irrational—self-interest. The freedom to choose one's own life-style, to control one's own destiny, releases the individual from the constraints of traditional norms. It is the essence of what we call "individualism."

Rooted in Greek tradition is the concept of philotimo mentioned before, which touches the core of the Greek personality. It literally means "love of honor." It implies that respect is given to one's honor by others, and includes self-esteem. Any insult, either direct or indirect, inflicted through family members constitutes a serious offense and calls for retaliation. In the traditional village, community honor depended upon certain sex-linked virtues, strength in number of relatives, a well-ordered household, and wealth in land to support one's family. In the contemporary village, honor is reflected in the display of a style of life that emulates an urban sophistication.[33]

Anthropologist Ernestine Friedl illustrates this point in her study of hospital care in provincial Greece. Hospitalization, a recent innovation in the countryside, initially met with trepidation since it was viewed as a form of abandonment by family members. She writes:

I believe what is of commensurate importance is the latent function hospitalization fulfills in the perpetual rivalry for prestige among family members. Hospital care is believed to be the sophisticated urban way of caring for serious illness and childbirth. Hospitalization therefore can enhance family prestige.[34]

Despite this changing definition of honor, it is still the status of the family as a collective unit that forms the core of philotimo, not the individual who, in actuality, has little importance apart from the group. Protection against the violation of one's honor continues to motivate the actions of Greek men. Recently, a father in rural Greece killed his prospective son-in-law for abandoning his daughter on the grounds that her dowry, a furnished apartment, was not adequate. The father turned himself over to the police explaining that he was not a murderer, but a father who had to protect the family honor and that he could now live with his conscience. The father's reaction was not uncommon in Greece, particularly in the rural areas.[35]

According to traditional values, male members of a family are obligated to assault those who are responsible for a dishonor. A former professor of criminology points out:

The crime of honor is not only Greek but a generally Mediterranean and Latin American phenomenon, the offended person even resorting to murder to avenge an insult against a sister, mother, daughter, or to settle a dispute over property.[36]

The murder rate in Greece, however, continues to be low: 1.3 percent per 100,000 of population in 1979, compared with 8.8 percent in the United States and 3.8 percent in Italy.[37]

There are strong rural-urban differences regarding the ideal of honor. It has widespread family implications in the rural areas, whereas it tends to be more restricted and individualized in the cities. For example, desertion or divorce were never considered alternatives for the rural population, although they are now gaining ground among urban people.

Traditional men, however, still cannot accept the "misconduct" of their wives, should they elect to leave their husbands. The male feels that this casts an aspersion upon his masculinity and that he has no recourse but to take retaliatory action, either toward his wife, the man involved, or both.[38]

Another illustration highlights the role of honor in the general orientation of Greek life. A recent report in Western Europe indicated that Greece had twice as many traffic deaths than any other Western European country. In 1979, Greece incurred 195 deaths per 100,000 cars, compared with Belgium's rate of 91, the Netherlands' of 64, Italy's of 58, and Britain's of 46. In the United States, there were 3 deaths per 100,000 cars. The Greek situation had reached such extremes that an International Medical Conference was held in Athens in 1979. At the conference, the undisciplined and individualistic character was cited as the main explanation.

"It is understandable that Greek drivers are extremely temperamental," said the general director of the Hellenic Automobile and Touring Club of Greece, a counterpart of the American Automobile Association. "They have the mistaken impression that everyone is out to challenge and demean them and, therefore, must be defeated."[39]

The rapid urban growth of Greece in the past three decades and its entry into the world of commerce and industry may have consequences in the future for modification of this behavior, but the core elements of the traditional value system still remain intact; what has changed are the different ways of interpreting them within the context of an evolving urban environment. A cultural lag is, of course, to be expected in any developing country; attitudes and values always tend to lag behind technological advances.

This ideal of honor and family cohesion have also for centuries supported the institution of the *prika* ("dowry") without which a marriage agreement could not be transacted. Both father and brothers are responsible for providing an adequate dowry, and the brothers are obligated to postpone their own plans to marry until their sister(s) has a husband to protect her.

The dowry, which had been part of the Greek civil code since 1946, is usually composed of trousseau, household goods, and furniture, which are the minimum requirements; the remainder includes agricultural property, money, and residential property. According to Greek law, both daughters and sons have equal rights to their parents' property. The underlying assumption of the dowry system is that a young woman is not able to make a contribution to the marriage as breadwinner; the dowry, therefore, constitutes her contribution to the expenses of married life. At the turn of the century, the dowry may have had a useful purpose by strengthening the weak position of the woman, particularly in the eyes of her in-laws. By the same token, however, an inadequate dowry placed her at a disadvantage in that it reflected her failure, and her family's failure, to live up to expectations as dictated by custom.[40]

Sociologist Irwin Sanders comments on regional variations in the dowry system:

Some villages, particularly those in the Peloponnesus and Central Greece, where the lure of the city is strong, set as the chief goal of the dowry a house in Athens to be provided by the bride. . . . One thing is attested to on every hand; the wife who brings a big dowry, particularly in cash, is not sent to the field by her husband except in most unusual circumstances. This privileged status, both in her own home and in the community, is assured her.[41]

Since cash has become central to a "successful" marriage, young girls will often leave their villages to seek employment in the cities as a way of meeting traditional demands. Educational achievement has now come to play a more prominent role in the assessment of a dowry, although it is still a secondary consideration. Its importance, however, may be gleaned from the dramatic rise of literacy in Greece. In 1907, it was estimated that 40 percent of the population aged ten and over was illiterate; that figure was 18 percent in 1961. Illiteracy among women showed a dramatic decline from 80 percent in 1907 to 27 percent in 1961.[42]

There is irony in the fact that women seek employment as a means of conforming to a traditional norm.[43] Two different ideological worlds are thus welded together, a nontraditional pattern reinforcing a traditional one, while at the same time acting as a springboard for social change in the options of women.

In addition to providing their daughters' dowries, parents were traditionally responsible either directly or indirectly for arranging suitable marriages for their children, sometimes through a *proxenetra* ("matchmaker"). The American ideals of romantic love and companionship marriage were alien to Greek life. Free choice in mate selection with its stress upon personal interaction and romantic love was viewed as deleterious to the solidarity of the family; it would have meant a diminishing control over the individual, particularly the female, and a weakening of the obligatory bonds that held the family together.

In short, love becomes dysfunctional for a family structure that subordinates the individual to the group. This family type is an "amoral family" in that it focuses primarily upon the immediate material interests of the nuclear family rather than upon communal concerted action for the achievement of some common goal. In a study of a southern Italian village, it was found that a climate of economic scarcity and fear of destitution bred mistrust and mitigated against collective action.[44] This applies to the Greek case as well.

The prophecy is self-fulfilling; mistrust tends to strengthen family bonds which, in turn, function to protect individual members against a potentially hostile environment. But what is it in the socialization process that causes the Greek villager to view the external world as hostile? What elements in the culture inculcate a sense of mistrust?

Writing in the late nineteenth century, Sir Rennell Rodd reported that the entire system of village beliefs was governed by a horde of maxims and superstitions which conditioned the individual from the moment of birth. It was believed that the child was surrounded by evil spirits who sought to control its destiny. The villager believed that soon after a child's birth, the *moira* ("fates") appeared to determine the direction of its life, a direction that could not be reversed. The parents, however, sought to propitiate the fates with gifts, as if they were amenable to bribery.[45]

Another report, published in the first decades of this century, noted that,

. . . the newborn infant is surrounded by perils. One of them arises from the Nereids (haunting spirits that take on the nature of mortals, but who can also make themselves invisible), who spirit the child away from the parent.[46]

It was thus the fates who decided which child would die and which would live, and that which was written (fate) could not be unwritten. It was a fatalism connoting a general sense of powerlessness.

Children, in this view, are particularly vulnerable to the whim and caprice of evil spirits of which the "evil eye" is a case in point. It may be conveyed unwittingly through praise or admiration by innocent bystanders. While several antidotes exist, exorcism through prayer is regarded as the most efficacious. The deleterious effect of admiration and approval may be closely connected with the old idea of Nemesis—a retribution in price for what excites the envy of others. Envy as the purveyor of misfortune tends to enhance mutual suspicion and to restrict trust and confidence to one's family. Every encounter is suspect; the individual cannot be too cautious; it is a war of all against all.

Indigenous to the culture is the idea of the world as a cosmic battleground where one must use all the resources at one's disposal to offset a constantly imminent calamity. Competition is an ever-present phenomenon; life is a series of struggles. While Orthodoxy plays a very important part in the life of the villager, it merges with folk philosophy and makes the individual the victim of irrational and impersonal forces, rather than the child of God, mediated and protected by the sacred presence of the Orthodox hierarchy. The villager believes that the world created by God is always in conflict with the Devil, who sends out demons and evil forces such as the evil eye to torment man who stands between the Devil and God.[47]

Because the environment is always testing man, always trying to defeat him, precautionary measures are taken to protect the individual. A baby is helpless against the evil forces of human envy, and "under these circumstances, external spiritual or even magical forces are believed to be necessary."[48]

Friedl notes that when a mother wraps her infant with its swaddling cloth she makes the sign of the cross three times, followed by a spitting gesture three times toward the infant; finally she pins the blue bead that is supposed to protect the child against the evil eye on its swaddling band.[49] The belief in the evil eye is general throughout Greece, whereas the practices of telling fortunes from the patterns of coffee grounds at the bottom of a cup, from beans dropped on the floor, or by means of cards are regionally determined. Of all divinations, the one regarded as least serious is that of reading coffee grounds.[50] These strategies for controlling the unknown are understandable in a country whose people have not experienced, until recently, the benefits of education, technology, and medical service.

Some of the traditional features of village life, however, have been modified by urban elements, and the old and new remedies are often used simultaneously. An antibiotic drug may be used along with a wise woman's exorcism of the evil eye. "For some illness is caused by 'microbe' and other illness by 'people's envy.' "[51]

The residual features of traditionalism may serve latent functions by sustaining those village values that stress group dependence. As long as evil remains external to the individual, one is not responsible for it, and the family continues to remain a potent force in providing protection and mutual trust. As we noted, the priority of the group over the individual is an important element that runs through the larger Greek culture.

The political instability that has characterized Greece derives from the primacy given the group. The absence of individual autonomy negates the very principle upon which democracy is predicated.[52] One's expectations of political figures parallels the hierarchical ranking found in the village, with its concomitant obligations and rewards. Failure on the part of the authoritative figure to meet expectations results in personal attacks for disloyalty, betrayal, and compromise; there is no focus upon policies or programs, only upon political personalities.[53] This, in turn, leads to further alienation from the public sector and a reinforcement of the family clan as a primary reference group. In line with this anthropologist Dorothy Lee writes:

Obedience is very important and taught to a child almost from birth; but again, this obedience is within a structured whole, to the parents, older siblings, and to people who stand in this relationship. Authority comes only from this structured whole, and *obedience* is only to people. Government is not personal, and the law is external to the organic, structured whole.[54]

Honesty in abstraction is not a virtue and may even be regarded as foolish. Loyalty is never to something abstract like the government which is equated with impersonal law. Responsibility is not social responsibility; rather, it is given to the family, sometimes to friends, and to the village. To take care of one's own, irrespective of merit, is one's duty.[55] This attitude complements the concept of *meson* ("contact"): the use of an intermediary in order to exact from the government a specific favor or advantage, such as securing a job, gaining admission to a university, settling property disputes, and so forth.

Family roles and the clientage system have their roots in centuries of Turkish rule, when it was customary for a local notable to intercede with the authorities on behalf of the villagers. It gave him prestige and power, while the villagers gained a sponsor as well as security.[56] If a villager has a relative who can help, he will turn to him; in fact, part of the motive for wanting to educate a son is the need to secure protection.[57] The respect for educated persons is quite marked in Greece; these individuals are sought out for information and for their opinions about current news. A study of pattern communications in a rural village reported the concern that illiterate farmers showed with regard to education and the news. One informant told the interviewer, "People who can read are better than us. It's a big thing to be able to read and write. I admire my son who can. If I wasn't afraid that they would laugh at me I would go, at this age, to school."[58] He had to turn to the teacher and the priest in the village for information and news.

The question that arises is, why should an illiterate farmer in a remote village with an illiteracy rate of 90 percent be so concerned with education and the news? There may be several reasons, but interviews with the villagers pointed most clearly to a concern with status. To be sufficiently informed about the news and to be able to discuss it with the teacher or priest of the village engaged one in a type of intellectual discussion, through which one gained prestige in the eyes of the villagers.[59]

Two discernible patterns emerge with regard to Greek culture: on the one hand, the deference paid to authority as determined by the kinship structure and the extension of this pattern to the larger context of Greek culture; and on the other hand, the ideal of honor which makes the individual vulnerable to the opinions, actions, and innuendos of others. It is the "others" who have the power to inflict ridicule and embarrassment, it is the "others" who have the power to expose the fragility of one's ego, a situation that must be avoided at all costs.

This sensitivity to the opinions of others is reminiscent of sociologist David Riesman's typology of tradition-, inner- and other-directed types of social character. The tradition-directed person accepts the legitimacy of existing norms and knows no alternative social rules; deviation from the rules results in shame. However, during a period of early industrialization, a less compliant personality is needed. This type of person is expected to pursue alternative patterns and tries to follow them no matter what others may say or do. This inner-directed type is more independent and more competitive. Deviation from the stipulated goal produces guilt. As a country becomes more economically developed, people learn to adapt by changing their attitudes and behavior in response to the expectations of those around them. The controlling mechanism in such a milieu is anxiety.[60]

In an industrialized society cues are always changing. The result is a chronic anxiety over misinterpreting others and thus making inappropriate responses which, in turn, tend to increase one's anxiety. The tradition-directed society socializes its members through shame, brought either upon themselves or the group, although the two are indistinguishable. Others are important to both tradition- and other-directed types of social character. The latter, however, are left alone to interpret the constantly changing norms of their society, while the former's family and community govern the appropriate responses of its members.

Riesman's typology comprises ideal types; they are approximations of what exists in the empirical world. They also tend to overlap, so that all three categories may be found in combined form in any historical period. The Greek view of self reflects the tradition-directed type (conformity through shame); the inner-directed type (self-assertiveness); and the other-directed type (sensitivity to the opinion of others).

How does socialization of the Greek child reinforce this orientation? Scott G. McNall's ethnographic study of two villages in the late sixties notes that when he asked villagers how many children they had, they invariably answered, "Two children, and one daughter."[61] The ethos of egalitarianism is conspicuously absent in Greek culture. The conviction that men are superior to women finds its justification in the Biblical story of Adam and Eve, which the Greeks believe relegates each sex to its appropriate role. Villagers believe that the Bible story documents the vulnerability of women to sensuality and thus their weakness, a weakness that is part of their nature and therefore unchangeable. In addition, the perceived power of a woman to contaminate through menstruation restricts certain of her activities during that time. For example, she is not permitted to light the candles in church, receive Holy Communion, or bake certain breads for the holy days. The male, however, is always clean, and because of this, more responsibility accrues to him. Physical strength becomes a third, albeit less symbolic, reason for the assertion of male superiority.[62]

It is interesting to note that the woman, in her maternal role, cautions her son to beware of three basic evils of the world—fire, woman, and the sea. The internalization of both reverence and disdain for women cannot help but create ambivalence and mistrust for mother and son. In addition, the woman not only is regarded as essential to the formation of a household, she *is* the house. "Without a woman there is no house." Absence from her house for an extensive period of time constitutes a type of spiritual infidelity, because her absence damages the unity of the house.[63]

However, it is the attribute of weakness by which she is identified, and it is the norm of *endropi* ("shame") that serves to enforce honorable behavior. This constraining norm is intended to protect her against her basic feminine sexuality. If she fails to live up to traditional expectations, it is attributed to a defect of nature, whereas a man's weakness is attributed to a defect of character.[64]

The code of endropi still retains force; young girls in the village are still expected to be modest and chaste. Their eyes, however, "are no longer downcast." Modern-style dresses tend to be more revealing than the traditional homespun clothing which was intended to conceal their sexuality, but "a violator is still in mortal danger from the girl's family if he is not immediately arrested."[65]

When, therefore, the villager equates children with sons, it is because the weakness of the girl places a heavy burden on the family, in terms not only of the dowry that has to be provided, but of the constant vigilance that must be kept to see that she does not bring dishonor to the family. Her very nature has to be protected, which is one of the major reasons for her dependence upon men. A man does not require such surveillance, since he is free from inborn weakness.[66] It is through a man, therefore, that a woman is validated and through motherhood that she is revered.

Regardless of sex, however, children are socialized to learn the strategies that will ensure their survival in a milieu where total unmasking is what the individual seeks to avoid. The child learns, through the stories he hears from his mother and father about "others," that his membership is part of an "in-group" as distinct from the "out-group." He learns that, in protecting the sanctity of the family, self-interest is upheld as a moral good; it is the value that assures self-preservation. He learns that he must never become the object of ridicule, he must avoid being laughed at, avoid being the butt of another's jokes, for it is not only self-demeaning for him but ego enhancing for the one who has initiated the joke. The child learns that masks must be worn in public; the presentation of the self keeps others at a distance, preventing them from seeing one's shortcomings, failures, and weaknesses. Total unmasking exposes one to diminished prestige. A child is told, "Don't do such and such, people will laugh."[67] The public self will tend to be aggressively assertive; it will outtalk others, outdo others, outwit others, in a game in which the peril is loss of philotimo, even if only temporarily.

Males and females are expected to develop skills in using "guilefulness" and detecting it in others.[68] Although one has to circumvent possible deception by others, one lies oneself in order to gain a superior stance or, at least, to maintain the status quo. Lies are also told to conceal unintentional failures, careless mistakes, cheating on a deal; lies may be told in defense of a friend or relative.[69] "Villagers," writes Friedl, "are not humiliated because someone tries to deceive them; they become angry only if the deception succeeds."[70]

On the other hand, the ideal moral state is to be above reproach, to be self-sustaining, to tell the truth, to possess honor, to avoid shame, and to be accorded prestige; it is this standard that is used in judging others. But it is not possible to give complete loyalty to one's family and at the same time be scrupulously honest in one's dealing with others. Yet, according to the ideal, this is what is required. The two values remain irreconcilable.[71]

Self-assertion is a behavior that allows no one to rise above you. It is a device that prevents others from discovering that you are not all that your public persona purports to be. This self-assertion is translated *egoismos* in Greek (*ego* = "I"). The overt manifestation of egoismos is competitive, even at times, bombastic and vitriolic; it presents a picture of the individual that is larger than life and acts as a buffer when the person is pressed into an untenable position in regard to self-esteem. The value of self-assertion, or egoismos, is that it is linked closely to the family, so that although an individual may have to resort to "lies" to make his point, his personal integrity with respect to his family remains untarnished.[72]

Being on guard so as not to fall victim clearly can be the cause of much tension in interpersonal relations. The child who is able to avoid being duped is regarded as a "cleverly bad" boy.[73] In trying to nurture skills of social survival, the mother is the most important person in shaping the child's self-image. She is especially interested in inflating her son's ego by telling him what an important man he will become. This socialization process has been termed the *Alexander complex*. The kingdom is there, the son need only take it, and if he does not get it, it is because someone tricked or deceived him.[74] Thus, the cause of his failure is external to him; individual responsibility and guilt, which are not features of Greek culture, do not plague him.

In a study exploring the self-concept of fifth-grade schoolchildren in the Greater Athens area, it was found that regardless of children's intellectual ability, they wish to be, or think they are, intellectually able. This may be due to the cultivation of a nonrealistic self-concept. In analyzing the child-rearing practices in Greece, psychologist Harry C. Triandis writes the following:

Parents in Greece tell their child that he is the greatest, bravest, the nicest on earth. Consequently, the child develops certain sensitivity toward criticism. Deep down he knows his parents exaggerate and are worried for his possible weaknesses but he must show the world a face of confidence and to behave completely according to the image that his parents create for him.[75]

Given this deeply imbedded need to prevail, one is moved to ask what role, if any, is played by empathy in the sturm and drang of Greek life. The ethnographic literature infers that this phenomenon is confined to familial transactions. A study conducted among a sample of Greek and United

States children revealed that middle-class Los Angeles children scored higher on empathy than middle-class Athenian children.[76] Excessive competition, which is imputed to the Greeks, coupled with the stress on the public self would seem to inhibit the development of empathy. In addition, the dominant power assertiveness employed by Greek parents, particularly with regard to sons, may explain why boys had lower empathy scores than Greek girls. The high achievement expectations placed upon sons engenders competitive behavior from an early age and discourages what are stereotypically regarded as feminine traits, such as empathy, from surfacing.

In summary, we have been considering a code of moral behavior governed by honor, and its reciprocal, shame. These moral and ethical norms are also intrinsic in other Mediterranean countries and seem to have their origin in certain ecological factors, religious beliefs, the terrain of the country, and economic scarcity, as well as political fragmentation.[77] In the case of Greece, these conditions sustain a strong autonomous nuclear family, with the head of the household assuming responsibility for its survival and enhancement. Sons are a decided asset in terms of the manpower needed by the father to protect the family against encroachment from other families similarly situated and to sustain his authority in the village. Protecting the patrimony, of which the daughter is a part, lies completely in the hands of the family, which ideally functions as an integrated unit for its own integrity and prestige. Loyalty is turned inward to the family and to a specific locale, rather than toward the nation.

Given this fragmentation, honor and shame evolved as adaptive mechanisms, as ideological tools, to strengthen the identity of the family and to enlist the loyalty of its members. One's resources may be challenged by others who are more clever or stronger, but honor functions to define the limits of action and reduces appreciably acts of violence that would erupt if each were left to pursue personal interests without stipulated limits. Guilefulness, deceit, lies, cleverness, mockery, joking—all represent ways of releasing on a more harmless level the fears, insecurities, and threats that are endemic to a highly competitive environment.

Over the years, this pervasive feature of Greek life, along with its norm of patriarchy and the concomitant sex-role stereotyping that it encouraged, has served to define the individual's limits beyond which both honor and shame could be violated. Recently, however, women's groups in Athens have successfully agitated for reforms that would abolish the legally sanctioned institution of the bridal dowry, equalize the age of consent (currently fourteen for women and eighteen for men), usher in civil marriage and divorce by mutual consent, and depose the husband as legal head of the family. Greece has a very low divorce rate, and the church and government feared that reforms would destroy the traditional Greek institution of the family. The women's groups deny that it was their aim to revolutionize society or to challenge cherished social values; their goal, they argued, was not militant revolt, but "democracy in the family."[78]

Patriarchy was an accepted fact for the immigrants who came to American shores in the first half of this century; their departure in no way challenged the essential values of rural life, which is to say, Greek life. On the contrary, their departure symbolized an affirmation of those values. They had no other standards by which to judge themselves except those shaped by the reference group of which they were a part. It was only in the decades following the Second World War that the status of peasant took on a pejorative meaning, a meaning established by the standards of a developing urban society.

But, first, let us turn to the early immigrants who were plunged into the unknown, bereft of family support and without the assurance of village security.

Chapter Two

The Immigrants

The Early Phase

Very few Greeks had arrived in the United States prior to the twentieth century. In 1848, there came 91,061 Irish, 51,973 Germans, and 1 Greek. In 1858, there were 2 Greeks among the counted immigrants, and from 1847 to 1864, the total number entering the port of New York was 77.[1] Despite the sparse industrial development in Greece, chronic crop failures, and the need for dowries, Greek village farmers did not yet see America as a solution to their economic problems.

A number of young Greeks were adopted or sponsored by Americans during this immigration period. In the nineteenth century, the struggle for independence had gained Greece a large number of philhellenes, both in America and Europe, and some of them were instrumental in bringing young, orphaned boys to this country. Among them was George M. Colvocoresses, orphaned in the massacre at Chios in 1822, who made a distinguished career as a commander during the Civil War. Lucas Miltiades Miller was adopted by Jonathan Miller of Vermont. He was elected in 1853 to the Wisconsin legislature and in 1891 became the first American of Greek descent to be elected to the United States Congress.[2]

Ioannis Celivergos Zachos was brought here by Samuel Gridley Howe to become curator of Cooper Union, an institute for the advancement of the arts and sciences in New York. Howe also brought Michael Anagnos to the United States in 1861. After Howe's death, Anagnos became director of the Perkins Institute and developed a program for the deaf and blind. His most famous student was Anne Sullivan, teacher of Helen Keller.[3] Some of the New England Perkinses, usually regarded as Anglo-Saxon, are said to be descendants of a Greek merchant named Perkentzis who came to the New World, via London, in the 1780s, and whose family later changed the name to Perkins.[4]

In addition, there was the itinerant adventurer to be found in any country at any time, spurred on by inner restlessness. John Griego, a Greek sailor, is said to have accompanied Christopher Columbus on his first voyage to America. Another was Petros, the Cretan, who was active with the Spanish in their exploration of the New World. One, Don Teodoro, is reputed to have been the first Greek known to have set foot on American soil in 1528. Some sources claim that the Spanish explorer, Juan de Fuca, who, in 1592, discovered the straits south of Vancouver Island that bear his name, was a Greek sea captain named Ioannis Phocas from the island of Cephalonia.[5]

Besides the widely scattered Greeks who were brought to the colonies or came voluntarily, a large number, approximately 400, came under the auspices of Andrew Turnbull to cultivate the land he owned about seventy-five miles south of St. Augustine. The Greeks were part of a larger Mediterranean contingency which exceeded the number Turnbull had initially planned to bring from Europe. The Greeks seemed to him well-suited for the job because of their work habits, their religious affiliation, and the salubrious climate, which was similar to that of Greece. He named the settlement New Smyrna, after the birthplace of his wife who was the daughter of a Greek merchant in Smyrna, Asia Minor.

Not knowing that they had been brought here as indentured servants, these early settlers nevertheless were compelled to work under insufferable conditions; instead of vast fields to be cultivated, they found vast swamp-lands infested with mosquitos. Instead of opportunity and opulence, they encountered starvation and malaria to which many lost their lives. In 1777, the survivors fled to St. Augustine where they prospered as merchants and established a place of worship which was recently designated a shrine to their memory by the Greek Orthodox Archdiocese of America. One, John Geannopoulos, became a teacher in St. Augustine and founded a school in his own house, a school now held to be the oldest wooden schoolhouse in the United States. The total Greek population by this time was extremely small so that, slowly, they were absorbed into the larger community of St. Augustine.[6]

Mass Immigration

The vast flow of Greek immigration did not begin until the 1880s when economic scarcity showed no sign of abating. Emigration to the United States seems to have been triggered by an obscure young man from a village in Sparta named Christos Tsakonas, born in 1848. This "Columbus of Sparta," after completing two years in the village grammar school,

A Village in the Peloponnesus   *Photograph by Jean Carlisle Vavoulis*

Piraeus for work and then to Alexandria, Egypt; in 1873, he leave for America, an unusual venture for a man of his station. Apparently he found life in America congenial, for after returning to Greece in 1875, he decided to leave again for America, this time with five compatriots. This group seems to have constituted the nucleus for succeeding waves of emigration from Sparta.[7]

It was from the Peloponnesus and Tripoli, both agricultural and pastoral regions, that the early immigrants came. Although after 1890, they began arriving from all parts of Greece, those from the Peloponnesus kept coming in greater numbers.[8] It is difficult to arrive at an accurate estimate as to the number of Greeks arriving here prior to the Second World War, since the American census tends to consider one's place of birth as one's nationality, thus excluding a large segment of those Greeks living outside of Greece proper. Nevertheless, it is estimated that approximately 500,000 arrived during this period, a total that includes those arriving from non-Greek territories who nevertheless identified themselves as Greeks. About 95 percent of the immigrants from 1899 through 1910 were males.[9]

The economic situation of Greece was so desperate that the Greek government encouraged emigration of their young men during this time in the hopes that they would send back enough money to help the economy. And, indeed, their hopes were fulfilled. Greek immigrants sent some $4 million to $5 million to their families in 1905.[10] In 1906, it was noted that the districts from which the largest number of immigrants left were also the most prosperous because of the money being sent by both fathers and sons.[11] Writing in the early part of this century, anthropologist Henry P. Fairchild observed:

> The principal incentive for the industry of the men of the country is to secure enough money to make good matches for their sisters. In this respect men show a really admirable devotion to their sisters.[12]

There was a temporary lull in emigration when news of the 1907 financial crisis in the United States reached Greece; this was accompanied by letters telling of unemployment and suffering among the immigrants. But once the crisis had passed and despite discouraging letters still being received in Greece, the pace of emigration picked up. However, it was halted by the Greek government in 1912 during the First Balkan War, but resumed again in 1913.[13] During 1914 and 1915, a total of 10,969 and 17,804, respectively, emigrated. The next major outflow occurred right after the First World War when an estimated 26,386 left from the port of

Piraeus.[14] Saloutos refers to the period through World War II as the "pioneer years" of Greek emigration.[15]

For those peasants who did not have the money to make the trip, steamship agents began to circulate in the villages, exciting their imagination with stories of the opportunities to be found in America and advancing them their fares. Many families sold part of their land and farm animals or used up whatever savings they had; some solicited loans from moneylenders or mortgaged their property, so eager were they to embark on this promising experience in America.[16]

The benefits of this early migration were clearly visible in Greece, where village improvements were testimony to the rewards of migration regardless of its hardships. In some villages, the cancelation of mortgages was one of the most significant results of emigration.[17]

But what was life like for these early immigrants in America? How did young, unskilled males with little education and no knowledge of the English language adapt to the demands of the New World? Having traveled by ship for approximately thirty days in cramped and less than hygienic conditions, they encountered their first traumatic experience when confronted with the medical examiner at Ellis Island. One story is related of an immigrant whose eyes were troubling him as he moved with dread toward the doctor who was to examine him. As the man's turn came, an official called to the doctor, distracting him and thus permitting the immigrant, Evangelos, to flee past the gate toward a side alley into Brooklyn. For a whole year after that, he dreamed he had been sent back to Greece.[18]

After leaving the port of disembarkation, the new immigrant would usually seek out a relative or *patrioti* ("compatriot") who had preceded him. If he had no one to turn to, he might stay in a large northern city and work in a factory or a restaurant as dishwasher, busboy, waiter, or on the street as bootblack or peddler; he might go west to work in a mine or on a railroad; or he might end up in a New England mill or a textile or hat factory. Other Greek communities developed in the South, especially in Tarpon Springs, Florida, where the sponge industry was created by Greek immigrants.[19]

Despite the fact that the Greeks were an agricultural people, they did not seek this occupation in America. There were several reasons for this: the Greek saw his stay here as a temporary one; his experience with farming had not been a positive one in Greece; and after 1882, the United States was already a settled land, and consequently, no free land was available. The immigrant had no money to buy land, so that a majority settled in the large industrial towns and cities.[20] Moreover, Greeks are a gregarious people who do not find solitary farm life congenial. Farming in Greece is not characterized by isolated farmhouses separated by great distances; the farm land is some distance from the house, but the houses are built in close proximity.

The Old Immigrants: The Pioneers

One early immigrant, now in his seventies, remembers going through Ellis Island, which he said was referred to as "the zoo." From there he went to meet his father who had emigrated earlier. He was a boy of fourteen when he left Greece and was never to see his mother again. He left primarily to earn money for the dowry of his three sisters.

I came here when I was fifteen years old in 1912. I had two years of education in my village. I came from the Peloponnesus. I was a vendor selling peanuts. In New Jersey I lived with six other peanut men, and I was the only boy there. We lived in one big room and put all the peanut wagons on one side of the room and slept on the six beds on the other side of the room. It was an agonizing time; we were beat up just for being Greek.

I became a dishwasher in a hotel in Brooklyn, and then I worked in a hat factory. The following year I got a job in a restaurant as a counterman. At that time I used to sleep in the kitchen of the restaurant so I wouldn't have to pay rent. I succeeded in sending 100,000 drachmas to my oldest sister; a lot of money in those days. Eventually I became manager of the night shift.

I then went to work as a waiter in a restaurant owned by a relative. Non-Greek employers refused to hire Greek waiters. The boss would say, "What are you?" When I said, "Greek," he would answer, "There's no job." They would hire Scandinavians, Germans, and English. So we had no choice but to depend on Greek employers for our jobs. Meanwhile, I was sending all the money I made to my sisters so that they could get married.

In the 1920s, while I was working as a waiter, my boss made me sign a statement which said I was being paid a certain wage even though I wasn't. I had no choice but to sign it in front of his lawyer. Meanwhile, I had to live on the tips I could make. I remember always feeling a great deal of insecurity; always afraid that one of the boss's relatives would come from Greece and replace me. And I had no place else to go.

Often workers had to pay for their jobs. I remember, George, an agent or padrone who got us jobs, and then we had to repay him with high interest rates. He used to bring many young boys over to shine shoes, usually from the Peloponnesus, and they had to work to pay the agent for their passage; having no money, they slept on the floor like sardines and ate only bean soup every day.

Some of the men I knew had very abusive bosses, and they decided to return to Greece; and many did, saying they would rather spend the rest of their lives "eating bread and onions" instead of working like slaves for fifteen hours a day.

Some bosses, of course, were worse than others. One in particular wouldn't let us [waiters] sit together at meal time or even talk. He supervised what we ate and kept us apart so that we wouldn't become friendly.

That's why I was determined to be my own boss. In the 1930s I bought my own coffee shop, followed by a tea room, and then a restaurant. I remained in my own business until I retired. I learned English well enough to become Assistant Physical Director of the YMCA during the Second World War. I didn't make money doing it, but it gave me a lot of satisfaction.

My father returned to Greece before the Second World War, and I never saw him again. In 1959, I returned to Greece, but Greece was altogether different from the way I remembered it as a young boy. In my village, all the trees were cut down and the wood was made into charcoal; I didn't even recognize my village. I had gone there to stay for six months, but after three months I came back to America.[21]

Because the Greek male intended to return to Greece, there was a great discrepancy between male and female emigration to the United States. In 1910, the men numbered 93,447 and the women 7,835; in the decade 1910–20, the number of foreign-born males was still greater than females, but the proportion was changing; and by 1930 these proportions had been reached: males, 195,192, and females, 108,559.[22]

An informant elaborated on the effects of this sexual imbalance:

We were very lonely in the United States; we did not have any Greek women here, and the kafenio [coffee house] used to provide us with a place to meet and share our day's experiences, talk about the old country, our families, and, of course, to discuss Greek politics. We also became very busy trying to raise enough money to build our own church. We used to hold services in a Protestant church, but in 1914 we succeeded in building St. Constantine in Brooklyn. It's something we were proud of. There couldn't be any Greek life without the church.

I remember that most of the marriages were arranged through letters, and pictures were exchanged. Usually, an intermediary helped arrange a good match. Sometimes the girls would come, and after seeing them, the men decided that they didn't want to marry them. In one case this happened, but the girl had a relative who had been in the United States for a while, and he knew enough to get a lawyer and take the man to court. She won the case, and he had to pay for all the expenses the trip cost her.

Greek Female Immigrants

There has been a tendency in social scientific literature to view the immigration experience as primarily a male experience; the female has been regarded as an appendage, a passive component in the cultural transposition that took place. The classic model of the "marginal man" has stressed the fact that immigrant life was male dominated and male focused. The underlying assumption was that once the immigrant made the proper adjustment to the host culture, marginality would be overcome, the male being the key to the understanding of the necessary adaptations.

The woman's role in the process has not been considered, nor has the impact that the new culture had upon her been examined. Greek women not only were wives and mothers, but also possessed valuable skills which they used productively in the process of adapting to American values. They were a genre, a type, who share some similarities with Greek women emigrating today, but who, as a type, were unique never to be replicated in their subtle nuances. Not all survived the challenge, any more than all the men did, but we may glean something of their resilience and skills from the following experiences related by first-generation women themselves:

I was eleven years old when Smyrna was destroyed by the Turks. My mother, sisters, and I escaped to Athens, but we were destitute. We all had to work, and I did what I could at eleven; I sold cigarettes at a store stand for half a drachma a day. As a child in Smyrna I was very comfortable; my father was a successful merchant and had many men working under him. But after the disaster there was no one to support us.

We lived in Athens where I learned sewing and embroidery. Then I was married, and my husband emigrated to America. I was pregnant and had to leave Greece to join him. A separation from my mother reminded me again of the atrocities we had been through. I remembered the Turks pulling my sister out of my mother's arms; my anxiety at being separated from my mother was very painful. But I was seven months pregnant, and my place was with my husband. When my family took me to the ship that would take me to America, I walked up the plank alone; it was getting dark, and I got to the deck of the ship as fast as I could so that I could see my mother one more time and wave good-bye to her. When I finally got to the rail and looked down, I saw no one. There was only darkness. I screamed for my mother, but no one answered. I knew instinctively at that moment that I would never see my mother again. I remember saying to myself, "You'll never see her again."

When I arrived in America my husband made a living by painting, but later he opened a small grocery store, and we worked it together. He died twenty-seven years ago, and I ran the store alone for nine years. My two sons are educated and doing well.

My agony is that I did not go to school. I learned to keep the books for my husband's business; but I always felt the lack of an education.

Another first-generation woman who had emigrated at the age of fifteen from a village in the Peloponnesus related the following experience:

I came to America with my father in 1920. I was the eldest child. I left from Patras on an American ship that was filthy; the stench was terrible, and the food and bread tasted of gasoline. I kept thinking, "Is this what American food tastes like? Is this what we're going to be eating when we get there?"

When I arrived I worked in a factory in New Jersey and after that in a cigar factory. I wanted to go to school, and my father was willing to let me go, but my uncle with whom we lived persuaded my father not to send me. I will never light a candle for that uncle. When I brought my cousins from Greece in the 1950s, I sent them to night school immediately. I said, "Don't be like me, ignorant; learn English, be educated." And they were. But I'm getting ahead of my story.

My father was a street vendor; he sold peanuts. An old man who worked with him noticed my cousin and I. One day he came to our apartment to look at us closely, and then he asked to speak to my father alone. He had chosen me for a young man he had in mind. He went to the young man and said, "Costa, I found a nice girl for you." And it was agreed with my father that I would marry him.

When I met my husband, he worked in a leather factory. In 1922 he opened his own restaurant business. He had two sisters in Greece, and he worked very hard to send money for their dowry. He also helped his brothers, and built a house for his father in Greece. He was very proud of that. That was his aim, to make money and help his family in Greece. He brought his brother to the United States with three children and helped him to set up his own business.

In 1922 when my husband opened a restaurant I worked there at night for twenty years. I traveled by subway to get there. My husband worked during the day; he did all the cooking. We had four children, and my husband vowed that none of the children would be in the restaurant business. Our two sons are professionals which my husband was always proud of. We worked hard so that our children could have a better life, and we succeeded. My years of work did not go to waste, and I've forgotten that I worked so hard; I don't feel tired because our children turned out so well. I'm very satisfied. I always loved America. I never had a desire to return to Greece to live.

When I took my first trip to my village in 1950, I didn't recognize it. I didn't even recognize my mother. When I left in 1920 my mother was a young woman, and when I went back I found an old woman. I felt I was in a strange country.

But the fabric of the past comes not only from the immigrants themselves but also from their progeny whose marginality and ambivalence was tempered by the passing of time. One second-generation woman related the story of her mother's journey as told to her:

My mother was not quite twenty-two when she managed to escape from the Turks in Asia Minor with her two younger sisters, fifteen and eleven. My grandmother put them on a boat to Mytiline expecting to follow them with the rest of the family. The boat left them on the wrong side of the island, and the three of them had to walk to the capital. My mother was wearing high heels which she broke in order to walk. When they got to the capital, she did not have enough money for passage to Athens. She saw a sewing machine in the window of a store, and she used the money she had to rent it. She sewed in order to earn enough money to get to Athens where she knew they would find relatives. She managed to get there and went to a hotel owned by one of her compatriots. He was taking care of other refugees from Asia Minor at his hotel. She worked there as a seamstress. My mother spent four years in Athens, from 1922–1926, and was the sole provider for her two younger sisters. Their family, whom they thought would follow them to Athens, never came. Her mother, two sisters, two brothers, and grandmother were all killed in the Asia Minor holocaust. Only one brother, with whom she was united, survived.

While she was in Athens she met a patrioti [a fellow countryman] who had a brother in America, and he decided that my mother would be an ideal bride for his brother. He wrote to him and said, "I found the perfect woman for you." My father was a custom tailor in America. He emigrated in 1916 with twenty dollars in his pocket. He used to sleep on one of the tables in the shop where he worked so that he wouldn't have to pay rent.

My father got his citizenship papers and went back to Greece to marry my mother in 1926. They returned to America and were very happy. In 1931–1933, when the tailors were trying to become unionized, my father was on strike for eighteen months. My mother decided to go to work, and she did for a French seamstress. However, she made very little money. She then heard that the fur industry paid well, and so she became a finisher. I can remember her cooking at night for next day's dinner, sewing all the clothes my sister and I wore, and, as if that wasn't enough, she was active as president of Philoptochos. [Philoptochos is an organization of Greek Orthodox women whose aim is to help the needy in the community. Its name comes from philos, "friend," and ptochos, "poor," thus "friend of the poor."]

My mother always stressed education, and both my sister and I always had piano lessons. I remember, so clearly, that on the first day of each school year she would always make new dresses for us to wear. It was something we looked forward to.

Something that stands out very vividly in my memory is the Second World War when my mother went shopping and came back stocked with groceries and said to me, "When you haven't been hungry, you can't know what it's like; but I vowed that my family would never go hungry again."

I wish I could remember more; wish that I had listened more carefully when my mother talked about these experiences. I now realize how strong she was and what courage she had to come through her hardships, still able to enjoy life and do so much for us.

Salt Lake City, Utah

Following the tragedy in Asia Minor and the subsequent exchange of populations, many women from relatively affluent homes were left with no option but to emigrate. Again, the pressing demand for dowry provided a major impetus. The eligible women were usually brought here by a relative, or they formed part of a contingent accompanied by one man whose passage had been paid by young bachelors eager to marry and raise a family. Many of these young women arrived in Salt Lake City with tags tied to their clothing, their prospective grooms not able to do more for them. A poignant story is related of a young girl who was stranded by the railroad track not knowing where to turn for help and was fortunately discovered by a passing stranger who happened to be Greek. He escorted her to a section gang a distance away where her future husband worked, and they were united.[23]

This is not to imply that Greek immigrants went to the West in large numbers. Actually, they were the least numerous of the early arrivals who sought out the Great Plains and the Rocky Mountain West as a place to earn a livelihood. It is not known whether Greeks crossed the Great Plains in covered wagons, although we do know that in 1860 there were at least two Greeks in Texas and one in the Territory of New Mexico. During the nineteenth century, Texas attracted more Greeks than any other territory in the West, probably because of its accessibility by water to sailors and others visiting its port towns.[24]

Approximately 220 Greeks lived in the western states and territories in 1890, about two-thirds of them in Texas. At that time they operated saloons and grocery stores, and marketed and ginned cotton.[25] Their numbers remained small until mass migration began in the 1890s.[26]

The census of 1920 showed Nebraska to have a Greek population of only 1,504, less than half of what it had been in 1910.[27] This has a special significance and may be explained by the anti-Greek riot that took place in South Omaha in February 1909. South Omaha's Greek Town was burned down, driving 1,200 Greeks away. What precipitated the event is described below.

In South Omaha, one of the most shameful riots ever known took place because of prejudice against the foreigner. A Greek went into the house of a young lady of questionable character and a policeman, following the man, arrested him without any overt cause whatsoever. The Greek resisted and, in the scuffle which followed, the officer was shot. That was Saturday night. The following Sunday morning as the bells were ringing, calling men to worship, a mob assembled and, under the leadership of disreputable fellows, began storming the Greek quarters, smashing windows, breaking doors, and pursuing the terror-stricken and defenseless Greeks in all directions. On the corner of L Street and 24th Avenue was the firm of the Demos brothers—superior men in every sense of the word, one of them being married to an American girl. This store was several blocks away from the Greek quarter, but on came the raging mob as the surging tide, lashed by gusts of rage and passion. They attacked the store at a time when the white-haired mother of the Demos Brothers sat quietly at the soda fountain. They smashed windows, tore to pieces the soda fountain, strew on floor and street the contents of windows and cases and left the place, which represented an investment of more than $7,000, a mass of ruins. The brothers and their families fled for life. They had other stores in Omaha, which they immediately gave up, for they knew not how far this wave of fury, fanaticism, and savagery would sweep, and in a week they found themselves reduced by mob violence in Christian America from the position of prosperous merchants to paupers. Instances of mob violence against the foreigners are also found in the East, and even the South is not exempt.[28]

The violence in Omaha occurred after the arrival of large numbers of Greeks seeking employment during the winter months when little work was available on the railroads. At the same time, a large number of Greeks were living in Omaha when the meat-packing industry was experiencing labor unrest. In 1909, the workers struck for higher wages, and the packers brought in Greek strikebreakers willing to work for lower wages.[29] Needless to say, this generated wrath and resentment toward the Greeks. Equally as threatening were the ambitious, hard-working Greeks who operated small businesses. The more prosperous Greeks had invested in an estimated thirty-four to fifty grocery stores whose value was placed at a quarter of a million dollars.[30]

Other western states also saw hostility toward the Greeks as well as fears of competition from their businesses. In Montana, mass meetings were held to organize for the purpose of ridding the city of Great Falls of its Greek population, its "undesirables, the ignorant, depraved, and brutal foreigners."[31] A committee was formed in 1909 for the explicit purpose of ridding Montana of its ethnic blight.

Greeks remember when a hundred of them, who had cleared the land of sagebrush near Mt. Home, Idaho, and expected to be paid the following day, were, instead, taken from their tents by fifty masked men on horseback and herded, half dressed, down the railroad tracks clutching their few belongings.[32] Further threats and hostile acts came from the Klu

Klux Klan who viewed the immigrants, in general, as eroding the moral fiber of American society.

Such incidents reflected a period when Anglo-Saxon megalomania was at its height; the Greeks in response turned inward, becoming more clannish and xenophobic with each confrontation. This anti-immigrant sentiment was eventually to culminate in an Immigration Commission's report, which advised that immigration be curtailed on the grounds of the immigrants' presumed inherent inferiority. This resulted in the Johnson Act of 1921 which limited Greek immigrants to 100 a year; the number was raised to 307 in 1927.[33] The commission's findings had a long-lasting impact, not only upon the immigrants, but upon their children as well who grew up in an atmosphere of ethnic intolerance.

As Greeks continued to work their way across the country, laying rails, digging sewers, clearing land of sagebrush, they were always fearful of being caught by railroad detectives, always alert for town officials who would charge them a three-dollar head tax and then jail them if they could not pay. As they traveled west, they heard about the burning of Omaha's Greek Town; in trepidation, they arrived at Salt Lake City's rail yards where Leonides G. Skliris, a padrone, provided them with work in exchange for a fee. In addition, each worker was forced to shop only at stores owned by Skliris's agents. To be sure, the Greeks were furious that Skliris was living an affluent life at their expense, but there was little they could do about it. It was, after all, Skliris who had the connections, and the men accepted his exploitation of them in America as they would have in Greece.[34] Since the mines paid twice as much as the railroads, the Greeks gravitated to them and became the largest immigrant group in Utah's mining towns.[35]

A major function of the padrone was to supply strikebreakers for the mines and railroads. Being the authorized labor agent for both the Denver and Rio Grande and the Western Pacific railroads, the Utah Copper Company, and the coal mines in Carbon County, Utah, Skliris was able to provide work for unemployed Greeks readily. The Greeks were never told that they were to function as strikebreakers, although it is doubtful that this information would have deterred them. They were astounded that laborers complained so vociferously and behaved so aggressively toward their employers. Unlike the northern Italians and southern Slavs, Greeks did not leave their country for seasonal employment in northern countries where radicalism was prevalent among the workers.[36] Further, their own role as landowners in Greece, despite meager returns, was the basis of their sense of individual proprietorship.

While it is true that the Greeks became involved in the 1912 Bingham strike in Utah led by John Leventis, their primary concern was to rid themselves of Skliris and his extortion practices. Once that was accomplished, they were prepared to return to work, but were persuaded that the problem of Skliris was secondary to the need for unionization.[37] In 1922, the Greek miners joined a strike in Salt Lake City that had national repercussions. Again, they were not so much concerned about unionization of the mines as they were about the insult to their philotimo, their self-respect. They discovered that they were being cheated on the coal-weighing machines,[38] and it was this inequity they sought to correct. The primary aim of the union was not achieved.

During these initial years of struggle, the living conditions of the Greek workers remained insufferable; their living in shacks and crowded tents fostered unsanitary conditions, their diet was deficient in essential nutrients, their hours of work were long and dangerous. They lived in constant fear of losing an arm or leg, always suspicious that the company doctors were indifferent and negligent in their treatment, sometimes amputating a limb that might have been saved. Dejected in spirit and often in poor health, they were without the traditional folk remedies administered by the women of their villages.

They were sustained by two goals: furnishing their sisters with an ample dowry for a suitable marriage and finally returning to Greece with enough money saved to ease their families' economic burdens. It is estimated that some 40 percent of the Greeks in Salt Lake City accomplished their goal; the other 60 percent continued to work with the aim of establishing their own businesses. Of those who remained, many married non-Greeks, but the majority brought "picture brides" from Greece.[39]

One can only imagine the fear and apprehension these young women endured coming alone to a country whose language they did not know while fearing, at the same time, that they might be suspected of violating the moral code of shame and honor of their people.[40] With a clear sense of right and duty, they married only to find themselves in a paradoxical situation. On the one hand, they had lost the support of family and kin, but on the other, they were confronted with a new freedom; for the first time in their lives, they did not have to defer to parental supervision in their day-to-day activities. In a sense, they were left to chart their own lives in a social context wherein women enjoyed a freedom unknown in the provincial world from which they came.

But the familiar supports that the villagers knew so well were suddenly in disarray. All about them they saw new patterns of life, and the more they saw, the more convinced they became that the Old World had to be re-created anew. The camaraderie of the men, their social refuge in the kafenio, their establishment of a Greek church in 1905 which served the Greek, Serbian, and Russian people, and finally the building of the first Holy Trinity Greek Orthodox Church in 1912—all marked the beginnings of Greek Town in Salt Lake City.

By the 1920s the presence of Greek women in America made it possible for the male immigrant to think of it as a permanent home. Family life now evolved along the closely knit patterns of their homeland, enveloping the Greek language, Orthodoxy, and cultural traditions. With the zeal of pioneers, Greek women stabilized family life and made possible the growth of Greek communities. The observance of holy days, the presence of the church as a social and religious center, the celebration of name days, the founding of Greek afternoon schools, and the continued interest in the affairs of the old country tended to reinforce Greek nationalism. Adults who grew up during that period remember that as children they were taught to say, "A Greek I was born, and a Greek I shall die."

In the 1920s, the immigrants were young, ambitious, and optimistic as they moved from the ranks of manual labor to become proprietors of confectionery stores, flower shops, restaurants, and shoe-shine parlors. The economy was expanding and opportunities seemed limitless for those with entrepreneurial skills—and some luck. The immigrants' children were still young and tractable; they spoke Greek at home and attended Greek schools where they performed in plays that either extolled the grandeur of Greece or mourned the years of oppression under the Ottoman Turks. Overall, a harmony prevailed that concealed the inevitability of acculturation and future generational conflict.

Dissension, to be sure, existed in the community of Salt Lake City as it did in other Greek enclaves following the First World War and the beginning of the Great Depression. As we have noted, the problems of Greece were the problems of the Greeks in the diaspora. The constant shifting of political power in Greece, as in the twenties between King Constantine and the liberal political figure Eleutherios Venizelos, divided the Greeks in this country and created ideological camps of Royalists and Venizelists. Members of the church hierarchy were also ideologically split, creating a schism in the church and the community that took many years to heal. Priests were hired and fired according to their political sympathies, and religious services were intermittent. We shall have occasion to explore the church schism more fully.

Despite the tensions created by Greece's political problems, continuing national identification was encouraged by fraternal organizations, newspapers, Greek schools, social gatherings that excluded non-Greeks, and the continuing commitment to the Orthodox faith. The Greeks in Utah were confronted with another group equally as clannish and equally as defensive: the Mormons. Each group viewed the other as inferior and considered it arrogant in regarding itself as possessing the only true religion.[41] The Greek woman could not understand the frugality and "coldness" of the Mormon woman. Helen Papanikolas writes:

> Among the Greeks, kisses and embraces were perfunctory rituals on greeting people, leave taking, namedays, and church celebrations. They were shocked to learn that Mormon children were punished by being sent to bed without food. Love and food were synonymous to the Greeks. A person could be sick, he could be grief stricken, but to be hungry was the worst evil to befall him.[42]

The animosity between the two groups was not concealed. The Mormon practice of polygamy was especially repugnant to the Greek people. Although both Greek and Mormon women subscribed to the value of self-sacrifice and both viewed themselves fundamentally as appendages to men, there did exist some significant differences. Unlike the Greek Orthodox church with its ordained clerical hierarchy, each Mormon male could become a holy agent invested with the privileges and power of priesthood.

> In the Mormon view of man, not only is he a spirit child of God, but he is capable of achieving Godhood himself. In the process of becoming a God, a man must enter into the "new and everlasting covenant of marriage by which he and his wives will be married for all eternity."[43]

Mormon men held a special kind of dominion over women, and polygamy, or more properly, polygyny, played an important role in their religious orientation. In 1853, Brigham Young, a leader of the Mormons, announced the legitimacy of the doctrine of "plural wives," based upon a vision of the Mormon's former leader Joseph Smith in 1843. According to Mormon theology, it was not possible for women to benefit from spiritual progress without a man. It was possible for her to find a spiritual mate in the afterlife, but this was hardly a practical solution to a woman trying to make her spiritual and economic way in the world of here and now. Mormon women arriving in Utah throughout the nineteenth century had no choice but to enter polygamous relationships in order to assure themselves of spiritual guardianship. If, on the other hand, a man had a wife who was not supportive of his spiritual progress, she could live through her husband's good works as he continued to take on additional wives if he wished. In the Greek case, the woman was protected in life by males of her immediate family through marriage; her eternal protection as a member of the Orthodox faith was provided by the church.

Although both the Mormon and the Greek Orthodox churches held motherhood to be the most crucial experience in a woman's life, the Mormons did not invest the role of the mother with the tender, mystical, and exalted qualities exemplified in the Virgin Birth. The icons, the venerated statues that stressed the intrinsic feminine nature of religion, were lacking in the Mormon church, and its chapels echoed the austerity of the Puritans' New England church of masculine order and intellect. A Mormon woman of Utah relates the following:

I cannot recall anything feminine about the majority of meeting houses except an occasional vase of flowers on special occasions. The colors in most were flat and somber, the furniture solid and functional, and any pictures displayed were invariably of the male leaders of the church—I cannot recall a picture of any women gracing those beige plaster walls.[44]

The Greek women found their Mormon neighbors *analates* ("bland, without salt").[45] Their different religious doctrines affected relations between them for many years. Convinced of the intrinsic rightness of their religious views, both sought refuge in their respective ethnic enclaves. While time has tempered feelings of ill will, one still finds expressions of these historic, unresolved conflicts. Recently, for example, the ecumenical patriarchate of Constantinople issued a directive that:

. . . the blessing of a marriage of any Orthodox Christian with a Mormon is not permitted. [Such marriages can be blessed] . . . if before the marriage, the person belonging to the Mormon faith is accepted into Orthodoxy through the Sacrament of Holy Baptism.[46]

Clearly religious lines are still being drawn, but for many second-generation Greeks whose children married Mormons, the directive unnecessarily reactivated bitter memories. The once dramatic differences between the two religions now seem less pronounced. This may be part of a general secularizing trend reflected in the fact that Greek customs and practices once so revered have diminished in intensity. English has gradually replaced Greek as the language spoken in the home, Greek-school enrollment has declined, the nonethnic media prevail, and the coffeehouses, once the refuge of the older male, are gone. The Greek church remains the center of any collective sense of Greek identity.

In this transitional phase, the Second World War confirmed the primacy of America as the locus of identity. While sympathy, support, and pride reached out to the Greeks fighting on the side of the Allies, it was the destiny of the second-generation young Greek American men that preoccupied their parents. The ultimate sacrifice was being made to their adopted country—their sons. All else paled by comparison.

Milwaukee, Wisconsin

While the central themes of conflict and accommodation run through the immigrants' experience, the singleness of their purpose emerges as salient in community after community. In their efforts to meet familial responsibilities, some situations proved more calamitous than others, depending on the particular region of settlement and economic conditions.

In Milwaukee, the Greeks settled primarily among the German population, and again their origins and religious differences set them apart. They arrived in Milwaukee around 1905 and worked in urban areas throughout the state, although the largest settlement remained at Milwaukee. The vast majority had emigrated from the Peloponnesus, especially from Arcadia, but also from Rumeli and the Aegean and Ionian islands.[47] There were about eighteen nationalities working in the tanneries by 1910; the Greeks employed in 1898–99 were the last to be hired. The Germans came first, then a few English people and Scots, the Poles, Russians, Italians, Croatians, Slovaks, Lithuanians, and finally the Greeks. What attracted the Greeks to the tanneries of Milwaukee was probably, very simply, the availability of jobs that apparently were not choice ones.[48]

Greek immigrants worked in the tanneries owned by the German families. In 1916, the manufacture of leather ranked third in Milwaukee's economy, with iron and steel and heavy industry ahead of it.[49] Tannery labor required no knowledge of the English language and no prior experience. Other Greeks worked in iron and steel mills, in restaurants as dishwashers and waiters, and in factories of various types. Paradoxically, it may be that their lack of education and skills facilitated their adjustment to the exigencies of the economic situation. Their expectations for money and higher status as well as their desire to return to Greece could be realized as they went from working in tanneries to owning small grocery stores, confectionery shops, coffeehouses, restaurants, and shoe-shine parlors. By 1920, at least forty such businesses were owned by Greeks in Milwaukee.[50]

Interestingly enough, the second generation did not, as a rule, follow in the businesses developed by their fathers; they sought advanced degrees in the professions. The jump from blue-collar to white-collar status in one generation can perhaps be explained by the strength of the primary group, the fear of bringing shame to one's family, the approbation accorded the achiever by the community, and, finally, the reluctance to accept assistance from charitable organizations. All these factors helped develop individual and group resourcefulness which facilitated occupational mobility.[51]

This resourcefulness is found in the building of the formal structure of the ethnic community. The church in Milwaukee was organized in 1906; its purposes were not only to function as a place of worship but to establish a Greek school, provide burial grounds, and care for the destitute. Greek Orthodoxy is a group-centered religion; all believers contribute as best they can to the preservation of the church. With Greek nationalism so strong during this period, the transmitting of the values of Hellenism to the younger generation became of paramount importance. The fiery patriotic passion of the Great Idea, reactivated during the Balkan War of 1912–13, caused three hundred to six hundred Greek men to leave Milwaukee for Greece. It is estimated that more than thirty thousand Greeks arrived in New York from every corner of the United States to return to Greece and help unify the motherland.[52]

With the advent of the First World War, the Greek community in Milwaukee, along with other communities, was divided in its loyalty between the pro-Western policies of Eleutherios Venizelos and King Constantine's neutral stance. The formal organization of the community was administered by lay people in charge of hiring and firing priests, Greek teachers, and other personnel, and their decisions were dictated by ideological stance rather than by the survival of the community as a whole. The ecclesiastical clergy as well were torn between loyalties that transcended theological considerations. This communal schism was causing strong antiforeign feelings in Milwaukee, and the city's priests appealed for greater civic concern and participation in the affairs of the Milwaukee community as a way of proving their loyalty to their adopted country.[53]

With the passing of time, however, the immigrants became more concerned with the welfare and education of their own families, their new status as naturalized citizens, and their realization that some balance would have to be achieved if the community was to survive at all, and this began to alter their thinking. During this time of emerging cooperation with the host culture, the American Hellenic Educational Progressive

Association (AHEPA) was organized in 1922 in Atlanta, Georgia, for the purpose of facilitating the immigrants' adjustment to their new home. In 1924 a chapter was organized in Milwaukee by a group of middle-class businessmen and students.[54] Those who feared the encroachment of assimilation and viewed AHEPA as disloyal to all that was Greek formed their own organization, the Greek American Progressive Association (GAPA).

Intergroup tensions on the one hand and shared sentiments on the other continued to sustain formal institutions such as the Greek-language school. It offered a nationalistic curriculum including reading, geography, history, grammar, and mythology.[55] The question as to what constituted ethnic identity in the transition from one generation to the next was subtly emerging. But, an inestimable number of reluctant second-generation Greek youths, to their dismay, found themselves attending Greek school. All their protestations could not deter their parents from sending them. Saloutos relates his boyhood experiences during the 1920s in Milwaukee's Greek school:

> I suppose one reason I hated Greek school was because it gave me little time to play or do the things I wanted to do as a youngster. Imagine a grade school youngster coming home from the public school in late afternoon, then having to ready himself for a school he had no desire to attend, and which he attended often under protest, haunted with the thought he would be reprimanded by the teacher for coming to school unprepared, taking with him often a piece of Greek bread or some other edible to curb his growing appetite, often sitting in bleak, uncomfortable and sometimes cold surroundings totally different from what he knew in the public school, and forced to have a late supper. . . .
>
> For a youngster, the Greek language school was a nightmare. I felt incarcerated in it, and I hated it; but I had little choice in the matter as long as the parental will reigned supreme. My parents kept insisting that I had to learn Greek, become better educated than they, and achieve a better station in life than they had. And one way of doing this was by going to the Greek school to learn the language, history, and achievements of the people who gave light to the world.[56]

With all its drawbacks, apparently the Greek school managed to preserve some semblance of Greek language and culture; it sustained communication between parents and children, and reaffirmed the values their parents held onto so tenaciously.

By the 1930s, Milwaukee's community, like that of Salt Lake City, had become reconciled to America as their permanent home. Greek political differences that had shaped the community began to erode, and the church was now under the administration of the Greek Archdiocese of North and South America with its offices in New York. Greece's role in the Second World War enhanced the country in the eyes of the world; American patriotism and pride for the Greeks of the diaspora now merged. A symbol of the melding of the two worlds was the completion in 1960 of a new church in Milwaukee designed by Frank Lloyd Wright. Architecturally, it expressed the New World experience combined with the culture of the Old.

Chicago and New York City

In 1907 it was estimated that of the 150,000 Greeks in the United States, between 30,000 and 40,000 were working as laborers in factories and railroad construction gangs. Others worked as bootblacks, waiters, vendors, and clerks in stores that catered to ethnic needs. An unknown number owned and managed their own businesses: grocery stores, coffeehouses, bakeries, carpentry shops, and barbershops. The legal and medical professions were represented in relatively small numbers.[57]

In 1913, out of a total of 253,100 Greeks estimated to be in the United States, New York State had 32,200 as compared with 30,000 in Illinois. In New York, the majority (20,000) were located in New York City and Brooklyn.[58] The first arrivals in Chicago and New York were the Spartans, followed by the Arcadians who eventually outnumbered them.

Most of the immigrants starting out in menial occupations were involved with the padrone system, which, as we saw earlier, operated in communities throughout the United States.[59] This was a form of indentured slavery whereby the immigrant was obliged to work three to four months before receiving a salary of ten to twenty dollars a year. In exchange for a job, the immigrant was provided with passage and money called "show money," which was necessary to declare at the point of entry to the United States. In return, the padrone extracted a mortgage on the village property of the prospective emigrant or a close relative for a sum equal to three or four times the cost of transportation with the assurance that the three or four months of work in this country would fulfill his obligations. The exploitation was reprehensible. Often the neophyte would arrive and find no job awaiting him; at times the job he did find was in violation of U.S. labor laws. As a solution to his problems, he often had to pay an interpreter's fee as well as a labor agent's fee. Even after acquiring a job, the immigrant would usually be approached to give the agent a further sum of money to ensure his job security.

One fourteen-year-old boy brought to Chicago by his father was left to work in shoe-shine parlors under the patronage of a padrone while his father returned to Greece to bring the rest of the family to the United States. The informant, now in his eighties, relates how he worked from six in the morning until nine and ten at night, only to work even longer hours during the weekends. After working, he was obligated, along with the other boys, to clean and prepare the shop for the following day's business. The time until his father's return seemed interminable. Feeling abandoned and having no one to turn to, he would seek some corner in which to hide so that others might not see the tears he shed.

Chicago was a city that could absorb many immigrants because their arrival coincided with the great fire that took place in the latter part of the nineteenth century. Construction work was readily available in rebuilding the city, and in addition, Greeks worked as street vendors and at other unskilled jobs that continued to draw larger numbers into Chicago than elsewhere in the United States. By 1882, a Greek settlement of several hundred had been formed. A decade later, the first resident priest officiated in a warehouse, and by 1893, the church was relocated and consecrated by the first Greek Orthodox hierarch to visit the United States.[60]

At the turn of the century, the Greek immigrants began to settle near the West Side at the "Delta," a triangular area bordered by Halsted and Harrison streets and Blue Island Avenue. This area became Chicago's first Greek Town and remained a self-sustaining ethnic enclave until the 1960s when the University of Chicago displaced it.[61] It is estimated that twenty thousand Greeks inhabited the area between the two world wars.

The Chicago community, however, was not without its internal tensions and resentments. The Spartans, the largest group to have emigrated to Chicago, found sodality in organizing the Lycurgus Society which also included Greeks from Arcadia. As the latter began to exceed the former in numbers, they formed their own organization and their own church, and hired a priest from Arcadia. The split seems to have been motivated by a desire on the part of the Lycurgus Society to impose a tax on "certain Halsted Street Greeks," namely the Arcadians.[62] As a result, a second Greek Town was formed on the near West Side of Chicago.

During this period of struggle and accommodation to their adopted land, the Greeks of Chicago had an important ally in Jane Addams, founder and director of Hull House from 1889 until her death in 1935. Through her empathy and understanding, she helped the immigrants adjust to their new environment and provided them with facilities for discussions, meetings, and Greek plays, continually encouraging them to be proud of their ethnic heritage.[63] Jane Addams was an ardent exponent of cultural pluralism when the melting pot concept was the prevailing ideology. Her respect for their ancestral culture undoubtedly enhanced the immigrants' self-image. The symposia and language classes she sponsored gave direction to their understanding of the new social milieu in which they found themselves. Very few immigrants had the advantage of such an experience in a country where hostility and rejection were the usual reactions.

As immigration increased, the Greeks became dispersed throughout the city, so that by 1930, eleven formal communities had been founded. The proliferation of these communities was instrumental in strengthening the bonds of Greek ethnic identity, as they established churches, Greek-language schools, voluntary organizations, and Sunday schools; each parish dealt with its problems on a local basis, tending to what it regarded as its own essential needs. An overall unitary community did not emerge. The issue of Greece's political struggle between Royalists and Liberals ignited and reignited dissension among parishes and members.

In 1915 the United Greek Parishes of Chicago sought to bring unity out of the chaos that separated Greek from Greek, parish from parish. The attempt met with frustration as each faction, obsessed with the issue of political turmoil in Greece, failed to meet the substantive issues confronting them as a marginal community in the United States. The local approach to ethnic problems continued to dominate each community down to the 1980s.[64]

The years throughout the twenties were years of disarray for the Greek church in both Chicago and New York City. In 1892 the Greeks of New York City established a pattern of church organization and administration that other communities followed. The first step was to organize a society (naming it after some classical hero) and enlist member support and money. In New York, it was the Society of Athens; in Chicago, as noted, the Society of Lycurgus.[65] Although internal unity did not prevail, New York City and Chicago were the only cities in which Greek Orthodox services were performed regularly from 1891 to 1899. Despite the repetitious scenarios of dissension within the church, it continued to remain the nucleus from which Greek ethnicity emanated and sustained itself.

In the early part of this century, these two cities also went in parallel directions in regard to economic activities. The earliest settlement for the Greeks in New York City was along Eighth Avenue between 14th and 15th streets and the South Bronx. Ironically, given the numerical majority of Greeks, New York City did not produce the ethnic enclave that was characteristic of Chicago until well into the twentieth century, following the legislation of 1965 when large numbers of immigrants began to arrive in the United States. Having arrived, they established Astoria, in Queens, as *the* ethnic enclave of New York. Despite the historic absence of the ethnic insularity that characterized Chicago, New York City was always regarded as the most important Greek American community in the country. This may be due to the facts that the Archdiocese of North and South America was established in New York City; the first national Greek American newspapers, *Atlantis* and *National Herald,* originated there; and also possibly that the entrepreneurial spirit was strong in a city representing not only the industrial center of the country but its cultural center as well.

A 1909 survey of Greek businesses in New York City reported 151 bootblack parlors, 113 florists, 107 lunchrooms and restaurants, 70 confectioneries, 62 retail fruit stores, and 11 wholesale produce dealers. Apparently very few Greeks worked in factories. Those who did not have their own business and did not work for their compatriots went through the pushcart-peddler syndrome.[66] In Chicago, the most prominent enterprises were the confectionery trade and shoe-shine parlors whose proprietors expanded their operations to include hat cleaning, shoe repairing, and the cleaning and pressing of clothes.[67] It was the florist trade, however, that made the greatest progress in New York, as happened later in Chicago and other cities.

The confectionery field was a natural for the early immigrant, because of his experience in making pastries and candy in Greece, and the fact that the local ethnic coffeehouses and other retail establishments used his products. The confectioner became the one who traded with the general public, and in this sense, his public esteem was enhanced.[68] Chicago was the site of the major candy business of the Greek community, and by the 1920s, Greek immigrants were among the foremost restaurant owners, ice cream manufacturers, florists, fruit and vegetable operators, and confectionery merchants in the city.[69] Serving the public in this capacity made the Greeks aware of the need to become Americanized, having realized that antiforeignism was an obstacle in their drive for ascendancy. Their efforts to organize were aborted in the late 1920s and early 1930s when many confectioners went out of business because of the Great Depression. Nevertheless, Chicago remained the center of the candy industry, and in 1947, an estimated 350 to 400 shops and 8 to 10 candy manufacturers were still located there.[70]

It has often been said that when two Greeks meet, they open a restaurant. Be that as it may, the business represented a firm step on the ladder of entrepreneurial success for those who had been engaged in menial jobs. The Greeks started in the restaurant business about 1900, catering mainly to the ethnic palate of their compatriots. In New York, the original fast-food service was provided as Greeks took to the streets and sold frankfurters and other items. The current street vendors, who fill the streets and parks of New York, are but a replication of an earlier immigrant scene. For many, it is still the first step in acquiring capital with which to open a luncheonette, diner, or other business.

In Chicago, the Greeks entered the restaurant business in large numbers. Originally they sold food from lunch wagons to factory workers, but an ordinance forbade the selling of food on city streets, thus forcing them to pool their resources and open local restaurants. Most of these enterprises were, of course, family operated. Attacks from their competitors and the local newspapers compelled the Greeks to organize on a collective basis to defend their interests. One of the first attempts to organize occurred in Chicago, but the inability to reconcile personality and regional antagonisms of Old World origins sabotaged any productive plans.[71] In 1919, one out of every three restaurants in Chicago was operated by a Greek. Anglicizing the names of their restaurants brought them a larger clientele.

However, the success of the Greek restaurateur only incurred the wrath of the non-Greek engaged in a similar enterprise. Having the support of city newspapers through which they vented their hostility, non-Greeks confronted the reader with advertisements that read, "John's Restaurant, Pure American. No Rats, No Greeks."[72]

The fruit and vegetable peddlers in Chicago and New York City also faced obstacles from neighborhood merchants as well. At times, it was a Greek peddler versus a Greek merchant. The peddlers were subject to legislation that discriminated against them but that also alerted them to the fact that in order to protect themselves from future victimization, it was necessary to become citizens and use the franchise for their interests. The plight of the small businessman did not dissuade him from making a success of his enterprise, whatever its size. Prominent Greek names in the restaurant business, at one time or another, included Raklios who operated a large chain in Chicago, and Foltis, Stavrakos, and Litzotakis in New York City.[73]

The fur industry in New York drew many Greeks between the two world wars and represented one of the most politically radical groups of the working class. Starting in 1941, the newspaper *Greek American Tribune* represented the voice of Greek labor. Its publication continued until after

World War II, with support largely from the Fur Workers Union, Greek Maritime Union, and the Greek branch of the Industrial Workers of the World. Parenthetically, one thing should be mentioned with regard to the conservative ideology that is generally ascribed to the Greek people. Greek American studies is a relatively new academic area of research. The extent of radicalism among Greeks in the American labor movement has not been subject to rigorous investigation. The failure of Greeks to become a viable part of the labor movement in the United States has seldom been linked to the policies of the unions themselves which were antiforeign and discriminatory.

In 1909, the editor of the conservative *Atlantis* newspaper announced that it sought "to get all Greek workers to join the different labor unions." It fought hard whenever Greeks were induced by false promises to replace strikers and pointed out to them the meaning and disgrace of a self-respecting man becoming a scab. The editor told Samuel Gompers, leader of the American Federation of Labor, that his efforts were being frustrated by the union's policies. He protested to Gompers that "the Greek workers are forming societies for mutual protection and are taking an interest in the affairs of the labor movement in general, and from records it will be shown that the Greeks are good, honest workmen and would be desirable members of the trade unions once they had the opportunity to prove it. But how can they ever prove it if so little continues to be done by your organization to bring them within the fold of the trade unions?"[74]

Education. The illiteracy rate of the Greek immigrant between 1900–1908 was approximately 27 percent. In 1910, 24 percent were unable to read and write, but by 1920, the rate dropped 3.2 percent. This decline is attributed to the change in compulsory education practices in their native land.[75] Following World War I, Greek children in the United States began to be enrolled in public schools with greater regularity than before the war. Usually, they were placed in classes for the retarded, since they had insufficient knowledge of the English language. By the 1930s, however, increasing acculturation made adjustment to the American school system easier, and by the 1940s and 1950s, assimilation was the norm.[76]

In Chicago, as in New York City, the desire to counteract the alienating effect of the American schools caused individual parishes to increase the number of Greek-language schools already established during the first decade of this century. By the 1930s, concern over the erosion of the Greek language spurred the community of Chicago to pressure the Board of Education to restore Greek to the school curriculum. The Hellenic Education League was formed in 1935 and succeeded in its mission. In 1961, the program was discontinued, but by that time, the legitimacy of Greek as part of the educational curriculum had been established.

Later, with an influx of immigrants, the Chicago community, as well as New York, pressed for the reinstitution of Greek. Those in favor of teaching the language were supported by the new ethnicity of the sixties and seventies; their concern extended beyond the language component to that of the legitimacy of ethnic survival in a pluralist society. In Chicago and New York City, bilingual programs have been established, funded by federal grants from Title VII—the Bilingual Education Act of 1967. The Greek communities are divided, as is the population at large, in regard to the viability and success of the bilingual programs.

Up to World War II, each parish had its own school, and as the new immigrants went to Chicago, the need for ethnic schools increased. Unlike the Roman Catholic parochial schools, religion played a secondary role in the total curriculum. Essentially it consisted of learning the Greek language, Greek literature, history, geography, and church history. Currently, Chicago has three day schools and New York City twelve. The major vehicle for transmitting Greek education has remained largely the afternoon language schools. The Sunday school, unknown in Greece, provided another avenue for socializing the young in their ethnoreligious heritage and was organized in every parish after 1920.

Voluntary associations. In both Chicago and New York City, the regional organization continues to play an important role in the lives of many Greeks. AHEPA (American Hellenic Educational Progressive Association), one of the largest organizations, claims a membership of 500,000 with its auxiliaries, the Daughters of Penelope, Sons of Pericles, and Maids of Athena. An estimated sixty regional societies exist in New York City. Other associations include the Modern Greek Studies Association, the Hellenic University Club, Filiko, Krikos, the Greek American Lawyers Association, the Hellenic American Educators Association, and the Parnassos Society of New York. The various groups reflect the educational and class gradations of their memberships as well as the myriad ways in which ethnicity has been sustained.

New York City had no Hull House, no Jane Addams, but in 1972, a group of concerned citizens formed the Hellenic American Neighborhood Action Committee as a way of meeting the problems of adjustment confronting the recent immigrants to New York. It has formed service facilities for the young, the elderly, and the unemployed. Counseling services are provided to help the individual and family toward a workable adjustment in an urban context. It provides conferences, symposia, museum exhibits, and films which help clarify the Greek experience in America on a variety of levels. The Hellenic Foundation of Chicago offers similar services to its Greek community.

Accurate numerical figures are difficult to come by regarding the two largest Greek communities in the United States. New York City is estimated to have approximately 500,000, with 60,000–80,000 in Astoria, Queens; Chicago's Greek population is 125,000–150,000, with 20,000–30,000 centered at Western and Lawrence avenues, the new Greek Town of Chicago.[77]

The Greek Orthodox Ladies' Philoptochos Society. The first Greek women's group to be established was in 1894 in New York City. Apparently other concerned women's groups existed in the city; one called the Sorority of Ladies tended to the needs of disadvantaged immigrants in the first decade of this century. They raised funds by collecting at churches and among the Greek shop owners and by holding an annual ball.[78]

In 1931, these independent chapters or groups were consolidated under the late patriarch, the then-Archbishop Athenagoras, as the National Philoptochos Society. At the present time, the organization has over 50,000 members and 575 chapters, compared with 14,000 members and 375 chapters in 1960. The goals of the society have remained unchanged: preserving the Orthodox faith; educating the young; and helping the less fortunate. To accomplish these aims, Philoptochos women continue to raise funds through a variety of methods: social functions, fashion shows, bazaars, publication of ethnic cookbooks, and other events that might appeal to the community.[79]

In 1937, the society helped in establishing the Holy Cross Seminary in Pomfret, Connecticut, as well as St. Basil's Academy, an educational institution for the young.

They responded to the needs of war-torn Greece during the Second World War and of victims of the earthquakes that plague Greece periodically. Through the Foster Parent Plan, they help orphaned and needy children in Greece.

Recognizing the growing problems of the aged in the Greek American community, Philoptochos helped establish St. Michael's Home for the Aged in Yonkers, New York. This project is an ongoing one and plans for expanding present facilities are being implemented in Hartsdale, New York.

The organization has supported the Hellenic College and Holy Cross School of Theology in Brookline, Massachusetts, and has instituted support of the Greek Children's Cardiac Program at New York Hospital, New

York City, as a national project. The society also contributes regularly to all hospitals that provide cardiac medical services to Greek children free of charge.

During the Cyprus tragedy of 1974 and under the project Caress, more than 5,000 displaced Cypriot children have received approximately $1.2 million in monthly payments. Besides contributing to other major causes, they functioned as a pressure group in protesting the Turkish invasion and illegal occupation of Cyprus.

After more than fifty years of community involvement, the organization has grown from a small group of women effectively organizing their resources and energies in pursuit of goals that transcend local concerns to a large group concerned with projects of an even wider scope—influencing in the process the communal sodality of Greek Americans throughout the United States.

Spartanburg, South Carolina

An interesting variation in the adjustment pattern of the Greeks was their settlement in Spartanburg, South Carolina, a mill town.[80] The population of Greeks was sparse until the late thirties or early forties. As late as 1928, there were only 25 families living there, but by 1948, there were 256 Greek residents, comprising 50 families in a total population of 40,000.[81]

Unlike their counterparts in other cities, Spartanburg Greeks bypassed the route of peddler and pushcart by establishing confectionery stores and restaurants. This is not to say that peddlers were unknown throughout the southern states; indeed, they would occasionally come to Spartanburg as early as the 1890s. Apparently, one Nicholas Trakas did so, and sensing the need for a confectionery store in Spartanburg, he opened the first one in 1900. This provided the impetus for compatriots to follow suit. There seemed nothing in the background of these newcomers, originating from Sparta, Greece, to have led them into small businesses except that of chance.[82]

Proprietorship status provided them with a reasonably good living, so that they were not conspicuously distinguished from the native-born.[83] Their businesses were oriented to the community at large, and as residents, they were dispersed throughout the various neighborhoods; because of this, ethnic enclaves did not develop in Spartanburg. They were accepted as both businessmen and neighbors.[84] In addition, the Greek was valued as a civic-minded person, always prepared to contribute to the betterment of the community with tangible financial support.

One study relates this civic-mindedness to the values of the old country in which Spartanburg Greeks took so much pride and supported monetarily. Civic involvement, however, did not include political involvement which they eschewed, largely because of their small numbers. Many businessmen also feared a loss of their customers, so it seemed best to avoid controversial issues.[85] While most other Greek communities were vociferous about the political affairs of Greece, the Spartanburg Greeks avoided becoming embroiled with its conflicts.

Cohesiveness among Spartanburg Greeks was sustained through social and religious ties. Since 1910, they had used non-Greek churches where services were held by visiting Greek priests. When a priest was not available, they attended non-Greek churches, particularly the Episcopal church with which they felt a religious affinity.[86] It was not until 1941 that the Greeks in Spartanburg had sufficient numbers to pool their resources for the purpose of building their own church. Once built, it became synonymous with Greek society in Spartanburg. No family was excluded from contributing to its maintenance, both spiritually and financially. Worship, social functions, a Greek school program, emergency relief for the needy, all administered by the church, made it the center of Greek life.[87]

Education, particularly its utilitarian aspect, was valued by the Spartanburg Greeks. One writer refers to them as a very materialistic and economically oriented people. The administrators of the local colleges attested to the fact that their Greek students chose medicine, dentistry, engineering, teaching, business administration, law, and journalism—in that order.[88] In educating their children, sons were accorded preference. However, while the Spartanburg study was in progress, three young women opted to pursue careers and although their parents supported their decision, their action was still regarded as deviant in the Greek culture.[89]

While retaining a low profile, the Greeks remained a cohesive group. They did not experience rejection by the host culture nor a sense of inferiority in relation to it. Non-Greeks, in general, spoke well of the Greeks, while businessmen remarked, "They were shrewd, but likable."[90] It should be noted that the Greek businessman and worker were not regarded as economic threats to the native population of Spartanburg. The opportunities sought by the Greek immigrants were not in competition with the economic strivings of the non-Greek, which partly explains why the Greek was never an object of attack.[91]

An interesting trait of the Spartanburg Greeks is that they did not criticize or undermine each other, which would have weakened the position of the whole group. They were united and presented a solid front.[92] This factor may have made them less prone to internecine envy.

The acceptance of the Greeks may be due to several factors: the immigrants found reasonable economic stability in Spartanburg; there were fewer unattached males among them than in the larger cities; they enjoyed homogeneity of class (which minimized intergroup conflicts); and they seem to have had a higher educational level than Greeks in other communities. The Greek men and women who emigrated gave fifth- to eighth-grade education on the school records of their children, indicating that the parents had a higher rate of literacy than those in New York City.[93]

It is a sociological axiom that among the members of any dominant group, the greatest incidence of open conflict toward a given minority will be found among the strata that are most vulnerable to competition from the minority. The researcher states it succinctly:

He [the Greek] did not become a serious competitor of the native population and, hence, not an object of attack by them.[94]

Tarpon Springs, Florida

It is said that the name Tarpon Springs, Florida, was given to the area because of the large number of fish called tarpon which were seen jumping in local waters, followed by the exclamation: "See how the Tarpon Springs!"

Tarpon Springs stands as a unique Greek community in the United States because of the industry the Greeks were engaged in and because of their large numbers. The two people responsible for the sponge industry in America were John K. Cheyney and John M. Cocoris. Cocoris came to New York City initially in 1895 and went to work for the Lembesis Sponge Company. The firm sent him to Tarpon Springs to buy sponges that were at that time harvested by the "hooking" boats: men would go out to the sponge deposits in boats using hooks attached to long poles. Cocoris was to change this technique. His family operated a sponge business in Hydra, Greece, and when Cheyney offered Cocoris the job of handling sponges in Tarpon Springs, he accepted with the proviso that his five brothers, who were in Greece at the time, join him.

Cocoris convinced Cheyney that more and better grade sponges could be obtained by importing skilled men and diving equipment from Greece. In 1904, the first Greek spongers came to Tarpon Springs, bringing with them the newly invented pressurized diving suit, unknown in this country, which allowed the diver to go deeper than any "hooker" could and collect enough sponges to supply any demand.

Along with their diving skills, the Greeks introduced a new way of life to Tarpon Springs, changing it from a spa center for the wealthy into a brusque business town. By the end of the first year, 1,500 Greeks, mainly single men, arrived from the Dodecanese Islands, Halki, Clymnos, Symi, and others. In two short years, the spongers had approximately fifty diving boats and fifty-five new "hook" boats, and the flourishing industry engendered animosity from non-Greeks. They resented the disruption of the city's leisurely tempo and were jealous of the dramatic economic success of these vigorous foreigners.[95]

Tarpon Springs was founded in 1882 and was incorporated with a population of fifty-two residents in 1887. Initially it was dominated by northern aristocrats when the city was a vacation and health center for the very wealthy. The black population at that time were servants to this elite group. Not long after the Greeks came, the aristocrats began leaving their once peaceful retreat. The relationship between the Greeks and the black population was, from the beginning, a friendly one. Their interaction increased as the blacks were employed by the Greeks in the sponge industry. This collaborative effort led to a political bond, so that the Greeks who became active in local politics could rely upon blacks for their votes. Their interdependence was mutually reinforcing. Many of the blacks learned to speak Greek, even acquiring the dialect of their employers and co-workers.[96]

For many years the Greek community at Tarpon Springs had the distinction of being the only settlement where Greeks constituted a large majority of the population. By the end of 1905, 1,500 Greeks made Tarpon Springs the largest sponge center in the country. In 1940, there were 2,500 Greeks compared with 3,402 non-Greeks.[97] The economic impact of the industry was dramatic. Between 1910 and 1940, the income from spongers ran between $500,000 and $1 million per year; during World War II, it rose to $3 million. In this unprecedented situation, the Greeks were the innovators, the leaders, the dominant force in building a major industry and a self-contained ethnic community.[98] And, yet, while sponge diving was a lucrative business, it also exacted its toll in the lives of divers who suffered the bends, a danger inherent in their occupation.

In 1907, they established a church, the still-present St. Nicholas's, which was followed by Greek-language schools and the usual Greek associations based upon one's island of origin. The Greek church, the political clubhouse, the coffeehouses with outdoor tables, the Greek signs on the stores along the streets—all served to make the visitor feel that a bit of Hellas was established here. The Feast of Epiphany, always celebrated on January 6, draws, even to the present day, spectators numbering over 35,000.[99] The Epiphany celebration recalls the discovery of the true cross by St. Helen in A.D. 325 and observes the historic importance of the sea to the Greek people. The parishioners are sprinkled with holy water and fill bottles to take home to bless their houses. Following the church service, a procession winds to the sea, where young men anxiously wait to compete in swimming for a cross that has been tossed into the water by the Greek prelate.

During these halcyon years, a Greek community was built that was not merely a replica of the Mediterranean; as the Episcopalian prelate Thomas Burgess wrote, "It is sunny Argolis itself." Those were prosperous times for Tarpon Springs, with Greeks raising their families, buying real estate, and investing in other business enterprises. Holidays, namedays, Greek cuisine, and Greek gregariousness shaped the environment, and before long the Greeks became the most influential group in Tarpon Springs. Even the conductors of the trains would announce the arrival at Tarpon Springs as "Greek Town—Tarpon Springs." Blacks appropriated many of their customs, including the Greek "pascha" Easter celebration.[100] Gradually, some of the Greeks began to gravitate into banking and developed an interest in local government. Although they did not control the city, they headed the fire and police departments.

The Greeks experienced about forty-three years of this affluence, and many thought it would continue indefinitely. But between 1948 and 1954, the sponge industry underwent an abrupt decline. A biological blight called the "red tide" killed the sponges at a time when synthetic ones were being introduced on the market. A new source of income had to be found, but the ethnic insularity of the immigrant had not encouraged learning the English language, and this became an obstacle to finding employment. This had an extremely adverse effect upon the older sponge divers who, while they took pride in not going on welfare, suffered the indignity of watching their wives go to work to support the family. This destroyed the natural order of things, and it was difficult for the Greek male to adjust to it. On the other hand, his long absences from home during the sponge-diving years prepared the Greek woman to be independent and resourceful. The younger generation of men became electricians or auto mechanics, and others became educated to enter the professions. The skills their fathers and grandfathers had brought from the Aegean were slowly being lost. In 1954, when the sponge beds started to come back, younger Greek men were no longer interested in the work.[101]

In seeking the boundaries that defined ethnicity for the Greek in Tarpon

Springs, one must look at the variables of mixed marriages, language, and the church in relation to the three generations who have lived there. Each of these variables carries an unequal weight, of course, in the retention of ethnic identity. The marginality of the second generation still shows adherence to Greek customs, language, and even marriage within the group. Their progeny, the third generation, however, follows a more acculturated pattern. Marriage to non-Greeks, for example, has increased. The records of St. Nicholas Church show that during the years 1922 through 1941, out of a total of 213 marriages, only 2 were with non-Greeks. In the year 1958, out of 27 marriages in the church, 18 were with non-Greeks. Emotional storms over intermarriages still occur and the tendency is to draw the non-Greek into the community, but the feeling lingers that "there is a difference." Greeks in Tarpon Springs have felt that they were descendants of the classical Greeks with little or no foreign "blood."[102] There is apprehension in the community that if mixed marriages continue to increase, the extinction of the group is imminent.

Unquestionably, changes across generations are taking place in Tarpon Springs as they are elsewhere. Because of the decline of sponge diving, the town has turned to attracting tourists, and many Greeks now earn their livelihood through curio shops, restaurants, and a variety of retail shops, tavernas, and nightclubs. The young remain upwardly mobile, constituting about 40 percent of the students at the Tarpon Springs Center of St. Petersburg Community College, a percentage higher than that of Greeks in the total population.[103] At the same time, Greek women make up 55 percent of the enrollment at the local colleges.[104] The use of the Greek language shows a precipitous decline among the third generation, and factionalism marks the community with regard to the use of Greek in church services. Although less Greek is heard on the streets of Tarpon Springs, nevertheless the forces of language and church remain intrinsic to ethnic boundaries, for the church seems to be the last symbol or identifier of the Greek group. Ethnic loyalties, based upon island of origin, have always been a viable part of the community, and a strong sense of community still prevails. At a recent fund-raising event sponsored by AHEPA to raise money to build new facilities for the Greek community, one second-generation male expressed the following sentiment:

> The second generation never really had an interest in the sponge-diving business; although it provided a good living for our fathers, it kept them away from home for months.
> We're very proud of our Greek heritage and intend to do everything we can to keep our children part of it. When they marry non-Greeks, we make every effort to draw their spouses into Greek activities.

We have never felt like a minority; in fact, we always felt ourselves an important part of the whole community; in fact, we are the community.

At this time the Mayor of Tarpon Springs was an American of Greek descent.

A second-generation woman volunteered these comments:

We all want our children to be educated, but we try to keep our daughters as close to home as we can. The majority of them are enrolled in local colleges.
We have had newcomers arrive from Greece and they tell us that we are more Greek than they are; if we are, we're proud of it. We plan to continue maintaining our Greek heritage; we're proud of the values our parents brought with them from Greece.

Tensions exist between the more recent immigrants who have come to Tarpon Springs and the older residents. In part, this can be explained by their conflicting attitudes regarding America. The established families are Americanized and loyal to the United States, whereas the new arrivals are quite critical of America's foreign policy and resent the unskilled jobs they are forced to take. Tarpon Springs' Greeks see nothing wrong with this since they feel their parents had to work extremely hard when they emigrated. Be that as it may, the new immigrants do infuse a heightened Greekness into the community life; this is inevitable given their still close identification with Greece and their command of the language. They also appeared on the scene when the new ethnicity was in vogue, so that their strong sense of Greekness is compatible with the prevailing ethos.

Bilingualism, a byproduct of the new ethnicity, has been established in the public school program. The aim is to preserve both the American and the Greek cultures without one assuming dominance over the other. One would, for example, observe Oxi Day as well as Columbus Day, study Pericles as well as George Washington.[105] Greek afternoon classes are still attended, but the stress is placed upon traditional Greek culture and religion. Recognizing that ethnicity covers a wide spectrum, the community offers programs in Greek music, dances, cuisine, and the like. Greek Americans earnestly believe that a bilingual and bicultural approach will absorb the spouses of those who marry out.

There is talk of a resurgence of the sponge industry in Tarpon Springs because of the ecological movement in the country, which, it is argued, has created an appreciation of the natural sponge—one that is far superior to its synthetic counterpart. Apparently the sponge beds in the gulf are bountiful; whether the Greeks of Tarpon Springs will be willing to take up diving again, however, is questionable. Meanwhile, the Cuban immigrants have taken up the trade and sell sponges to the Greek merchants. Whether there will be a renaissance in the industry remains to be seen. But one thing remains constant—the fond nostalgia shared by the Greeks in Tarpon Springs for those who were in the vanguard of the sponge industry; they were independent, resourceful, and proud of having made Tarpon Springs the largest sponge center in the country. The local priest put it well when he said, "Every time we bury one of the old ones, it is as if a little bit of our heart perished."[106]

Lowell, Massachusetts

While the Greeks of Tarpon Springs were playing a major role in the economic viability of Florida, the Greeks of Lowell, Massachusetts, experienced what can be described only as culture shock as they flooded Lowell to work in the mills. By 1894 some 125 Greeks were employed as factory workers and immediately posed an economic threat to the Irish and French. Harassed by them, the Greeks devised a method of walking in packs in order to avert physical attack.[107]

They were extremely vulnerable; not being able to find living quarters, they were forced to sleep on the rooftops of the tenements. Finally, they earned enough money, pooled their resources, and moved into single-room tenements. As in Salt Lake City, Utah, they were exploited by the padrone system, but its practice in Lowell was brought to an end by a prominent Greek who contacted the appropriate official at the mill.

The pattern of nonfamily groups prevailed as men sent money to needy relatives in Greece and to encourage others to come to Lowell. The mill owners preferred to hire Greeks because of their sobriety, which only intensified antagonisms among the Greeks, the French, and the Irish.[108] The Greeks also proved more congenial to the owners because they showed little concern for union organizations. During the strike of 1912 in Lowell, the Greeks struck with the workers, but through their own organization and had to be dealt with separately.[109]

From 1901 church services were held in the basement of a building the Greeks had bought. However, in 1904 the church committee tore down the building and began to build one costing nearly $80,000.[110] Why build such an extravagant church? The committee argued that a church of such magnitude would discourage splinter groups from forming and building a second church. The quarrels centering upon the support of King Constantine or Venizelos in the pre–World War I years had split the communities of New York, Boston, and Chicago; the Greeks of Lowell were intent upon avoiding their mistake.[111]

Throughout the twenties, the men began leaving the mills and going into their own businesses, and a Greek Town servicing the needs of the Greek population evolved.[112] The characteristic network of fraternal organizations, newspapers, social activities, and Greek schools that welded together the Greek communicants was repeated in Lowell, Massachusetts.

Summary

In summary, immigrant groups have differed in their possession of skills that proved adaptive within an industrial society. The Greeks were rooted in rural and peasant backgrounds and, on the surface, would seem less likely to possess the attributes necessary for achievement in America. We have seen that economic necessity as well as the need to meet the pressures of a rural society were compelling forces in their emigration.

The impetus to accomplish, to achieve, requires an orientation to sacrifice and work. If the acceptance of such values presupposes a validation of the self vis à vis the group, then conformity will tend to govern behavior. This is not to suggest that disintegrative forces were not at work, that they did not engender delinquent or criminal behavior in some instances, but the survival of Greek American communities points to the predominance of conformity over nonconformity. Indeed, it can be argued that the very institutional arrangements established in each community to support the status quo provided the skills for moving beyond it.

This point is made in a study of "Formal Organization and the Americanization Process with Special Reference to the Greeks of Boston," published in 1949. It was observed that the formal organizations of the Greek community not only cushioned the shock of transition from a simple village society to a complex urban one but functioned to reward the successful climbers as well.[113] Initially, rising within the ethnic structure was of paramount importance, but at the same time it prepared the first generation and their progeny to transfer that upward striving to the larger culture. The ethnic community in Boston permitted members to develop leadership techniques which were transferable—fund raising, building churches, disbursing monies, securing church members and keeping them active—all functions that are typically American.[114] Although, usually, ethnic communities have been viewed as retarding assimilation, they paradoxically facilitate it as well.

Not unlike other ethnic groups in the New World, the Greeks were excluded from full participation in its social system; they were held in low esteem more often than not, and were subject to physical violence, suspicion, and contempt. In reaction they formed their own communal space. Insulating themselves from the disruptive forces of the larger society, they sought to sustain a strong ethnic consciousness across generations. Although many made significant advances economically, others did not. But the larger picture of mobility among Greek Americans reveals that their progress has been impressive.

The mobility trend reflected in Greek American communities is consistent with the 1970 census data which reveals that the second generation had a median income of $12,487 as compared with the national median of $5,509, thus more than doubling the national figure.[115]

In terms of occupational mobility, 18,107 native-born Greek men, from a total of 84,537, were listed in the professional and technical category, followed by 17,900 managers and administrators.[116] Of the total female population numbering 47,525 of foreign or mixed parentage, the largest number, 21,294, were in the category of clerical and kindred workers, an increase from 16,650 as of 1950.[117]

Chapter Three
The Changing Immigrant: Community Perspectives

We have been exploring the experiences of the large number of Greeks who emigrated before the Second World War. Mention was made of the quota laws of 1922–24 which precipitated a decline in Greeks entering the United States.

Despite the quota system, however, many Greeks entered the country because of a provision in the law that permitted American citizens to petition for certain relatives. From 1925 to 1929, when the quota law allowed only 737 Greeks to be admitted, actually a total of 10,883 Greeks entered, and this trend persisted throughout the 1930s. The number of Greeks arriving from 1941 to 1950, however, was the lowest since the 1880s, only 2,308.[1]

The New Immigrants (post-1945)

From 1946 to 1970, slightly more than 141,000 Greeks entered the United States as a result of specially enacted legislation, but the legislation did not really benefit the Greeks during the postwar years. On December 22, 1945, President Harry Truman granted some 28,000 displaced persons visas to the United States until December 1947; however, only 7 Greeks were among them.[2]

The McCarran-Walter Act of June 27, 1952, offered no relief to the Greek quota which was raised from 307 to 308, and in point of fact, the fundamental immigration policy of 1924 was operative until 1965. The Refugee Relief Act of 1953, however, affected the quota of entering Greeks significantly; 17,000 Greeks were admitted under this act, and another act of September 11, 1957, permitted another 1,504 Greeks to enter.[3]

Beginning in the early 1960s, emigration was motivated, as in the past, by the lack of economic opportunities in Greece and by the general impoverishment of the country. From 1961 to 1965, emigration fluctuated between 3,002 and 4,825, annually.[4]

In reviewing the international migration of Greek scientists, George Coutsoumaris, professor of political economy, reports that between 1957 and 1961 Greece lost over one-fifth of all her first degrees in engineering to the United States.[5] According to a National Science Foundation study from 1962 to 1969, 1,066 scientists left Greece for the United States. "Of them, 586 were engineers, 271 scientists, and 209 physicians and surgeons."[6] Thus, the fifties and sixties introduced a category of emigrants significantly different from their predecessors and from the majority of new émigrés.

The year 1965 was a turning point in Greek emigration. The national-origins system was ended by the Immigration Act of 1965, taking effect completely on July 1, 1968. From 1966 through 1971, a total of 86,344 Greeks entered the United States. The period ranks closely with those of the years immediately preceding World War I and after in the number of arrivals.[7]

Social change in Greece since the Second World War influenced the importance of education and altered traditional expectations. Improved communications in the provinces, towns, and cities sensitized both men and women to alternative options. Most of those who emigrated after the Second World War did so as family units without expecting to return to their homeland. Although many who came were students and professionals and some were in skilled occupations, the vast majority were still of peasant origin and of limited education.

According to the Annual Report of 1977 of the United States Department of Justice, 7,838 Greeks were admitted to the United States in the year ending September 30, 1977. The largest category, 4,360, were classified as housewives, children, and other, with no occupation reported. The other largest category of 900 were craftsmen and kindred workers, while 565 were classified as service workers. Only 334 were classified as professional, technical, and kindred workers.[8]

The Current Population Reports, issued in March 1982, is the first report presenting information on ancestry, language, and literacy of the U.S. population. The ancestry question was open-ended, that is, no prelisted categories were provided; it was based upon self-identification. The report, based upon a 1979 population survey, did not ask for religious affiliation. Bureau officials indicated that population estimates may differ only slightly with the counts from the 1980 census. Some respondents reported a single ancestry, others reported more than one. Among the Greeks 567,000 (57.3 percent) reported a single ancestry, while 423,000 (42.7 percent) reported multiple ancestry, yielding a total of 990,000 (0.6 percent). Spokespersons for various organizations and institutions in the Greek American community regard the number as underrepresentative, maintaining that their calculation, ranging from 2 to 3 million, is a more realistic one.

Emigration Flow: Generational Confusion

Up until the Second World War, it was relatively easy to identify the Greek population in the United States in terms of first and second generations, the old and the young, but this rather simplistic picture was complicated by the continuing flow of arrivals from Greece, Cyprus, and other areas of the world where Greeks of the diaspora had made their home. In addition, marriages across generations, as well as intermarriages, now blur the once clear distinctions.

A look at the literature dealing with Greek ethnicity will only disappoint those who are looking for a clear and simple definition as to what constitutes ethnicity for the Greek in America.

One reads, on the one hand, that the church has been remiss in providing its parishioners with an understanding of Hellenism and, as a result, has led Greek Americans to view Hellenism in parochial and tenuous terms. Because of this, runs the argument, Americans of Greek descent have been so brainwashed as to regard ritualistic religion, along with Greek music, Greek cuisine, and Greek dances, as comprising the alpha and omega of Greekness. On the other hand, one also reads that the church has provided solidarity and inspiration without which a Greek American community would be impossible.[9] Its supporters maintain that the church has succeeded despite the inveterate factionalism that has plagued it throughout this century. In 1970, when the delegates to the Clergy Laity Congress approved the substitution of English for Greek in the Liturgy, it was viewed by many as the only realistic action that could be taken in the light of the fact that a new generation of Greek Americans was emerging without a competent knowledge of the Greek language. It was regarded as a genuine effort to reconcile Hellenism with the demands of American society.

This seemingly innocuous attempt to salvage the younger generation by making the church more relevant to them represented a long delayed response to the grievances of the second generation who found the church's role alien to their secular experiences. The recent introduction of English in the church was spurred by the belief that this alienation could be overcome by providing a basis for communication on a variety of social issues including abortion, birth control, and mixed marriages. The underlying rationale was that the application of long held concepts such as the *logos* was no longer viable in a society dominated by scientific modes of thought.

Simultaneously, one also reads articles that report that the third generation of Greek Americans feel affinity for neither the church nor their Greek heritage, nor do they identify strongly with folkloristic values. These authors suggest that the locus of identification for the younger generation has changed, that they have opted for class rather than religion or nationality as the locus of belonging. They have done this, runs the thesis, because they are far more psychologically secure in their Americanism than were prior generations. As a result, class and status have become the sine qua non of their identification.[10]

Some Greek Americans identify ethnically with a popular fare of music, dance, and food, only to have it demeaned as trivial by others who impose a hierarchy of values that alienates most of the population of Greek descent. Since a pecking order functions to affirm one's own worth in most societies, this need to rank groups from Brahmins to Untouchables should not strike us as too unusual. It is true that the cultural appurtenances that are deemed trivial are, in and of themselves, meaningless. Yet, in the collective sharing, they are transformed from something profane to something sacred by providing the esprit de corps so essential to a sense of belonging and community.

Clearly, ethnic identity is extremely difficult to pinpoint. The concept is a fluid one and changes along a continuum of such variables as generation, education, occupation, and class. For example, as we saw, the first generation of Greek immigrants who came to this country in the early part of this century viewed nationality and religion as part and parcel of their identity. For this reason, the church became the major vehicle through which the immigrants' world was protected. Language, religion, Old World customs, and endogamous marriages were the accepted indices of Greek identification.[11] Any deviation by their children constituted a threat to their security, self-image, traditional role, and well-being.

Their children, the second generation, experienced the parents' definition of ethnicity as a liability. Despite this, the Greek church, the Greek school, and the Greek language became integral parts of the self-image of these reluctant participants. They became the hyphenated Greek Americans bordering two worlds. The collision of these two worlds reversed the natural order of things, so that the children became the culture bearers and the social arbiters for their parents. Use of the English language, one of the most important indices used in measuring adjustment to American culture, was hampered by the fact that, for the second generation, Greek had to be spoken at home, albeit limited to a vocabulary dictated by the exigencies of day-to-day living. Ethnicity for this generation was still identified with language, tradition, and religion, but was modified in conjunction with the American ethos of success and upward mobility.

By the 1950s, a third generation of Greek Americans was emerging, and a new definition of ethnicity was in the wind. This new definition was articulated by social scientists who believed that ethnicity based upon nationality and language was gradually being replaced by religion in the lives of all Americans. They measured religiosity by a belief in God and attendance at religious services. Belonging to a religious institution was not only a new way of determining one's ethnicity, but also a legitimate way of being an American, because while one was expected to give up the ways of the Old World, one was never expected to give up one's religion. However, the three religions having institutional status were Protestantism, Catholicism, and Judaism.[12] Obviously, Greek Orthodoxy was excluded. What did this mean for the third generation of Greek Americans? Was being Greek different from being Greek Orthodox? Given the above thesis, it would seem not.

In the mid-1960s, we sampled seventy-one third-generation Greek Americans in the New York Metropolitan area and found that religion continued to provide the context of self-identification for them. Indeed, although identification with language and customs, and a preference for endogamous marriages persisted, it was with a marked ambivalence. For example, on the one hand, they wanted the church to substitute English in the sermon, but on the other hand, they did not want all Orthodox churches to merge into an American Orthodoxy.[13]

In a recent study of 160 first-, second-, and third-generation Greek Americans living in the New York City Metropolitan area, it was found that there was less Greek school attendance with each subsequent group; fewer of the third generation spoke Greek; and increased identification as Americans was noted among the youngest generation, as was a significant increase in the number who approved of non-Greek marriages as compared with the first and second generations.[14]

Further data derived from the study is given below. Respondents were asked to fill out a questionnaire, the first part of which was a personal data sheet on which subjects designated their age, sex, education, and other census information. The second part consisted of items measuring the rate of assimilation. Indices included language, church attendance, religious attitudes, identification with cultural values, and exogamy, all of which permitted the respondent to be placed in either of two categories: ethno-religious or ethno-cultural. The first reflected the ethnic identification associated with the first generation—religion, language, and nationalism; the second reflected a wider range of cultural values—Greek history, dance, music, cuisine, and social organizations.

The sample, fixed by circumstance, was drawn from several sources including religious and secular organizations. Of the 160 individuals, 46 percent were males and 54 percent females. The age groups represented were 13–22 years (N = 76), 23–45 years (N = 52), and 46–68 years (N = 32).

A significant index of assimilation is the declining use of the ethnic language. We found that erosion took place across the second and third generations. Of the second generation, 96.7 percent indicated they spoke Greek, whereas 57.8 percent of the third generation spoke Greek. Of those not speaking Greek, the second generation comprised 3.3 percent of the total, and the third generation 21.9 percent.

Should English replace Greek in church?   The individuals in the first generation unanimously responded in the negative. The second generation was divided, and the third generation was unanimous in wanting the sermons delivered in English. Both the second and third generations, however, demonstrated a more traditional response when asked if English should replace Greek in the Liturgy. Of the second generation, 58.3 percent preferred the Liturgy in Greek, and the third generation was divided. One explanation for their split attitude toward the sermon and the Liturgy may be that the latter represents the sacred, the transcendental aspect of the religious experience and does not require knowledge of the language, whereas the sermon represents the church's position on issues ranging from religious ones to secular.

Attendance at Greek school.   The Greek school has traditionally been a most important vehicle for transmitting ethnic identity. First-generation parents knew instinctively that their children would be quickly Americanized without supportive institutions to counteract it. Attendance at Greek school differed significantly between the second and third generations. Ninety percent of the second generation had attended, whereas 70.3 percent of the third generation did. The second generation had Greek classes every day, the third only once or twice a week.

Intermarriage. The ethnic background of one's friends is an indicator of prospective mates from which one will choose. The respondents were asked if they would marry someone who was not of Greek extraction. With each successive generation, there was a greater tendency toward marrying outside the group. Of the first generation, 51.6 percent reported that they would prefer to marry someone who was Greek, and 30 percent of the second generation expressed similar sentiments compared to 25 percent of the third generation.

Contact with Greek mass media. The question covering involvement with Greek mass media indicated a decline from the first to the third generations. Of the third generation, 55.2 percent said they had no contact, whereas 7.4 percent in the first generation reported a similar response.

Attendance at church. Respondents were asked if they attend church: (1) every Sunday, (2) every other Sunday, or (3) several times a year. Thirty-eight percent of the first generation, 61 percent of the second, and 65 percent of the third generation go to church at least every other Sunday. The second generation is inclined to go to church more often than the first generation. When education is kept constant, those in the first and second generation seem to attend church less frequently.

Clearly, religion continues to provide a measure of identity for many born in a pluralist society. The recent arrivals differ from the first generation pioneers in that they found an established Greek community and, therefore, did not have to fight for preservation of an ethnic self, at least not in religious terms. It was a given. The ties of the second generation to the church have their roots in a continuing identification with the world of their parents. Much of this has been transmitted to the third generation.

The church has taken the initiative in organizing activities, both secular and religious, for the young. Further, the pattern of church attendance is colored by the factor of age; the life cycle is a critical consideration in each generation.

Attitude toward the church. The respondents were asked to indicate their attitude toward the church, coded as follows: (1) strongly favorable to the church, (2) neutral, or (3) strongly against the church. The three generations were strongly favorable to the church or at least neutral. The second generation was significantly more favorably inclined toward the church. Only three individuals in the sample were strongly against the church: one from the first generation and two from the third generation.

The first-generation college graduates tended to be more critical of the church than their second generation counterparts. They were opposed, however, to the use of English in the church, did not support an American

Orthodoxy, and chose friends of similar ethnic background. Sixty-one percent indicated their friends were Greek, compared to 25.3 percent of the second generation and 14 percent of the third generation.

Ethnic identity. The respondents were asked to identify themselves as either: (1) Greek, (2) American, (3) Greek Orthodox, or (4) Greek American. The second and third generations tended to identify as either Greek American or Greek Orthodox, but a trend was discerned for the third generation to identify as American. The first generation identified as Greek or Greek Orthodox. A further inquiry was made as to whether there was a difference between being Greek and being Greek Orthodox. Fifty-eight percent of the first generation, 55 percent of the second, and 64 percent of the third feel there is a distinction. As for a merging of all Eastern Orthodox churches: the first generation was opposed, the second generation was divided, and the third generation was strongly opposed to a merger.

A final question dealt with impressions held of Greek people. The responses were coded as follows: (1) positive, (2) negative, or (3) indifferent. No generation held negative attitudes, although a hint of indifference was discerned in the response of the third generation.

Conclusions. The findings of this study showed that both U.S.-born and foreign-born Greeks in America have retained a relatively strong attachment to their ethnic background. It also indicated that the attainment of higher occupational status among the second generation did not result, as might be expected, in a denial of ethnic identity or an abandonment of the Greek community.

The first generation still remains strongly identified with an ethno-religious dimension, while the third generation showed a greater identification with the broader cultural values of the Greek American community. Confusion as to precisely what constitutes Greek ethnicity was reflected in the younger generation who, while they expected both the sermon and the Liturgy to be in English, were negative in their response to becoming part of an American Orthodox church that would unify all Eastern Orthodox churches in America.

A myriad of inconsistencies was revealed. Clearly, so much of ethnic identity is an unconscious as well as an ambivalent experience. The individual is reacting to judgments and responses of people within the group as well as those outside. Judgments, both positive and negative, can operate to pull the person toward or away from the group into which one was born. How these positive and negative forces are transmitted to the third generation vis-à-vis the second generation is something about which little is known.

The demographic imbalance between the old immigrants and the new immigrants has produced needs and demands that differ because of their respective vantage points. The Greek American community has been and will continue to be fractured by the different rates of adjustment each group makes to the surrounding environment. Therefore, it may be that Greek ethnicity can only be understood within a specific social context.

For the majority of new immigrants, identification is rooted in nationality and the church. If they do not find a Greek church, they build one. An unestimated number of Greek churches, not affiliated with the Greek Archdiocese of North and South America, have already been founded in the New York Metropolitan area. It should not be surprising that the recent arrivals from Greece expect a Hellenized church, thus repeating the pattern of earlier immigrants who sought continuity of experience and solidarity within the church. They view the introduction of English in the church as part of a conspiracy to "de-Hellenize" it. If the Greek language and Greek values are not the focal points of the established church, then other avenues for maintaining self-esteem and security will be sought as, indeed, they are. In time, the children of the new immigrants may react against the ethnic church their parents hold on to so tenaciously, and if so, a new ethnic identity may take form to be determined, in part, by the structure of the larger society.

The Melting Pot versus Culturalism Pluralism

There has been a plethora of literature and numerous approaches to the study of the ethnic component. Lacking an established, cohesive body of theory, each study deals with the many situational variables interacting in a given group by attempting to understand the direction these intergroup relations may take. For the most part, research has been guided by ideological assumptions, either of the melting pot variety or that of cultural pluralism.

Very briefly, the melting pot approach views the assimilation process as desirable and inevitable, that is, groups with diverse beliefs and behavior patterns become fused together in a common culture resulting from dominant-minority relations. Israel Zangwill, an exponent of this position and author of *The Melting Pot: Drama in Four Acts,* writes:

America is God's Crucible, the great Melting Pot where all the races of Europe are melting and reforming. Here you stand good folk, think I, when I see you at Ellis Island, here you stand, in your fifty groups, with your fifty languages and histories, and your fifty blood hatreds and rivalries. But you won't be long like that brothers, for these are the fires of God you come to—German and Frenchmen, Irishmen and English, Jews and Russians, into the Crucible with you all. God is making the American! The real American has not yet arrived. . . . He will be the fusion of all races, perhaps the coming superman. . . . Ah, what is the glory of Rome and Jerusalem, where all races and nations come to worship and look back, compared with the glory of America?[15]

Early sociologists believed that eventually all minority groups would pass through the evolutionary stages of contact, competition, accommodation, and finally assimilation. The ultimate assimilation of all ethnic groups, however, has been challenged by a number of writers. The sociologist Milton Gordon has made a useful distinction between "behavioral assimilation"—absorbing the cultural patterns of the dominant society—and "structural assimilation"—acceptance of the immigrant into the organizational, institutional, civic, and social life of the host society.[16] Gordon believes that assimilation in America has only taken place on the cultural level. In other words, acculturation without assimilation has taken place among ethnic groups. Do our studies of Greek communities bear this out?

Anderson, Indiana

In the mid-1960s, Anderson, Indiana, had a Greek community of approximately 125.[17] Utilizing the variables of exposure to American culture and the rate of assimilation among three generations, the researcher explores systematically the place of the Greeks in the structure or social order of the larger society. Assigning the criterion of nativity to generation, an investigation is made of seven institutional areas with regard to assimilation, that is, external participation in the larger social system, as compared with subjective feelings of becoming an American based upon internalization of new values.[18]

Anderson, Indiana, followed the traditional patterns of the Old World in establishing its community. It did not, however, succeed in building a Greek church in the city. The responsibility for this was placed upon the economically successful families of Anderson whose autocratic manner and leadership alienated the less prestigious members of the community. Ensuing disagreements over the location of the church and the economic burden it would entail for community members discouraged completion of any plans. The members continued to attend the Greek church in Indianapolis.

Over time, the second generation openly challenged the tactics and authoritarian rule of the leading families. Following the Second World War, a shift from community organization to disorganization took place. To be sure, the role of Greece in the Second World War enhanced the Greek sense of pride, but the changes wrought by the war experience and the changing economy tended to pull the community apart. Many who had become successful in a war economy no longer felt compelled to follow the once powerful families for leadership. They expressed their resentment by withdrawing from the social functions attended by these families and redefining the parameters of "significant others." In addition, the second generation had become disaffected by the chronic dissension they experienced as young members of the community. Their individual families of procreation became more important as a source of support and a base for ethnic celebrations and social interactions.

On the substructural level, the Greeks continued to be held together by close family ties, observance of religious holidays, and festive celebrations. Despite changes that took place after the war, the Greeks in Anderson continued to come together as a community, either for a wedding or in times of sorrow when their collective identity provided support for the grieving family.[19]

Whereas in many institutional areas, the relation of assimilation to generation was linear, it was nonlinear in some other areas such as the family and religion. Structural assimilation in the institutional areas of occupation, formal association, education, and language has been very rapid. To put it differently, we have a case of acculturation without assimilation. The core of identity continues to remain an ethnic one. If the third generation is more secure as Americans, the problem of belonging, nevertheless, remains a perennial one, and since the tie with family and religion has never been completely broken, it is within these contexts that the third generation of Anderson finds its ethnic identification and affiliation.

All three generations in Anderson present high structural assimilation in the institutional area of the economy. In addition, cultural assimilation has been equally high, thus internalization of both the ethos of business initiative and upward social mobility has taken place.

The first generation had its fraternal organizations as well as its regional chapter of the national organization of American Hellenic Educational Progressive Association (AHEPA). Following World War II, the second generation showed a growing indifference to Greek organizations. Part of this may reflect the lingering ambivalence toward the ethnic culture so characteristic of that generation; because members wanted to shed their marginality, they sought to lose as much of the evidence of foreign origin as they could shuffle off.[20] The third generation in Anderson seem less alienated, as judged by their presence in official positions of Greek organizations. An interest in things Greek was discerned in the third generation, a type of return to those communal activities that foster conviviality.[21] The third generation managed to get rid of the immigrant foreignness, the hopelessly double alienation of the generation that preceded it; it became American in a sense that had been impossible for the second generation.[22]

By the time of the second generation, the community's initial concern with the affairs of Greece had eroded. This decline of interest in Greek national politics indicates structural assimilation. Very few Greeks read Greek newspapers beyond the first generation. Both structural and cultural assimilation has been high. It is reported that the question of Cyprus in 1974 and the national claims of Greece were treated with indifference by the Greeks in Anderson. Not only was this so among the second and third generations, but many of the first generation shared this attitude. Their present political concerns involve only what is going on in the United States. Structural assimilation is indicated by the increased participation across three generations in American politics.

Between 1931 and 1939, the second generation received a Greek education in the afternoon schools. The third generation did not benefit from any systematic Greek education. Although an afternoon school did exist in Indianapolis, the extracurricular activities offered by the American school, as well as the inconvenience of getting to Indianapolis, left the third generation without training in Greek. As a result, language proficiency among them is practically nil. The unintended consequence of total exposure to the American school system facilitated structural assimilation. With each successive generation in Anderson, the pursuit of advanced education increased. Cultural assimilation took place with dire consequences for language maintenance.[23]

As we have mentioned, language is the most impressive indicator of assimilation. In Anderson, no third-generation member speaks Greek. People who were interviewed saw the importance of language to ethnic and religious preservation, but language interest showed a decreasing rate of concern through three generations.[24]

We can conclude that structural assimilation in the institutional area of the language has been complete. However, cultural assimilation has not been as complete since all three generations expressed a desire for the continuation of the teaching and use of Greek within the ethnic boundaries.

The Greeks of Anderson did not have their own church. The absence of an external symbol of spiritual unity worked against the establishment of a community that could engage itself in church activities like Philoptochos, the Greek Orthodox Youth of America, and so forth. In addition, the need to travel to Indianapolis curbed social interactions among the residents and opened the door to the assimilation process.

While many of the third generation attended Sunday school, they did so at the Episcopalian or Methodist churches. Indeed, many baptisms and other religious rites were performed in these churches by visiting Greek priests. Such exposure to other religious institutions obviously hastens both cultural and structural assimilation in that other faiths are viewed as viable alternatives. Some individuals interviewed saw the Protestant sects as status-enhancing and used them as vehicles for upward social mobility. Conversions, therefore, which were nonexistent in the first generation, occurred in the second and third.[25]

Moving from the first to the second generation, a change in attitude toward the church is seen. The first generation did not attend church ostensibly because of business schedules, and the second generation did not attend because of cynicism on matters of religion and a strong dissatisfaction with the long hours of the church service. The third generation showed a more positive attitude toward church participation. It is believed that the increasing adaptation of the Greek church to an American milieu has been responsible for this, that is, the introduction of English in the church, shortening the church service, introduction of large choirs, and the general appeal of the Eastern Orthodox ceremony to its congregants. These changes in the Greek church indicate the assimilationist trend of the church itself, both structurally and culturally.

We have noted the centrality of Greek family life both in Greece and in the United States. In Anderson, three basic types of Greek American families were identified. The first generation in which both spouses were foreign born was characterized by a patriarchal orientation, reciprocal obligations, and strong in-group solidarity resisting the forces of acculturation. The second generation consisted of two native-born parents or one who was born in America. The marginality of this generation resulted in continuing ambivalence to Greek and American cultural forces that created pressures of both an external and internal nature. In Anderson, some second-generation members sought a solution through complete abandonment of the Greek way of life; others overcompensated in their identification with Greek culture. In general, there was a decline in patriarchal control, increased mobility, less religiosity, and weakened solidarity within the community.

When both parents and offspring or one of the parents is American-born, a family type emerges that is typical of the families found in the larger American culture. To be sure, residues of Greek culture persist, but the move toward a more egalitarian and nuclear orientation point to an incline. Both cultural and structural assimilation have taken place over three generations of Greek family life.[26]

Third-generation members, while irrevocably American, continue to identify with the ethnic subculture, but not in a manner reminiscent of their grandparents nor in terms of the marginality that plagued their parents. Vestigial residues of both remain and provide them with a locus of identity and a sense of belonging in an American society that has come to accept the fact that ethnic worlds provide the boundaries within which the self is validated.

Intermarriage is one of the most significant indices of assimilation. Of forty-seven marriages in Anderson, 38 percent were with non-Greek spouses. Marriages of the third generation did not show any particular trend, although a general preference for marrying within the ethnic group was expressed across generations despite the fact that intermarriage has been on the increase.[27]

The factors responsible for rapid structural assimilation in Anderson are explained by the lack of any cohesive resistance to assimilation. The original settlers of the Greek community did not present a united front because of their political differences with regard to the old country; they disagreed over the jurisdiction of the Greek church in America; there was a lack of systematic reinforcement of Greek education among the second generation; a power struggle for leadership prevailed among contending affluent families; and, extremely important, the group never built a church in Anderson, making it necessary to travel to Indianapolis for church services, Sunday school, and afternoon Greek school. In addition, the absence of a community church limited social interaction and discouraged the development of church-based groups.

The Emerging Hybrid Culture

Over the years, socialization or secondary socialization led to a merging of both Greek and American cultural traits. The new Greek American culture is characterized by the persistence of rural speech, rural values, and customs that defy change and any transgressions. Visits to Greece, after extensive absences, highlight the changes that have taken place and present bewildering encounters between Greeks and Greek Americans, particularly in the urban areas. The years of social change have altered perceptions and expectations.

While hospitality, gregariousness, and family discipline form part of Greek life, America has contributed personal and business initiative, emphasis on punctuality, and a certain respect for individual merit to the Greek American's outlook. To some extent, a new Greek American language developed to interpret many of the things that the immigrants encountered and for which no word existed in their native rural villages. For example, *automobile* became *atmobily*, *bank* became *banka*, *basket* became *basketta*, *bill of fare* became *billoferry*, *carpet* became *carpeto*, and so on. Visitors to Greece complain that they often do not understand many Greek words spoken there. A woman who returned after fifty years told me, "I cannot understand what they're saying; they use words I never heard, but in the village I was able to have conversations more easily. After being there for a month, I was able to better understand them." Another said, "Their life is so different; their standards of cleanliness leave much to be desired, and they do very little; they talk, talk, talk—in America, we work." These remarks are not unusual in interviews with first-generation individuals. Memories of their youth may draw them to Greece, but years of acculturation in America highlight the sharp differences between the two sets of social perceptions.

Another aspect of the Greek American community has been the Anglicization of names, and although some may be changed without removing identification with ancestral origin, others change so as to pass. In Anderson, of forty-three different families, eleven retained their original Greek names and thirty-two Anglicized them.[28]

Moving from one culture to another involves, as we saw, a conflict among generations; another is the conflict within the individual who is torn between incompatible cultural goals and undergoes severe personality stress in trying to reconcile them. In the generational conflict, resistance may be tantamount merely to stubbornness, in which case, the first generation refuses to accept more than the bare minimum of American culture required for survival.

In Anderson, the personality maladjustment of the marginal second generation was handled in a variety of ways: the individual could conform to values of both cultures and be assimilated in the larger community, yet without rejecting ethnic ties and identification; the individual could refuse to be part of the Greek community but still be considered by others and himself as Greek; or the individual could give up contact with the Greek community altogether, holding the Greeks in disdain and rejecting ethnic distinctiveness. The cosmopolitan Greek American intellectualizes the problems of the community and, in so doing, functions as an important agent in transmitting the ethnic cultural configuration to the ethnic community and to the larger society.

Therefore, a major contribution that Anderson, Indiana, made to the study of assimilation was the idea that where factionalism and conflict exist, assimilation tends to be rapid.[29] The rate of assimilation cannot be explained in terms of any one variable such as education or intermarriage. The configuration of variables themselves must be analyzed as well as the various institutional areas within which assimilation takes place at varying rates. The categories of cultural and structural assimilation facilitate a systematic approach to the study of ethnic group assimilation, but it is deceptively tidy in that both, in reality, are simultaneously interacting and blur the points at which one begins and the other ends. As demonstrated, what has evolved from the assimilation process is a Greek American culture, a hybrid of two cultures providing a new basis for ethnic belonging.

Houston, Texas

In a study of the Greek community of Houston, Texas, in the mid-1970s, the focus was on the social boundaries of ethnicity rather than on generational changes and the perception of Greekness over time.[30] The concept of social boundaries, introduced by ethnographer Fredrik Barth, states that:

. . . the ethnic boundary defines the group, not the cultural stuff that it encloses. The boundaries to which we must give our attention are, of course, social boundaries, though they may have territorial counterparts. If a group maintains its identity when members interact with others, this entails criteria for determining membership and ways of signalling membership and exclusion.[31]

The writer proceeds to explore the role of *active* membership in the community, that is, those Greeks who provide the means for the continuing existence of Greeks as a viable ethnic force. The central question raised in the study was, "What are the criteria that signal membership in the Greek American community, what elements constitute its ethnic boundaries?"

The Greek population of Houston is estimated to be about 2,500 to 3,000, much less than 1 percent of the city's total population. They are uniformly middle and upper middle class and are dispersed throughout the residential area of the city. Greek Towns were never established around Houston. The host culture has not shown prejudice or practiced discrimination against members of the Greek community. Therefore, attachment of the Greek to his ethnic background is regarded as voluntary rather than a result of exclusionary patterns practiced by the non-Greek community.[32]

While the study was not primarily concerned with generational shifts in ethnic traits, the research findings disclose that the Greek language is becoming a less important aspect of Greek American life among second- and third-generation members. However, Greek organizations—religious, recreational, educational, and cultural—continue to provide an exclusively Greek world. Boundary maintenance is determined most importantly by religion, a religion that is based upon ethnicity. Converts are not regarded as "real" Greeks by other Greeks. Non-Greek women who marry Greeks attest to the fact that conversion, involvement in activities of the ethnic community, and in some instances, acquiring knowledge of the language does not make them bona fide group members. The result is exclusion, an exclusion based upon the fact that they were not born Greek. The investigator views the significance that community members place upon "Greek blood" as threatening to continuity of the group. Given the increase of intermarriages, blood, it would seem, must yield to other aspects that make up the social boundaries of Greekness, that is, social, cultural, and religious aspects.[33]

The boundaries that are maintained to keep the Greeks separate from other groups include strong family ties; the festive aspects of Greekness, such as Greek foods, music and dance; and the "community rules" of performance, especially as regards propriety and success, which tend to be somewhat different from those found in non-Greek groups. A certain propriety is expected, that is, the individual must behave in certain prescribed ways concerning deportment, conversation, appearance, and so on. For example, concern over what others will think remains effective as a group sanction. Respectability is measured by a successful job, material accoutrements, appearance, and one's contribution to the Greek community. Approval from one's parents is of paramount importance and extends to the larger Greek community. Deviations occur, but not without exacting their toll in shame and guilt. The object is to avoid making the parents look *bad* in the eyes of the community. It is not the intrinsic worth of the individual that has primacy but the person's success or appearance of it, and the way in which one achieves it is less important than its relevance for the community. Reluctance to comply with group expectations results in withdrawal of approval, loss of parental love, and threat of ostracism.[34]

There is also a persistent feeling of superiority in being Greek. Individuals expressed an ideology of differentness, based to a large extent on being born into a heritage and a religion that is something special.[35] Therefore, marrying a *xeni* ("outsider") immediately places the spouse outside the pale of Greekness, even though the spouse may contribute more to maintaining the Greek ethnic boundaries than many who are born Greek.

The most salient feature of ethnic boundaries is the Greek Orthodox church, which reinforces a group cohesiveness and segregation. It is the strongest and most clearly defining of the social boundaries that separate the Greek American from the non-Greek.

Bergenfield, New Jersey

In another study of an ethnically mixed Orthodox church in Bergenfield, New Jersey, it was found that the parish of St. Anthony was composed of Greeks (45 percent), Syrians, Slavs, and converts. The parish was organized over twenty years ago by a small group of Greek and Syrian families who wanted an English-speaking Orthodox church. The most significant element determining social boundaries for this group was that of Orthodoxy, not Greek Orthodoxy. In assessing the ethnic factor with regard to the Greek language, involvement in Greek organizations, and Greek culture, music, and cuisine, it was found that the use of the Greek language, as might be expected, decreased with each successive age group. All those aged forty to sixty could speak Greek as compared with 20 percent of the teenagers. None of the sample (N = 67) belonged to Greek organizations. Intermarriages were inclined to increase with each successive generation.

Although ethnic parishes stress the traditional indices of Greekness, St. Anthony's concentrated her educational efforts solely upon Orthodoxy. The point was made that in Greek parishes the members who were most active in the church were the ones strongly attached to their Greek identity. However, St. Anthony's Greek parishioners showed no such correlation. There appeared to be no difference in church attendance or involvement in the church between those who identified strongly with being Greek and those who did not. The idea that perpetuation of Greek culture and identity were necessary reinforcements to Orthodoxy was not supported by this research. The social boundary established for community maintenance was commitment to Orthodoxy, although a Greek ethnic identity continued to play an important role in the lives of first and even second generations.[36]

As research moves from an earlier to a more recent context, the whole problem of how ethnicity is to be determined becomes more confounding. Ideological differences between generations begin to overlap, and ethnic institutions themselves act and react to social changes both within and beyond its boundaries; it is to these institutions that we now turn.

Chapter Four

Ethnicity: Evolutionary Change

The Church

Community studies reveal a growing dichotomy between nationalism and religion, a dichotomy unknown to the first-generation settlers in this country. As we have seen, the Greek church grew out of the immigrant experience; it was organized by immigrants and sustained by their collective needs. Each colony of Greeks formed a *kinotitos*, or community, comprised of a *symvoulion*, or a board of directors, whose function was to raise money to build a Greek Orthodox church.

The earliest church in the New World was founded in 1864 in New Orleans by merchants representing commercial firms owned by Greeks in Greece. When the merchants liquidated their commercial interests in the southern states, the New Orleans church passed into the hands of the remaining Greeks, Syrians, and Slavs who used it as a common place of worship.[1] Established later were Holy Trinity Church in New York, 1892, Annunciation Church in Chicago, 1893, and Holy Trinity Church in Boston, 1903. By 1923, there were about 140 Greek churches in the United States.[2]

Each church was part of a self-governing community which was recognized as a legal entity by the state in which it was located. The church building, in turn, belonged to each governing community.[3] The kinotitos wielded a great deal of power; the hiring and firing of the clergy, for example, was in their hands. Generally, a priest would be sought through the patriarch of Constantinople, the Church of Greece, or from among themselves. Needless to say, disagreements were frequent among members of a board with regard to a priest's qualifications, his personality, or his political orientation toward the Old World.

The absence of any centralized authority left decision making in the hands of the boards, and although theoretically they conformed to a democratic pattern, personality clashes and ideological differences proved disruptive. It became clear that a central authority would have to be recognized if institutional legitimacy was to be established. There were some attempts to consolidate the Greek church with other Eastern churches into an American Orthodoxy, but this did not materialize—the church seemed inextricably intertwined with its role as transmitter of the Greek heritage. Moreover, a single autonomous church was perennially challenged by other Orthodox leaders.[4]

The Greek immigrants came from the ecclesiastical jurisdiction of the church in Greece; they were part of the diaspora, which was under the control of the ecumenical patriarch of Constantinople (Istanbul). Russian Orthodoxy, having come to this country in the eighteenth century, wanted the patriarchate to transfer its jurisdiction over the Orthodox in America to the Church of Russia.

A word about the administrative structure of the Eastern Orthodox church is in order. It is composed of many autonomous churches which include the churches of Constantinople, Antioch, Serbia, Rumania, Georgia, Russia, and Greece. As self-governing churches, they are not held together by either a single prelate or a centralized organization. There is, in Orthodoxy, no one with an equivalent position to the pope of the Roman Catholic church. The patriarch of Constantinople enjoys a position of special honor among all Orthodox communities, but he does not have the right to interfere in their internal affairs.[5]

In an attempt to bring unity to the church in America, the ecumenical (universal) patriarchate transferred its jurisdiction to the Church of Greece which exercised theoretical, if not actual, control over it from 1908 to 1922.[6] Meanwhile, the Church of Greece became embroiled in a political struggle between the Royalist and Venizelist factions which persisted from 1915 to the 1930s. At this juncture, a brief historical recapitulation may prove useful.

Conflict between King Constantine and Venizelos of the Liberal faction flared after the outbreak of the First World War, the latter favoring the Allied cause which the pro-German king opposed. Venizelos was forced to resign in 1915, only to return and then to resign again. This pattern of intermittent leadership continued when he became premier for the third time in 1917, only to have the king restored to the throne in 1920. In 1922, Venizelos again regained leadership but retired from that office in the same year. In 1924, he returned to power again. Between 1924 to 1928, political chaos continued to reign, and yet again, in 1932, growing Royalist opposition forces caused Venizelos to resign. Fearing the restoration of the monarchy, he made a last attempt to stem the Royalist tide by organizing uprisings in 1935. The rebellion was soon put down by the army and Venizelos fled to France where he died shortly after. These political struggles were transposed to the United States.

The Greek communities identified with the bitter struggles of Greece which ignited conflict and hostilities, ravaging entire communities. The atomistic nature of community life, however, threatened the very ethnic survival they wished to maintain and for which they worked so valiantly. The ethnocentrism that characterized the immigrants made it impossible for them to take a broader look at the issues confronting them and the growing number of second-generation Greek Americans.

Since the church was the focal point of community life, its stability was imperative. In order to function effectively and survive, certain basic needs had to be met and certain problems identified and solved. In any organization, these functional requirements tend to be located in the social relationships that comprise the group to which individuals are linked by virtue of a common interest. It was precisely this broader range of commonality that eluded both church and community leaders during those pioneer years.

Meanwhile, the Church of Greece, realizing that it ran the risk of losing the Greeks of the diaspora, saw the need for uniting the fractured communities of this country. In 1918, therefore, Metropolitan (an ancient Orthodox designation for bishops of major cities holding important positions) Metaxakis, archbishop of Athens, visited America with the purpose of taking constructive measures toward solving the administrative problems of the Greek church in America. However, politics being what they were in Greece, the archbishop, who was supportive of Venizelos, was deposed when the king came to power. He, in turn, appointed an archbishop with Royalist leanings. Unwilling to comply with the decision of the Holy Synod of Greece in their appointment, Metaxakis returned to the United States and assumed what he regarded to be his rightful responsibility—to administer the Greek churches in this country. Needless to say, the Church of Greece was not about to countenance this rebellious act and sent its own bishop to America with the purpose of recruiting support for the Royalist position. And so the push and pull of disputed power was set in motion in America.

In 1921, Metaxakis organized the diverse communities by calling together the first clergy-laity conference and establishing the Greek Archdiocese of North and South America under statutes of the state of New York. Quite unexpectedly, at this juncture, he was selected to be patriarch of Constantinople. Once this was accomplished, he immediately transferred the jurisdiction of the Greek church in America to that of Constantinople.

The patriarchate's next act was to appoint Archbishop Alexander Rodostolou, an ardent Venizelist, to be the first archbishop to serve in the United States. As expected, the Royalists opposed his appointment vociferously. At the same time, they also objected to the transfer of the church's jurisdiction to Constantinople. The new archbishop was confronted not only with a hostile community but with opposing rival bishops for leadership. One such rival was Archbishop Vasilios, a Royalist, who fought an aggressive battle to win the support of the Royalists of the Greek American community. Archbishop Alexander's tenure was marked by chaos. One writer notes:

> Unfortunately the eight years reign of Archbishop Alexander was literally a nightmare. During this interval our churches and communities had become divided battlegrounds in which Venizelists and Royalists used physical violence even within the sanctuary of the Holy Altar. Police were stationed at strategic positions within some of our churches to actually prevent bloodshed.[7]

The church, it should be remembered, has historically been the leader of its faithful in matters both religious and secular; under Islamic rule, it was the Patriarch Germanos of Patras who sanctioned the struggle against the Turks in 1821 by raising the banner of revolution. It is through this religiopolitical lens that clerical behavior in the United States during this period must be viewed.

By the 1930s, the communities in America were divided in their loyalties; most were followers of Archbishop Alexander while others supported the rival Bishop Vasilios. The communities were demoralized and confused; their extinction seemed imminent. At this time, the Church of Greece, the patriarch, and the Greek government saw clearly that Hellenism would be destroyed in the New World if consensus was not reached immediately. In 1930, therefore, it was agreed that an emissary be sent to deal with a seemingly hopeless situation so that the Greeks of the diaspora would not be lost to them.

In May 1930, therefore, the metropolitan of Corinth, Damaskinos, was dispatched to this country on a mission of peace. His first step was to silence the embattled bishops by having them reassigned to Greece and to select the metropolitan of Corfu, Athenagoras, as the second archbishop to the United States. Meanwhile, the warring factions of Royalists and Venizelists continued their disputes unabated. The difficulties confronting the new archbishop were formidable. During his long tenure (1931 to

1948) as head of the church in America, a period of constructive church organization took place.

It would be a misstatement to say that his reign was without opposition. Certain of his administrative reforms ran counter to community leadership, and local power was to a large extent usurped. But despite objections, Athenagoras enforced uniform by-laws in all parishes and appropriated the right to regularize the discipline and selection of the clergy, thus divesting the local boards of this power. He further placed the bishops under his authority, thereby curtailing the independent dioceses of the bishops. In addition, he imposed membership dues in order to regularize the archdiocese's revenues. Both laity and clergy objected strenuously to these changes, the latter feeling that better trained priests might replace them. Indeed, some felt so threatened that they would not permit the archbishop to officiate in their churches, treating them as their personal property.[8]

While these innovative changes were taking place, Christopher Kontogeorge, a priest of Lowell, Massachusetts, proclaimed himself archbishop of America. For fifteen years, he and his followers challenged the authority of Athenagoras—a challenge that resulted in countless court battles. Kontogeorge died in 1950, and the struggle for decentralization was finally put to rest.

Despite obstacles, Archbishop Athenagoras continued to unite the Greek Orthodox communities under a centralized archdiocese; he diplomatically pacified the political factions; recognizing the need for a native-born American educated clergy, he established the Theological School of the Holy Cross in 1937; he founded an orphanage (the Academy of St. Basil) and a school for the training of teachers for the afternoon language schools. In addition, he organized the Philoptochos Society in nearly every community, thus bringing women officially into the structure of the church.

Although initially the archbishop's presence in this country was met with resistance and apprehension by many, several factors facilitated his eventual acceptance: the political climate of Greece had become less turbulent, the native-born Greeks found the politics of the Old World irrelevant, their parents were beginning to view their adopted country as their permanent home, and their concern with the future of their own nuclear families created an atmosphere conducive to the archbishop's reforms. His tenure ended in 1949 when he was selected to be ecumenical patriarch of Constantinople.

With the stabilization of the church as an institution, another era began with the arrival of Archbishop Michael on December 1, 1949. The new primate continued to build upon the foundation that had been laid. He strengthened the Greek Archdiocese's revenue by increasing the annual contributions of church members, and he founded the Greek Orthodox Youth of America (GOYA), an organization intended to bring the young under the aegis of the church. He also promoted a campaign for national recognition of Eastern Orthodoxy as a major faith in America, created an Archdiocesan Office of Information and Public Relations, and secured acceptance of the Regulation and Uniform Parish By-Laws of the archdiocese by almost all the Greek Orthodox communities under its jurisdiction. The primate also gained membership for the Greek Orthodox church of America in the National Council of Churches and the United States Conference for the World Council of Churches. Mindful of the inevitable problems of an aging community, he established a home for the aged, in Yonkers, New York.

The archbishop was a scholar and a linguist who enhanced the prestige of Orthodoxy among Americans and strengthened the effectiveness of the Greek archdiocese. The structural and cultural assimilation of the church was evidenced when he was invited by the president of the United States to deliver an invocation as the leader of the Greek Orthodox church in America in January 1957.[9]

After the death of Archbishop Michael on July 13, 1958, the former Metropolitan (James) Iakovos of Melita was elected archbishop on April 1, 1959. At the time, he was serving as the representative of the ecumenical and other Greek Orthodox patriarchates in the headquarters of the World Council of Churches in Geneva, Switzerland. As exarch of the ecumenical patriarch, Iakovos had been a strong proponent for ecumenical unity and had served as president of the World Council of Churches. Over the years, his leadership was recognized by invitations extended to him to give one of the prayers at President John F. Kennedy's inauguration, President Johnson's inauguration, and both of President Nixon's inaugurations.

On the administrative level, he has created a New Laity Department of the Greek archdiocese, established an Orthodox Liaison Office of Interchurch Relations, strengthened the church's educational system, and expanded the organization of Greek Orthodox Youth of America. He also founded the archdiocese camp in Greece, Ionian Village, where the young, and adults as well, learn of their personal faith and their heritage in the land of their ancestors.

Under his guidance, Holy Cross Seminary was reorganized in Brookline, Massachusetts, and brought up to standard for full accreditation by the Association of Theological Schools in the United States and Canada. Archbishop Iakovos initiated plans for Hellenic College, an undergraduate school accredited by the Association of Colleges and Universities in New England which functions in connection with Holy Cross. An educational center for the training of church lay professionals seemed, from an early date, an imperative for the archdiocese's training of its own priests and bishops in America.

Concerned with closer cooperation within Orthodoxy, he has been instrumental in organizing meetings of the Eastern Orthodox bishops, which resulted in the establishment of a permanent body known as the Standing Conference of Canonical Orthodox Bishops in the Americas, with the purpose of effecting closer cooperation and understanding among Orthodox groups and other denominations.

In 1978, a process of decentralization was initiated by His Eminence conferring upon the bishops full episcopal authority over their respective dioceses, thus replacing the diocesan districts with auxiliary bishops, formerly under his authority.

More recently, a Communications Commission of the Greek Orthodox archdiocese was formed to serve as a "think tank" in the communications field. Its purpose is to give direction to the newly established Archdiocesan Department of Communications whose function is to "shape and convey the Church's image in the Americas."[10]

In the area of human rights, the archbishop actively involved himself with the civil rights movement in the 1960s and was especially supportive of the late Dr. Martin Luther King, Jr., with whom he marched in protest against racial segregation in Selma, Alabama. In recognition of his humanitarian concerns, Archbishop Iakovos was honored with a Medal of Freedom from President Carter, who said in his presentation,

His life is one which has been dedicated to the broadest possible realm of basic civil rights, basic human rights, not just in this country, but throughout the world.[11]

Each religious leader faced varied social and psychological exigencies in trying to reconcile the ethnic church within an American milieu. The transition from a homogeneous immigrant group to a more heterogeneous one compounded the problems of the church. The formation of the church, as an objective structure composed of different organizational units, symbolized and maintained a pattern of Greek religious life; this is the function of any religious institution.

In writing on the subject of the organizational viability of the church, the Reverend Dr. Nicon Patrinacos lauds the success with which the church was led from institutional disorganization to organization. For, in the process, it provided support and solidarity for the immigrant and a locus of religious identity for their progeny. However, he adds, the church has become overconcerned with organizational efficiency at the expense of its primary function, "of bringing Christ to the lives of the people they shepherd."[12] The failure to translate Orthodox precepts into an intelligible guide for the individual making moral decisions has left the Orthodox spiritually impoverished, he argues. The goal of Orthodoxy should be none other than the strengthening of a religion based upon "personal strength." Whereas a group-oriented religion may have been functional for the immigrant and a source of guidance in the past, it becomes dysfunctional when subjected to the vagaries of a pluralist society.

Historically, Greek Orthodoxy was so firmly entrenched in the lives of its people that it was taken for granted. Lee's observation is instructive:

> Religion is so firmly entrenched and unquestioned that it can be taken with casualness and a lack of self-conscious effort. One talks about the Masses and the preparation for litanies, but not about religion. Religion is not a personal matter, nor is it a guide to conduct. . . . Young men do not talk about the meaning of Christ in their lives nor do young girls dream of entering a convent.[13]

This taken-for-granted attitude no longer pertains in a pluralist society where other religions and ideologies compete for one's loyalty. Indeed, modernity gives way to questions about the adequacy of religious beliefs acquired from tradition. In writing about the social construction of religious reality, sociologist Peter Berger notes:

> The typical premodern society creates conditions under which religion has, for the individual, the quality of objective certainty; modern society, by contrast, undermines this certainty, deobjectivates it by robbing it of its taken-for-granted status, *ipso facto* subjectivizes religion. And this change, of course, is directly related to the transition from fate to choice.[14]

The role of choice in the lives of contemporary believers and nonbelievers was empirically demonstrated in a Gallup survey undertaken by the Greek Orthodox archdiocese of North and South America in an effort to ascertain the religious belief, practices, and attitudes of the Greek American community toward a number of moral issues in the hope that the church could better augment its efforts to enrich the spiritual lives of its people. The Gallup organization found that "the young are searching for spiritual moorings" and are highly susceptible to the influence of other religious groups. When asked, "Have you ever been approached or spiritually influenced by other religious groups?" 36 percent said they were approached and 11 percent reported that they were influenced.[15]

When asked, "Do you feel that experimentation in occult activities such as astrology and fortune telling conflict with your faith?" 28 percent answered in the affirmative, 44 percent in the negative, and 28 percent had no opinion.[16] The researchers suggested steps toward clarifying the tenets of Orthodoxy as a way of strengthening personal religious growth. Concrete efforts in promoting religious education, encouraging retreats, providing counseling, and other endeavors have been underway in an effort to counteract the pressures of an anomic society.[17]

The suggestion of an "inner gyroscope" that would provide a mooring for individuals of Greek descent is an interesting one and illustrates the inroads that both structural and cultural assimilation have made in the church. It is well to remember that Orthodoxy has never undergone a Reformation, so that emphasis upon the individual person as against the corporate body never took hold. This point is aptly made by the theologian Georges Florovsky:

> The corporate worship of the Church plays a far larger part in his religious experience than in that of the average Western Christian. . . . Nobody is a Christian by himself, but only as a member of the body.[18]

In Protestantism, the Scriptures became the touchstone of Christianity, and the individual had to judge for himself. One sociologist observes:

> . . . the emphasis was not on the preservation of a tradition of values common to the members of the community, even to all Christians, but on the safeguarding of the freedom of conscience of the individual in his differences from others.[19]

Like Protestantism, Orthodoxy believes that the Christian church is a Scriptural church, but "it is the church alone which can interpret Holy Scripture with authority."[20] Further, "it must not be regarded as something set up *over* the Church, but something that lives and is understood *within* the Church; that is why one should not separate Scripture and

Tradition."[21] The contrast between Protestantism and Orthodoxy in its perception of the individual is dramatic; therefore, the incursion of subjective religion is bound to create tensions and strains within Orthodoxy.

The religious boundaries of Orthodoxy have not developed the flexibility to accommodate different rates of assimilation of its members. Unlike Judaism, it has had no Hassidic, Conservative, Reform, or Reconstructionist movement that would permit diverse expressions of Orthodoxy without loss of a religioethnic identity. For the Greek Orthodox, a polarity is imposed between "believer" and "nonbeliever." It must be understood that the very word *orthodoxy* by definition has historically precluded diversity, for it carries the double meaning of "right belief" and "right glory" (or "right worship"). This unity of resistance to change has had the advantage of maintaining the church when survival, under Ottoman rule, was its only goal. Theologian Timothy Ware has written the following:

> The Orthodox, therefore, make what may seem at first a surprising claim, they regard their Church as the Church which guards and teaches the true belief about God and which glorifies Him with "right worship.". . . The fundamental approach to Orthodoxy is a liturgical approach, which understands the doctrine in the context of divine worship; it is no coincidence that the word Orthodoxy should signify alike "right belief" and "right worship" for the two things are inseparable.[22]

A burgeoning problem for religious leaders is the role of ethnicity and its place in the life of the church. There is danger, writes Ware, "that excessive nationalism will alienate the younger generation of Orthodox from the church."[23]

The former dean of the Holy Cross School of Theology perceives the church as having a dual responsibility:

> Our faith, our worship, our sacramental experience creates a circle which binds us together . . . and as members of parishes we also share in another distinctive characteristic—our Hellenic heritage. . . . As a people we affirm our heritage. We do it with our language, our literature, our thought, our food, our music, and our dances. We do it with our hospitality, our patriotic feelings, our sense of kinship. We do it with our philotimo—our sense of self-respect and honor. . . . Our distinctiveness is above all a . . . distinctiveness of faith and belief in practice. There is a special sense of history and destiny for those who call themselves Greek.[24]

Critics of this dual-role approach find it untenable in the light of the language shift taking place along the generational continuum. For many, the preservation of language seems to have primacy over that of Orthodoxy; for others, a compromise solution is often sought through a bilingual church service that ostensibly provides for both a religious and an ethnic community.

Conversations with church leaders on the West Coast reveal an attitude favorable to an American Orthodoxy. Stressing "Orthodoxy" rather than "Greek," the following was volunteered:

> We need a return to Apostolic and pristine teachings, which means a return to Christ. Ethnicity is not important, social class is not important, occupational status is not important—only religious belief is important. The church is not a social center, it is a religious center. The only concern of the church should be religion. . . .
>
> We need to use English in the church service; but we need more than that, we need a focus on spirituality. We need an American Orthodoxy. It is the scriptures to which we should give our attention; to be a good Christian the Scripture must be our focus and not the priest.[25]

A lay member of the local church took issue with this point of view and dismissed it as "fanatic fundamentalism."[26]

Language

It is clear that language has functioned as one of the most significant symbols of ethnic continuity; it is the symbol around which groups construct their social organizations and preserve their uniqueness. The findings of the Gallup survey in regard to the use of the Greek or English language in worship services disclosed that "while church members are opposed to greater emphasis on the use of Greek, the Greek American group is fairly evenly divided in its views on the matter. As might be expected, persons in homes where some Greek is spoken are more than twice as likely to favor a greater emphasis on Greek as are persons in homes where only English is spoken."[27] Sixty-one percent of the less active members of the church preferred less emphasis on the Greek language compared to 17 percent of the more active church members. Seventy-two percent of the category opting for less Greek spoke only English at home, as compared with 14 percent of those preferring the use of the Greek language in church services.[28]

The decline in language maintenance removes a major obstacle to the unification of all Orthodox churches; for while language and a unique set of cultural values continue to make the Greek church distinct from the Syrian, Ukrainian, and Russian Orthodox churches, in matters of theological doctrine there is unity. The Gallup organization found in their research that 79 percent of Greek Americans would like to see closer relations between the Orthodox churches. Of that population, 83 percent reported English as the only language spoken at home. The same question was asked with regard to the Greek Orthodox church and the Catholic church, to which 62 percent responded favorably. When queried about closer relations with Protestants, 47 percent answered positively. When the same question was applied to Judaism, 30 percent favored closer relations with the Jews.[29]

In an interview commemorating his twentieth anniversary as primate of the Greek Orthodox church in the Americas, Archbishop Iakovos said that he was not as optimistic about further closeness with the million-member Orthodox church in America, which has accepted autocephaly—a total independence from the state-dominated church in Russia. The Greek church, which considers itself autonomous in terms of its ties to Istanbul, is not comfortable with the concept of one Orthodox church based in the United States.[30]

The primate, who is known as the leading exponent of Orthodoxy in this country and also as an authoritative spokesman for the ecumenical movement for Christian unity, believes that its aim is not to create one church or superchurch, but to unite the minds and hearts of all Christians.

In another context, the archbishop said this:

We have no intention, whatsoever, of abandoning the Greek language because most of the liturgical parts and the Sacrament are offered in Greek. Nevertheless, some parts of the Divine Liturgy and Sacraments, as well as of the teaching of the Church, are offered in English. But this, again, is dictated by the sense of our responsibility toward the Church membership, not because we would like to impose the English language upon anyone.[31]

The Liturgy of the church is conducted in the Greek of the New Testament and Byzantine times, not modern Greek; consequently, knowledge of it is limited to very few. Nevertheless, for many, it carries an attachment without which ethnicity seems barren. Speaking of the use of English in the church service, one woman contended that "the parishion-

ers do not want to be de-Hellenized; without a Greek liturgy," she asked,
"why bother going to a Greek church?"

One may gain insight into the nature of the language controversy
through letters written to the *Orthodox Observer,* the newspaper of the
Greek archdiocese.

> I agree that a certain amount of Greek contributes beauty and mysticism to
> the Liturgy, but English is also needed for the Liturgy to be an intelligent and
> meaningful vehicle of worship. Those who deny this are placing esthetics and
> Greek identity above Christ.
>
> The Liturgy should be the central act of worship, the focal point of parish life.
> But it's not. . . . The Liturgy has evolved into a ceremonial formality, with
> emphasis on theatrics rather than on spiritual nourishment. . . .
>
> Until more English is included in our Liturgy and Holy Week services, we
> will remain a religiously static institution, a Byzantine museum, a Greek social
> club, but not a really Christian church.[32]

Another expressed the following view:

> This letter is an appeal to stop printing letters from disgruntled Americans of
> Greek descent who are seeking banishment of the Greek language in our
> churches. . . .
>
> The Greek Orthodox religion is based on two principles: Holy Bible and
> tradition. I am shocked to read from people born and raised in this country who
> are so naive as to believe that by abolishing the Greek language we will somehow
> miraculously fill our churches with the youth.[33]

Another letter reads:

> In your issue of January 30, two letters held the position that it is time to have
> our church services in the American language and that adherence to our Hellenic
> language has adversely affected the spreading of the Gospel of Christ. . . .
>
> In my local church there are members who do not understand Greek; some are
> of Greek ancestry and some of non-Greek extraction. Yet, they welcome the
> perpetuation of the Hellenic language and state emphatically that with the help
> of all the aids we have in the American language one can follow every phase of
> the liturgy, and because the sermon is delivered in English they are adequately
> informed of our Lord's teachings.[34]

Disparate views also exist among those who support the use of English
in the sermon but not in the Divine Liturgy. Characteristic responses of a
sample of college students drawn from the New York Metropolitan area
included the following:

It's inspiring to hear the Liturgy in Greek. I would hate to have English replace it. In English the Liturgy would sound so ordinary, so commonplace. The Greek language adds something to the service. There's fascination in not understanding completely. It's mystical when it's in Greek.

I wouldn't like to see English replace Greek in the Liturgy; it would be like a Unitarian church.

No, I would never want Greek replaced in the Liturgy. The Greek language is what links all Greeks together. If we take it away, we remove one of the most vital characteristics; it's what makes us Greek.[35]

A second-generation woman, overhearing a respondent's support of Greek in the Liturgy, quipped:

For years we've been trying to get English used in the church, and now you young ones want Greek. I don't get it.[36]

She did not perceive that the Greek language no longer carried the stigma of inferiority as it did for her in her youth. The younger Greek Americans have, of course, less opportunity to feel "different," because their parents speak English, but the church has also changed in that it has become the organ through which differences, in a pluralist society, are legitimated.

Attitudes also differed with regard to the sermon. The consensus was that the sermon should provide moral and ethical leadership. The separation of the sacred and the profane in the church experience was reflected in the following statement.

It's inspiring to hear the Liturgy in Greek. English is too everyday. I see the Liturgy as a form of art. It's like looking at a painting, it's aesthetically enriching.[37]

Even when linguistic skills are absent, the Liturgy, as an experience of mystification, is undoubtedly efficacious in providing a sense of group cohesion and individual belonging. The inconsistency regarding language preference in different contexts becomes clearer when language is viewed from two perspectives—its communicative aspect and its symbolic aspect. Although obviously they may coexist, the progression of language shift in the United States highlights the role of the symbolic function of language as a unifying force.[38] Indeed, the persistence of language loyalty in the absence of functional utility can be interpreted as a positive attitude toward one's ancestral heritage.[39] Even grandparents lose the fluency they once had, and their children, in turn, forget the language they learned at home and in the ethnic schools.[40] It is rare for functional bilingualism to extend beyond the second generation; with few exceptions, members of the third generation do not use the ethnic tongue in conversation with their own parents, even when they are capable of doing so.[41]

The Greek Orthodox archdiocese continues to stress language as an indispensable link to ethnic continuity through its Department of Education and its implementation of programs in the community schools. The primate of the Greek Orthodox church has reiterated annually the promise he made in an encyclical letter of January 4, 1967, to the effect that "the Archdiocese has supported and cultivated and will continue to support and cultivate, for as long as it does exist, the Greek letters as an educational preparation and introduction to the spirit, tradition, and handing down of Orthodoxy."[42]

For the purpose of teaching the Greek language and Greek cultural history, several types of schools—afternoon schools, Greek American day schools, kindergarten schools, and classes for adults—have been implemented to meet the varying needs of different communities. The total enrollment as of October 1, 1982, in 21 Greek-American day schools and 416 afternoon schools was 38,771. Thirteen of the day schools are in the Greater New York area.[43] Two high schools are located in Astoria and Jamaica, New York. The number of full-time and part-time teachers is 1,160.

The Teacher's Training Department of St. Basil's Academy prepares many of its teachers for the various schools. Also, a seminar of three weeks' duration is held every year with the cooperation of the Greek Ministry of Education. The recent appointment of a counselor of education at the Greek Consulate General in New York City was intended to provide the Greek Ministry of Education with a clearer picture of the educational conditions in the Greek American community.

This continuing affinity with Greece was further evidenced by the Greek government's concern over the problem of de-ethnization among those of Greek descent living in the United States. On November 11, 1975, the Parliament of Greece debated the "de-Hellenization" of second and third generations and examined the possibility of "taking appropriate measures," that is, measures that would make it possible for the children, grandchildren, and great-grandchildren of Greek immigrants to remain Greek.[44] From their perspective, the issue of language maintenance is central to remaining Greek.

In December 1980, a conference on "The Teaching of Modern Greek in the Universities of the English-Speaking World" was held at the Panteios School of Athens. The keynote speaker, Harry J. Psomiades, director of the Center for Byzantine and Modern Greek Studies at Queens College of the City University of New York, outlined the complexity of the ethnic scenario and underscored the urgent need for Greece's substantive support in maintaining the teaching of modern Greek in the English-speaking world.[45] The vast majority of Greeks, after all, do not feel themselves to be transplanted Greeks, and even for those who presently do, the passage of time transmutes this experience both subjectively and objectively. Functional language maintenance, therefore, in the light of declining immigration remains a perennial problem for those who regard the mother tongue as central to Greek ethnic identity.

If the ethnic language functions largely as a rallying symbol for Greek Americans, can they be regarded as a sociolinguistic group? It seems not. It is well to remember that after the Greek War of Independence, there existed considerable cultural and linguistic differences among the inhabitants of the mainland territories and those of the islands. Further, the use of demotic Greek, the spoken language of the people, was eschewed for the pseudoclassic *katharevousa,* or purist language, of the religious, political, and academic establishments during the nineteenth century and well into the twentieth. Differences in communicative aspects of the language component among social strata were negligible. It was in 1976 that the government of Greece settled the language problem by recognizing the spoken language—the demotic—as the official language of the Greek nation, instead of the katharevousa.[46] In the process of evolving a sense of nationhood, other bonds, primarily the Orthodox faith, bound the people together into a single unit.

It is instructive here to consider Barth's study of the Pathans, inhabitants of Afghanistan and West Pakistan. He found that Pathan identity was defined by common ancestors, a common religion (Islam), and Pathan customs, and that while language could be included, it was not sufficient in itself.

We are not dealing with a linguistic group. Pathans have an explicit saying, "He is Pathan who *does* Pashto, not (merely) who speaks Pashto"; and "doing" Pashto in this sense means living by a rather exacting code in terms of which some Pashto speakers consistently fall short.[47]

It should be added that Pathan customs are consistent with, and complementary to, Islam. Criteria other than language play a more relevant role for group membership. In general, the central elements of ethnicity vary from group to group as well as within a group. At the same time, these elements are themselves subject to the forces of social change. It is, after all, not language but people who provide a sense of community and belonging.

As we have seen, community studies reflect a decline in the ethnic-language link, but not necessarily a diminishing of ethnicity. It has been suggested that some of the most important causes of the decline of the Greek language were as follows: (1) the Depression of the thirties led to a weakening of Hellenism; (2) Greek schools were inadequate in terms of qualification of teachers and limited financial resources; (3) Greek nationalism declined following Greece's defeat in Asia Minor in 1922; (4) the community was divided over Greek politics; (5) Greek organizations were English speaking, particularly AHEPA with its large membership, thus discouraging functional maintenance of the ethnic language; (6) the upward mobility of the Greeks expedited language shift; and (7) intermarriages and the limited educational background of immigrants proved an obstacle to linguistic survival, which is a "rather intellectual phenomenon requiring substantial schooling."[48]

How relevant is the educational level of parents in sustaining functional use of the Greek language? A sample of 260 academics of Greek descent, 30 percent of whom were born in Greece, responded to a questionnaire in which they were asked to evaluate their reading and conversational proficiency as well as that of their children in the Greek language. Forty-five percent assessed their own reading ability as excellent, 19 percent as good, 17 percent as fair, 14 percent as poor, and 4 percent indicated no proficiency. With regard to conversational ability, 46 percent indicated excellent, 33 percent, good, 14 percent, fair, 3 percent, poor, and 2 percent, no competence. In judging their children's reading competence, 1 percent evaluated it as excellent, 14 percent as good, 20 percent as fair, 26 percent as poor, and 38 percent indicated no competence. With regard to conversational ability, 5 percent considered their children's performance as excellent, 17 percent as good, 22 percent as fair, 26 percent as poor, and 30 percent reported no proficiency. In response to the statement, "Understand, but do not speak it," 18 percent responded positively, whereas 82 percent were negative in their reply. This was significantly different from their parents of whom only five academics of the total population responded negatively.

It is interesting to note that the erosion of language along the generational continuum is not related to disaffection with the Greek American community. For example, 60 percent of the academics surveyed are members of Greek-related organizations and 85 percent indicated they attend church at least "several times a year." At the same time, the majority identified themselves as Greek American, followed by American Greek and Greek, suggesting a persistence of ethnic identity despite the erosion of language.[49]

The Greek Press

Given the natural progression of Americanization, it was inevitable that the Greek press, long the sustainer of nationalism and language, should acquiesce to its inevitable demise. It is reported that over 730 American foreign language papers, nearly two out of three, have folded since 1940.[50]

Sociologist Robert E. Park, who viewed the assimilation of the immigrant as inevitable, wrote *The Immigrant Press and Its Control* in 1922 in which he ascribed an un-American role to the foreign press whose existence was supported by foreign countries; the press, he said, inadvertently and tacitly controlled the nationalistic outlook of the new settlers in America. Having been both a journalist and a sociologist, he recognized that the problem of the foreign press would be a temporary one; it would play a vital role in reinforcing language and nationalism, but it would also act as an organ for acquainting the neophyte with the laws and customs of the new country, thus facilitating assimilation.[51] The immigrant's dual motives, as Park saw it, of remaining foreign and becoming American— "problem and solution"—were to be found within the foreign press itself. External coercion, therefore, was not necessary to restrict the "un-American" press, since over time it would become, by its own momentum, de-ethnicized.[52] As indeed it has.

How did this happen? In the early years of this century, the Greek press played a prominent role in keeping immigrants in touch with the warm, familiar events of their villages and informing them of the happenings taking place in the Greek colonies. But it did more than assuage the loneliness and alienation they experienced; it became an educational vehicle for learning the Greek language, particularly among the women whose literacy rate was lower than that of the males. Women have reported in interviews their frustration and then, at last their success in merging letter with letter, word with word, phrase with phrase to complete a sentence that would yield some news of their homeland as well as of their adopted country, thus providing a measure of autonomy.

One important aspect of the Greek press was its publication of the Greek language in the demotic rather than the purist form, which would have excluded the vast majority of Greeks from its readership. Victor Papacosma, a historian, makes the point that it was the "first generation in economically trying times which transmitted a rich, centuries old legacy, despite minimum schooling and an alien environment."[53]

The first Greek-language paper printed in the United States was the *New World* published in Boston in 1892.[54] It was short-lived as were many others that followed. Two presses survived into the second half of this century. The *Atlantis,* which was founded by Solon Vlastos in 1894 in New York, eventually became a daily and was well received by the immigrant population eager to learn of the homeland.[55] Vlastos's political leanings were conservative; he was supportive of the king and an advocate of neutrality for Greece during the First World War.[56] His journalistic status remained unchallenged until 1915 when the *National Herald* (*Ethnikos Kiryx*) was founded; it was an antiroyalist and politically liberal newspaper. Demetrios Callimachos was its editor for twenty-seven years and was a dedicated advocate of liberalism among the Greek readership.[57] In the Greek community, the camps were clearly drawn between the readers of the *Atlantis* and those of the *National Herald.*

The Greek press was constructive in meeting the nostalgic yearnings of the immigrant; it reinforced ties with the homeland and provided useful services in perpetuating the language, reporting social events, publishing information on naturalization procedures, and so on.

However, the two papers played a divisive role in the community by placing ideological convictions above journalistic analysis. Instead of working together toward a united front in the community to help settle, for example, the schism in the church, they focused upon partisan politics rather than news based upon reason and objective reporting. This ideological conflict fostered dissension and undoubtedly alienated a large segment of the second generation.

Atlantis and the *National Herald* had their greatest impact in forming the social outlook of many immigrants. The Greeks did not develop an influential socialist or radical press despite the fact that they were initially in the lower socioeconomic stratum. Perhaps their commercial orientation prevented the development of a class consciousness, or their ethnic salience may have been responsible.[58] To put it another way, if ethnic salience and class consciousness provide two different reference groups, then for the Greek immigrant the ethnic salience was a more tolerable one than some abstract proletariat group.

Despite this, several socialist papers emerged from World War I and lasted until after World War II, but they never had the influence or impact that *Atlantis* and the *National Herald* had. In July 1918, the newspaper, the *Voice of the Worker (Phone tou Erghatou)*, established to advance the role of the worker, changed its name to *Embros* ("Forward"). In July 1923, it became the Greek news daily for the Communist party of the United States. Written in demotic Greek, *Embros* expressed the plight of workers in terms and words derived from the fabric of their lives. In 1938, *Embros* was superceded by *Eleutheria* ("Freedom"). In 1941, the *Helleno-Amerikaniko Vema* ("Greek American Tribune") replaced *Eleutheria* as the voice of Greek labor supported by the membership of various unions. Clearly, none of these had any significant impact upon the Greek American community. When the military ruled Greece from 1967 to 1974, *Atlantis* and the *National Herald* responded guardedly to this controversial issue. But journals with limited circulation such as the *Wire* (San Francisco), *Greek American Solidarity* (Minneapolis), *Demokratia* (New York), *Eleutheria* (Waltham, Massachusetts), *PAK Newsletter* (New York), and the *Journal of the Hellenic Diaspora* (New York) stood in opposition to the junta and continued to represent positions of the political left and liberal center.[59] However, when Cyprus was invaded, the Greek press, collectively, mobilized the Greek American community to effectively influence Congress.

The Greek press was responsive to the erosion of language proficiency as early as 1923 when the *Democrat* was published, billing itself as "The First Greek Newpaper Published in English." Since 1945 the English language press has continued to play an important part in preserving ethnic identity among second- and third-generation readers. The *Chicago Pnyx,* established in 1939 and still in print, caters to business and professional people; the *Hellenic Chronicle* (Boston), established in 1950, is dedicated to "American Hellenic and Orthodox Ideals."[60] In November 1973, the *Hellenic Times* (New York) was founded, and the biweekly *Hellenic Journal* (San Francisco) has appeared since 1975.[61] The preservation of ethnic identity is sought by all these English newspapers and journals, and ties to Greece remain of paramount importance to them.

The fate of the ethnic press, however, is clear. In October 1973, after seventy-nine years, *Atlantis* was forced to cease publication, citing as reasons costs and union disputes. By that time, both *Atlantis* and the *National Herald* had mellowed, and the vituperative editorial attacks on individuals rather than issues were now part of another era. They, too, had undergone Americanization. Today, the *National Herald* remains a major daily. In 1977, *Proini* began publication from New York City, but whether it can withstand the fiscal problems facing the publishing industry remains to be seen. Although the liberalized immigration laws of 1965 revitalized the ethnic press, it may be that they were a matter of "too little, too late," particularly when daily newspapers from Athens are available in major cities.

On the other hand, Greek radio programs have proliferated since 1955, going from 30 to 160.[62] By providing news, entertainment, and information with regard to community events, the radio and Greek television programs offer other avenues for ethnic reinforcement. The shift from newspapers printed in Greek to bilingual or English format strikes one as paradoxical—"a Greek paper in English."

An English press and a bilingual church have emerged as leaders within their respective institutional frameworks. Robert Park's prophecy of assimilation has not been fulfilled. He was correct, however, in stating that the foreign press would meet its own demise in the process of facilitating the immigrant's assimilation.[63]

The process is still an ongoing one. The two daily national newspapers, the *National Herald* and *Proini,* continue to draw from the immigrants of the pioneer generation and the more recent émigrés. However, the loss of a large readership potential that might have come from the second, third, and emerging fourth generation has reduced significantly the role of the ethnic press in Greek American life. Consensus regarding the circulation figures of these two newspapers is difficult to obtain.

Politics

We have noted that Greeks were inclined to eschew political involvement during their first decades in this country, focusing mainly upon their homeland until that focus was blurred by time. Other explanations may have been their small numbers, their traditional suspicion of government, and a commercial orientation that was resistant to the politicizing influence of union movements in the United States. In addition, the limiting boundaries of their religioethnicity discouraged an exchange of ideas with other groups, and they did not feel compelled to organize for self-protection as did the Jews. Being dispersed throughout the country, the Greeks did not pose a serious threat to social, political, or economic establishments.

Their limited numbers could be ignored by politicians who generally offered inducements to ethnic groups in hopes of winning their votes. In the past twenty-five years, however, a political foundation was laid which helped to make Greek Americans viable candidates for political office. While most Greeks remained politically passive, a substantial number recognized that the tangible benefits and rewards offered by the system would not be forthcoming to the Greek community or to individual members if political disaffection was not overcome. The traits that encouraged their representation throughout the economic spectrum might have the same effect in the sphere of government. The pioneering individuals who made their way to centers of political power have been termed the "insiders"; they provided the link between the body politic and the Greek American community.[64] In the main, they were Democrats, but Republicans were also represented. A few of these insiders include the following: George Vournas, AHEPA leader and liberal advocate who had the confidence of presidents; Tom Pappas, influential in national Republican politics during the Eisenhower administration; Dean Alfange, who ran for governor of New York in 1942 as an American Labor Party candidate; Charles Maliotis, a businessman and close friend of the Kennedys and Tip O'Neill; Bill Collins of Minneapolis, friend and supporter of Hubert Humphrey; Angelo Geocaris, who spearheaded the campaign for Senator Paul Douglas of Illinois and remains an influential figure in that state's Democratic politics; and William Helis, the New Orleans oil tycoon who also had considerable political influence.[65]

As acceptance at the structural level progressed, it paved the way for political participation by a younger generation of Greek Americans. In a relatively short period of time—from 1966 to the present—eight Greek Americans were elected to the House of Representatives and two to the United States Senate, and two were elected as governors, five as mayors, and one as vice-president. Many of these political victories were won without a broad ethnic base.[66]

Some of the "firsts" among elected officials include the following:

• George Christopher, a Republican in an overwhelmingly Democratic city, was elected mayor of San Francisco in 1955. He was the first Greek American to seek a senatorial seat and the office of governor (in which he was defeated by Ronald Reagan).[67]

• In 1958, John Brademas, a Democrat, was the first native-born Greek American to be elected to Congress from the state of Indiana. In 1977, he became chief majority whip, a position below only the speaker and the majority leader. After twenty-two years in the House, he was defeated in 1980. A Harvard graduate, he attended Oxford University as a Rhodes scholar and earned a doctorate in social studies there in 1954. Recently he was named as the thirteenth president of New York University.[68]

• In 1968, Spiro Agnew became vice-president of the United States. It is interesting to note that from the 1930s on, Greek Americans consistently supported the Democratic party, until Agnew established an affinity between himself and his fellow ethnics. The facts that he was an Episcopalian, did not speak Greek, and had nebulous ties with the Greek community did not deter the vast majority of Greeks from voting for him, proving once again that blood, *to ema,* will out.[69]

One study measuring assimilation and voting patterns demonstrated that the persistence of ethnicity resulted in the widespread support that Greek Americans gave to Nixon and Agnew in 1968. Upward mobility, as measured by education, did not influence affiliation with the Republican party very much. In 1968, 53 percent of the Greek Americans cast their votes for Nixon-Agnew; about 36 percent voted for Humphrey-Muskie.[70] It seems that primarily "because of identification with the Vice Presidential candidate, the majority of the Greek Americans supported the Republicans in 1968."[71]

• In 1970, Paul Sarbanes, a Democrat, Harvard Law School graduate, and Rhodes scholar, became the first Greek American elected to the Maryland State Legislature. Another impressive first was his election to the United States Senate in 1976.[72]

• In 1975, Helen C. Boosalis of Lincoln, Nebraska, a Democrat, was the first Greek American woman to win election as mayor.[73]

• In 1979, Olympia Bouchles Snowe, a Republican from Maine, was the first Greek American woman to be elected to the House of Representatives.[74]

• Another first was the achievement of Yorka C. Linakis, who was elected justice of the Supreme Court of the state of New York in 1979.[75]

Other appointments in the political arena were those of Michael Manatos from Wyoming, appointed to the White House staff as administrative assistant for congressional relations by President Kennedy; Peter Peterson of Nebraska, former president of Bell-Howell and the first to hold a cabinet post as secretary of commerce; John Nassikas, chairman of the Federal Power Commission; and Eugene R. Rossides, assistant secretary of the treasury in the Eisenhower and Nixon administrations.[76]

These political inroads made by relatively new immigrants occurred simultaneously with the rekindling of the new ethnicity, sparked by the social issues of the sixties. The Greek American community, in general, took a relatively passive role during this tumultuous decade, however, bypassing the hippie phenomenon and counterculture trends. While many students were turning away from middle-class values, arguing that the straight world was illusory, that if one were to open the hood of this seemingly shiny car, one would find it rusty and full of grime and muck, Greek Americans were pursuing the straight and narrow path. Indictments of contemporary society and identification with Vietnam dissenters were not part of their ideological framework.[77]

It is true that the counterculture was spurred by young rebels whose middle-class status was firmly established. An argument could be made that Greek Americans were too busy struggling to win status and recognition for themselves and their families; this end would not be served by a collision with the professed values of American life. Clearly, the issue is part of a larger value configuration associated with socialization and cannot be answered monocausally.

During the sixties and seventies, many Greek Americans were actively achieving positions in elected and appointed posts; it was a time when politics as a rallying point for ethnic salience seemed to have established itself as a potent force. It was in the sixties that black Americans became acutely aware that without retaining ethnic differences, political input was a moot point; ethnicity was viewed as the prime focus for political enunciation and action. The "roots" phenomenon symbolized the shift from the ideology of the melting pot to that of cultural pluralism and legitimized political action on the part of the ethnic group. Cyprus, Ireland, Africa, Israel are but a few salient examples.

According to sociologists Glazer and Moynihan, the immigration process is the single most important determinant of American foreign policy. Foreign policy responds first to ethnic composition, although, of course, it responds to other things as well. They add, "If other nations wish to lessen ethnic diversity, it is clear that this is not yet the view of Americans, certainly not of Greek Americans, whose numbers, militance, and congressional strength became evident with the onset of the Cyprus crisis of the summer of 1974."[78]

Cyprus, whose ethnic population is 80 percent Greek, was invaded by the Turks in the summer of 1974. Their contention was that the Turkish-Cypriot community, comprising 18 percent of the country, was in danger of becoming subject to Greece's political ambitions to unify Cyprus with Greece. With this as a justification, the Turks occupied 40 percent of northern Cyprus, and the Greek Cypriots became a displaced people in their own country. Forced to abandon their homes and belongings, they sought refuge in the south of Cyprus.

This situation unleashed two immediate issues: relief for the refugees and a cessation of military aid to Turkey by the United States. The use of American weapons in the invasion of Cyprus violated United States law and exacted an immediate response from the Greek American community. It was the first time that an estimated 2 million Greek Americans (negligible at the state and national levels, but a more viable voting bloc on the local level), although politically unorganized, marshaled their resources of formal and informal organizations to deal with an issue of foreign policy. The Greek Orthodox church, AHEPA, local organizations, the Greek American press, and Greek radio programs—all led in uniting support for Cyprus. In the vanguard were priests, traditionally conservative but now politically responsive to the threat to Hellenism. In their sermons, they articulated the issues of morality and legality with regard to continuing military aid to Turkey.[79]

At that time, the term *Greek lobby* came into existence. The two best known lobbying groups are the United Hellenic American Congress (UHAC), whose membership is made up of church supporters, both lay and clerical, with headquarters in Chicago; and the American Hellenic Institute located in Washington. The institute itself primarily promotes trade relations between Greece and the United States; only its Public Affairs Committee acts in a lobbying capacity. Following the Cyprus crisis, both groups organized and lobbied effectively for a United States arms embargo against Turkey.[80]

Support for the arms embargo in Congress was led by former Representative John Brademas, Representative Benjamin Rosenthal (D-N.Y.), Senator Paul Sarbanes (D-Md.), and Senator Thomas F. Eagleton (D-Mo.). President Gerald Ford and Secretary of State Henry Kissinger were opposed to an embargo, arguing that Turkey was militarily strategic to the national security of the United States. Congress maintained that U.S. arms had been used illegally by Turkey in the invasion of Cyprus and supported a military arms embargo against Turkey until progress toward a just settlement could be demonstrated. The embargo, despite the administration's strong objections, went into effect February 5, 1975.[81]

That the Greek American community was effective is evident from the imposition of the embargo. As Brademas expressed it:

> If we members had not been able to put together a compelling case, in terms of law, policy, and morality, we would not have been effective. But on the other hand, without the kind of support we got from the Greek community, our case might not have been sufficient to win the day.[82]

Nevertheless, their effectiveness was diluted. In responding as a panelist at an American Enterprise Institute forum entitled "What Should Be the Role of Ethnic Groups in U.S. Foreign Policy?" Eugene Rossides, chairman of the American Hellenic Institute, said:

. . . the foreign policy of this country has in the last fifty years been run by the bureaucracy, the executive branch, and that coterie of elitist members of the foreign policy establishment. We cannot have a situation in which the bureaucracy, a third force, not elected can try to develop a monopoly of facts and information, and of information flow to the media, to set the stage of the issue. The Cyprus question, for example, was presented as if it were a Greek-Turkish issue. It was a violation of the rule of law of our Foreign Assistance Act.[83]

As the Cyprus issue progressed, the media began to reflect the administration's position, asserting that the United States had to place a higher priority on national interests than on morality and legality, and that Turkey was militarily more strategic and important to NATO than was Greece.[84]

In becoming a major focus for action, ethnicity tends to become suspect because of its affective ties, raising questions of dual loyalty in the decision-making process. Clearly, when ethnic interest conflicts with national interest, the citizenry must choose the latter. The difficulty, however, lies in trying to define the national interest, the most important consideration in any foreign policy question.

In the Cyprus case, the implication was that Congress had acted irresponsibly, succumbing to the pressure of an ethnic group, many members of which comprised the legislators' constituencies. However,

The results of preliminary investigations would seem to indicate that Greek American attempts to influence members of the Senate or the House on the issue of aid to Turkey were not very effective. . . . Any relationships that do exist are small, more prevalent in the House of Representatives, and more apt to occur among Republican members of the House or Senate than among Democrats.[85]

Obviously, a legislative vote is an expression of many variables interacting simultaneously, but what is of interest here is that Greek Americans saw themselves as promoters of their own welfare. It is this tendency toward a more aggressive stance that prompts some critics to interpret ethnic politics as divisive for the larger society. And yet, if the argument against ethnic politics is carried to its logical conclusion, one would have to argue for the elimination of class, religion, denominations, education, and all those social phenomena that carry negative as well as positive attributes.[86]

Not all critics of ethnicity believe that it should be relegated to oblivion. They acknowledge that subcommunities have a place—but within the private sphere; the same applies to religious institutions, the foreign press, and ethnic organizations. If, however, these personal interests and concerns of a group of people are permitted to invade the public sphere, that collectivity is immediately transformed into a pressure group and threatens the fabric that binds all Americans together in a common goal. But, as we are reminded, "What being American means is a matter still being worked out in the process, and it will probably continue that way indefinitely."[87]

Until such a definition is reached, what is to be the role, beyond the franchise, of the individual citizen with regard to decision making in both domestic and foreign policy? The constriction of the world, its complex communication networks, tends to exacerbate ethnic aggression because people see instantaneously the moral and legal abuse as well as the inconsistencies of the ethnic's country of origin. The old ethnicity was far more compliant, far more insecure; the new ethnicity is more aggressive.

In an attempt to counteract this aggressive trend in the Greek case, Ford and Kissinger met with Archbishop Iakovos in October 1974. They recognized the potential that the archbishop and his priests had for involving their flock in an act of citizen participation. The aim of the meeting was to influence the archbishop by assuring him that aid to Turkey was not inimical to Greece's interest.[88] Had the archbishop's view, that the Cyprus question was a question of human rights, been altered, the schism within the Greek American community would have been critical.

The mediating structures of church, family, and voluntary associations function to stabilize the private sphere, which modernity continuously threatens with anomie and alienation. However, beyond that, the megastructures of modern society themselves are dependent upon the moral sustenance of the mediating structures. The larger structures are too remote to provide the collective moral consciousness without which society could not survive. Instead of discouraging subcommunities, therefore, public policy should protect them and recognize the invaluable role that ethnic diversity plays, not only in providing meaning and identity in people's lives, but in preserving social stability.[89]

The initial effectiveness of the Greek American community's response to the problems of the Greek Cypriots was not sustained. Many became demoralized, and a period of inertia set in. The administration's opposition to the embargo, supported by the media, blurred the issues and contributed to a sense of powerlessness regarding the solubility of the problem. To what extent interrivalries, basic ideological differences, and personality clashes played a role in diluting the Greek community's effectiveness is not known, but these characteristics, common to all ethnic groups, do not appear crippling among ethnic groups with more extensive experience and political sophistication. The need to gain the support and sympathy of others outside one's ethnic group cannot be overstressed. This, in turn, depends on the group's access to media control. The Greek American community did not have this.

What impact did this ethnopolitical involvement have upon the community? Only a general statement is possible. The community experienced a sense of ethnic pride in the unity it demonstrated for the first time on an international issue. It raised the political consciousness of ethnic organizations who have since increased their support for Greek Americans campaigning for political office, and it has increased campaign contributions to candidates for the United States Congress. "Before the invasion of Cyprus, probably only 5 percent of U.S. Congressmen had campaign contributions from Greek Americans," said Andrew Manatos, assistant secretary for congressional affairs at the U.S. Department of Commerce. "Now, it's more like 30 percent. Greek Americans are telling each other, 'We've got to pull together to help our friends.' "[90]

One of the most significant role changes occurred in the Greek Orthodox church; traditionally a conservative church, it had not bridged the gap between theology and social consciousness.[91] By the 1960s, Orthodox theologians had begun to assess this dimension in the life of the church.[92] The participation of the archbishop in the Selma march of the sixties was more symbolic than indicative of any widespread civil rights concern among the Orthodox.[93]

In the case of Cyprus, the role of the priest was both enhanced and changed by his generating collective support among his flock. In some instances, a more aggressive role was taken, as the following indicates:

During three hours of debate on the highly emotional issue today [the arms embargo on Turkey], Rev. Evagoras Constantinides, a Greek Orthodox priest from Merrillville, Indiana, sat in the front row of the House Rules Committee hearing room to make evident his opposition to the resumption of Turkish aid. Father Constantinides is a constituent of Rep. Ray J. Madden, Chairman of the Rules Committee. The Cypriot-born priest is in charge of lobbying among members of the Indiana Congressional delegation, but he said he had been prowling the halls of Congress pleading the Greek case to almost anyone who would listen.

His efforts have not been in vain. Mr. Madden acknowledged during the hearing that the effective presentations of such Greek Americans as Father Constantinides had won him over to their point of view.[94]

How widespread this activism was among the clergy is not known, but it dramatizes a departure from the traditionally conservative role of the religious functionary.

Outside the Mainstream

Painters. In general, studies of Greek life in America have dealt with those individuals who, in some way, have been affiliated with either the church or a voluntary ethnic association.[95] This identifiable entity has come to represent the sine qua non of the Greek experience in America. The picture tends to highlight the conventional occupations pursued and the success achieved vis à vis the Horatio Alger route and to ignore the self-motivated individuals intent upon expressing their individuality within the broader scope of the art world.

It is true that very few Greeks went into the arts. Perhaps this can be explained in terms of their rural and traditional backgrounds. The Greek, after all, saw himself initially as a sojourner—intent upon returning to his homeland after acquiring sufficient capital. His orientation was to the past, not to the future. This posture would discourage any ambition that did not fall within the folk definition of success. Undoubtedly, the arts were alien and a threat to the insularity of the Greek family and to the reciprocal relations embedded within it. Be that as it may, there were those who resisted the constraints of localism.

A number of potential artists found their way to the New World. One of them was Emmanuel A. Cavacos who came here in 1903. Jean Xceron (Xerocostas) emigrated in 1904 from his village in Peloponnesus. By 1911, Theodore Tsavalas, who had been studying art in Athens, came to New York City. In the same year, Polygnotos Vagis arrived and met George Constant who had come here two years earlier. While these men had to earn their livelihood through conventional menial work, they were all studying art by 1910. The painter Kimon Nicolaides is acknowledged as the first Greek American to pursue art as a career. He was born in Washington, D.C., in 1891.

In 1919, Basil Marros and John Vassos arrived in the United States. Vassos studied with John Singer Sargent and John Sloan. By 1920, Polygnotos Vagis had a piece of his sculpture exhibited at the Brooklyn Museum. A one-man show by Kimon Nicolaides in 1923 in Paris helped start his teaching career at the Art Students' League in New York. At the same time, George Constant was teaching and exhibiting in the Midwest and came to New York in 1922. In 1926, his work was on exhibit in

Munich, Germany. In 1927, Xceron moved to Paris where he remained for ten years, and in 1931, he held his first one-man show at the Galerie de France.

The two artists who seemed to be most prominently exhibited during the 1920s were Polygnotos Vagis and John Vassos. In the early years of this century, a very small number of Greek Americans entered the field of art to eventually develop their own artistic styles.

At the end of the 1920s, Theo Hios emigrated to this country followed by Nassos Daphnis. Hios worked in the restaurant business, which left him little time for artistic studies, but by the mid-thirties his decision to devote himself to art led him to the WPA (Work Projects Administration) project for which he painted a mural. Here he met George Constant who was working for the project at the time. Now a veteran of the school of abstract painters in New York, Hios is also a member of the art faculty of the New School for Social Research; he describes the twenty-five paintings of a recent exhibit that comprise "Works on Paper" as evolving from his conception of a "dual movement of forces which express horizontal and centrifugal movement as in the eye of a hurricane moving in and out of space."[96] Hios's work is represented in the National Collection of Fine Art, Tel Aviv (Israel) Museum, the Parrish Art Museum (Southampton, New York), and others. He has had many one-man shows, including showings at the North Carolina State Art Gallery, the Toledo (Ohio) Museum, and other renowned galleries.

Nassos Daphnis, the next to come to the United States, was another young immigrant seeking to actualize himself. Not knowing the language, he worked in his uncle's business in the wholesale flower district, a Greek enclave on Manhattan's 28th Street. There he met Michael Lekakis, then little known, who supported himself as a sculptor by working in his relative's flower business. Daphnis confided to Lekakis that he wanted to become an artist, and an invitation to Lekakis's evening drawing class started him on a career of art and a friendship with Lekakis.

Until then self-taught, Daphnis's primitive painting of the thirties created a wave of interest, and when he had his first one-man show at the age of twenty-four, three of his paintings went to museums. His primitive style gave way gradually to large-scale geometric abstractions which derived from the 1960s. At this time, he received several commissions for decorating large outdoor walls on New York buildings. His work is represented in the permanent collections of major American museums such as the Guggenheim and the Whitney in New York City. He has twenty-two one-man shows and forty group exhibits to his credit.[97]

Michael Lekakis, born in New York City, had his first one-man show in 1941 when he exhibited a series of small bronzes with a New York gallery; he created his first sculpture in 1930 at the age of twenty-three. In 1963, he was selected for an important group show at the Museum of Modern Art (New York City), "Americans 1962." He has had eight one-man exhibitions and selected group exhibitions at the Whitney Museum and the Guggenheim in New York, the Cleveland (Ohio) Museum of Art, and the Wadsworth Atheneum, Hartford, Connecticut.

In the early 1930s, Vagis was holding one-man shows at important New York galleries; in 1934 his work appeared at the Chicago World's Fair and Corcoran Gallery of Art in Washington, D.C.

Another artist beginning to gain recognition was Constantine Pougialis who held his first one-man exhibition at the Art Institute of Chicago in 1931. By 1933 he was exhibiting at the Museum of Modern Art and the Whitney in New York.

In 1937, Jean Xceron had a work from his New York exhibition purchased for the Guggenheim Foundation. Later he was to join the staff of the Guggenheim Museum where he remained for the rest of his life.

By the 1930s, a handful of Greeks were well represented in the mainstream of modern art. In 1944, William Baziotes, born in Pittsburgh, Pennsylvania, in 1912, was given his first one-man show by Peggy Guggenheim, and Theodore Stamos gave his first one-man exhibition in 1943. Stamos was born in New York City and grew up on East Eighteenth Street in Manhattan. His father worked in the wholesale flower business. He attended the academically prestigious Stuyvesant High School but left three months before graduation. He said, "I was the original drop-out. I suppose I left when I made the decision that I wanted to be an artist. Teachers never encouraged me; they don't know very much."[98] He won a scholarship to the American Artist's School, where he studied sculpture; he turned to painting because he couldn't afford the sculptor's material or space.

The postwar years brought together Kristodimos Kladis, Polygnotos Vagis, Xceron, Baziotes, and Stamos. The most prolific artist at the time was Theodore Stamos. Every year from 1947 to 1963, he held at least one one-man show in an important gallery; and from 1945 through 1970, he has been represented in at least one of the more important group shows in this country and abroad. Toward the close of the fifties, action painting, or abstract expressionism, in which Baziotes and Stamos had been prime movers, became the accepted style of painting, and in 1958, it received official confirmation in a show sponsored by the Museum of Modern Art in

New York called "The New American Painting." It included five paintings each by Baziotes and Stamos, and its impact upon the art world was
enormous. Stamos's work is to be found in numerous museums including
the Metropolitan Museum of Art, the Museum of Modern Art, the
Guggenheim, the San Francisco Museum of Art, the Tel Aviv Museum,
the Whitney, and others.

Stamos's father was from the island of Lefkada, and he took his first trip
to Greece in 1948. His ethnic ties are reflected in the titles of his work: *The
Three Furies, Demetra's Revenge, Greek Easter.* He has always signed his
paintings in Greek rather than English. "We spoke Greek at home. I never
felt resentful about being Greek; it was part of my life. I wanted to learn
even more about Greece, about Greek."[99]

From Stamos's point of view, "the Greeks here are pretty dead, even
with all their cultural organizations. It's a strange thing to say but the
Greeks in Greece are more advanced. Here, art is more accessible, but the
Greek middle class—doctors, lawyers, don't buy anything, don't support
art. Look at George Constant—he was finally given the Charioteer Award
[by the Parnassos Society of New York]. It's about time he got some
recognition from the Greek Americans. They don't do much. It's unfortu-
nate." This author well remembers the occasion of being asked to relate
George Constant's work to Greek ethnicity; Mr. Lekakis spoke on those
aspects of Mr. Constant's work that revealed the internal spirit of the
creator himself. Without doubt, George Constant was deeply moved by
the recognition accorded him by the Greek American community at this
event—although it was late in coming. George Constant was widely
exhibited and purchased for many years, and his importance as a trailblazer
cannot be ignored; the fact that he was well known allowed other Greek
Americans in the thirties and forties to see themselves as potential artists.

Greek artists had begun meeting and helping each other, and when
Michael Lekakis met Nassos Daphnis, he offered him the temporary use of
his studio and model for a few days each week until Daphnis could find a
place for himself. This mutual reinforcement enabled others to embark on
the mainstream of modern art.

Another potential artist, Lucas Samaras, arrived in this country at the
age of eleven. His father was a furrier, and he had been raised during the
German occupation. Samaras works with a myriad of objects and materials
which he assembles to evoke an emotional impact. Some of the titles of his
work illustrate this: *Box 82, Mixed media: Photo-Transformation, SX-70
Polaroid.* His work has been exhibited at the Museum of Modern Art, the
Guggenheim, the Whitney Museum, the Institute of Contemporary Arts

in London, and others. He has had at least twelve one-man shows. With reference to his ethnic background, Samaras writes in his "Autobiographic Preserve," "Greece is my prehistory, my preliterate past, my unconsciousness, my fantasy. America is my history, my consciousness, my adult life in reality."[100]

Dimitri Hadzi, a Greek American whose initial interest was chemistry, had a father who was a furrier and a mother who wanted her son to study art. As a youth he was taken to the studio of Michael Lekakis, not knowing that someday their sculpture would share an affinity in natural forms. The great bronze *K.458–The Hunt* (1964) was commissioned for Philharmonic Hall in Lincoln Center, New York City. There have been other significant commissions for Maryland, Boston, Minneapolis, Fullerton, California, and St. Paul's Episcopal Church in Rome, Italy.

Another artist, Chryssa, born in Athens of educated parents, executed in the mid-fifties what came to be called her "Cycladic Book Series." Chryssa has worked with slabs of baked clay with signs and symbols on them; neon lights are central to her design in expressing contemporary life. Her work is to be found in New York City at the Guggenheim, the Museum of Modern Art, and the Whitney Museum; Philadelphia Museum of Art; Museum Boyman Van Beuningen, Rotterdam, the Netherlands; National Galerie, Berlin, West Germany; and others.

Stephen Antonakos, born in Greece, emigrated here at the age of four. By the late 1950s, he was showing his collages in a New York City gallery. He worked with various materials in his collages, and in 1964, he began working in neon. Although his family was not opposed to his artistic ambitions, he feels no ethnic affinity with his Greek background. He has had at least twelve one-man exhibits, and his work is on view at the Whitney Museum, the Museum of Modern Art, and the Guggenheim.

Tom Boutis was born in New York City, studied at Cooper Union Art School, and later studied in Italy under a Fulbright grant. As an abstract painter, his interest is purity of design, shape, and color, all merging to form color fields of space. "My intention is to show how one can perceive depth on a two-dimensional surface within a quiet and intimate perceptive factor."[101] He does not feel that his Greekness has had any effect upon his career in art. He has had ten or more one-man shows and at least twelve group exhibitions. His work is to be seen at the Art Institute of Chicago, New York University, the Canton (Ohio) Art Institute, and elsewhere.

In the early 1950s, a young Greek American born in Montana, Peter Voulokos, was creating massive pots—something that had never been tried in the United States, and by 1953, his work was being shown at the

Museum of Modern Art. At the same time, Donald Odysseus Mavros was working with clay but not as a potter. Mavros was born in New York City, and his first encounter with ceramics was in the local high school, where an art teacher taught him to experiment with glazes.

Following his studies at a New York art school, Mavros found little interest in the United States in the medium of pottery; it was not considered a full-fledged art. By the 1940s, however, he was certain that this was to be his art form. He finally gained recognition in 1950–51 through the Syracuse (New York) Museum of Fine Arts exhibitions which toured the country for one year. In 1952, he founded his workshop in the midst of the Greek flower district in New York City. In 1951, he had his first one-man show at the Pietrantonio Galleries in New York. He has had seventeen exhibitions of his own here and abroad and has participated in more than 120 group shows.[102]

On a trip to Thessaloniki in Greece, Mavros saw prehistoric Greek pottery. "These forms, their color and shape, greatly impressed me, and this spirit I want to reflect in my own pottery." He has been influenced as well by early American Indian pottery and was responsible for establishing the ceramic section of the New School for Social Research.[103]

Sculptor Louis Trakas was born in Brooklyn, New York. After attending the High School of Music and Art, he received a scholarship to Cooper Union Art School. From there he went on to study anthropology and philosophy at Columbia University, New York City. He was awarded a Fulbright scholarship to Rome, which was subsequently renewed. He is currently a faculty member of Manhattanville College and of the New School–Parsons School of Design, both of New York.

His identification with Greek ethnicity is reflected in the titles accorded his works: *Minoan Recollection II* (1980), *Omphalos* ("Center") (1975), *Stele* ("Columns I") (1981), *Kima* ("Wave") (1982). Trakas works in semiabstract and abstract sweeping forms. His work has been exhibited and is to be found in private collections both here and abroad. His sculpture is on view at the Museum-Guild Hall, East Hampton, New York.

In 1980, he founded an educational program in Crete with the intention of linking America to Greece's cultural heritage, to build, as it were, a cultural bridge between Crete and the United States. The program centers on the study of the sculpture and ceramics of Crete, exploring the techniques used by the Minoans in 2000 B.C. The intent is not to replicate their style but to study their techniques, from there, following one's own potential, one's own creative inclinations.

The program is on the college level and is open to all students regardless of ethnic background; it is interesting to note that during its three years, it has attracted very few Americans of Greek extraction. In the first year (1980), no Greek American student attended; in the second year, one Greek American enrolled; and in the third year, four Greek American students joined the program. Enrollment usually includes eighteen to twenty students, but the paucity of Greek American attendance reinforces the prevalent concern about the Greek's indifference to and lack of support of the cultural and artistic world.[104]

Apparently, though, segments of the Greek American community are not insensitive to this neglect. In 1977, the Hellenic American Neighborhood Action Committee held an exhibit at the Brooklyn Museum of Art entitled *"Noemata"* ("a product of one's mind") in which fourteen contemporary artists of Greek descent were exhibited. In its brochure, it noted that "Greek Americans have, in general, been negligent in recognizing and encouraging and supporting the arts and the struggling artists." Again, "now after over half a century of establishing its place in American society, the Greek American community has begun to find the time and resources necessary to extend itself into the arts."[105] In addition to artists who have already been mentioned, the exhibition included Christos Gianakos, Steve Gianakos, Mary Grigoriadis, Aris Koutroulis, Nicholas Sperakis, and Theo Stavropoulos.

Writers. If the Greek American in the visual arts has felt ignored, the same can be said of the writer who has expressed a similar grievance. The complaint seems to be well-founded. Two publishers told this writer that books on Greeks don't sell. Why? Because Greeks don't buy books as do some other ethnic groups.

On the relation of the writer to society, Isaac Bashevis Singer, winner of the Nobel Prize for Literature in 1978, said before the Swedish Academy, "Strange as these words may sound, I often play with the idea that when all the social theories collapse and wars and revolutions leave humanity in utter gloom, the poet may rise up to save us all."[106] In another context, he said, "Literature is completely connected with one's origins, with one's roots. The great masters were all rooted in their people. No assimilationist can be a great writer."[107] And Alexander Karanikas has pointed out, "That so many Greek American authors do employ ethnic characters, actions, and situations means that they are following the simple dictum of writing about what they know best—families, friends, themselves."[108]

The first Greek American novel, *Gold in the Streets* (1945), was written by Mary Vardoulakis. It takes place around 1906 in the mill town of

Chicopee, Massachusetts, and describes the struggles of the Greek immigrants as they made the transition from peasants to industrial workers.[109]

Ariadne Pasmezoglu Thompson's *The Octagonal Heart* (1956) reflects the marginality of Greek life in America. It is not characterized by poverty and illiteracy, but represents the perennial saga of cultural conflict. It is the story of a girl's life in an affluent suburb of St. Louis, Missouri, during the First World War and centers upon her desire to become a doctor and marry a non-Greek; both desires are opposed by her family. In this case the heroine is triumphant in achieving both.[110]

It is to Harry Mark Petrakis that we turn to feel the pulse of the Greek experience in America. Fears, hopes, dreams, anguish of dislocation, frailty, love, joy, and humor are all portrayed in his ethnic characters. He is the storyteller par excellence. While his plots and characters are drawn from the Chicago of his boyhood, they tend to embrace and, at the same time, transcend ethnic boundaries.

In *Lion at My Heart* (1959), Petrakis depicts a working-class Greek family embroiled in generational antagonism between a patriarchal father and his son. The son is damned by the father for marrying an Irish girl, Shiela Cleary. The father becomes increasingly alienated from his son, feeling torn between his cultural identity and the boy.[111]

A Dream of Kings (1966) has as its central character Leonidas Matsoukas, a gambler, who is never able to raise enough money to return to Greece. He loves his dying son genuinely and wants to take him to Greece, but his own weakness prevents him from doing what is right. This novel was made into a major film in 1968.[112]

The Odyssey of Kostas Volakis (1963) traces three generations of a Greek American family from 1919 through 1954 centering upon the tensions brought about by the acculturation process. Kostas starts his pilgrimage to America, to Chicago, by marrying Katerina, not because he loved her but because he needed a dowry to buy him the passage to the promised land. Having worked through the usual acculturation process, their lives are marred by a tragedy between two of their sons—fratricide.[113]

In an autobiographical novel, *Stelmark* (1970), Petrakis draws a series of sketches about his family as seen through the eyes of one of the sons. *The Land of the Morning* (1973) is set, as are most of his novels, in Chicago's Greek Town and concerns a Vietnam veteran and the tragedies suffered by his family.[114] *Nick the Greek* (1979) deals with the life of the infamous gambler, Nicholas Andreas Dandolos.[115]

A Petrakis Reader (1978) contains twenty-seven short stories. The one students find most humorous is "The Journal of a Wife-Beater." The husband is convinced that he cannot maintain patriarchal rule unless he beats his wife. She, much to his consternation, hits back. After several such altercations, he decides that, indeed, he is not married to an ordinary mortal woman but to a goddess, albeit a fierce one.[116]

His sole work not related to the Greek immigrant experience is *The Hour of the Bell* (1976), which evokes the heroes of the Greek revolution. The first of a trilogy on the revolution, it covers the period from 1820 through 1821, culminating in the seige of Tripolitza.[117]

Tom Chamales's novels *Never So Few* (1957)[118] and *Go Naked in the World* (1959)[119] were on the best-seller lists and were made into major motion pictures. His first book dealt with his experiences in the war; the second focused on life with a Greek family following the war years, its internal stresses and the thrust to find his own identity. His career was ended by his premature death.

George Christy's *All I Could See from Where I Stood* (1963) centers upon a twelve-year-old boy living in western Pennsylvania on the eve of World War II. It is a place where Greek is synonymous with un-American. The icons, the votive lights evoke fear in the boy. The foods and celebrations are ethnic woes for Stephanos. Gradually he moves toward greater acceptance, greater tolerance.[120]

Another protagonist who despises Greek life is Daphne in *The Education of a Queen* (1962), a novella by Thalia Cheronis Selz. Her father is Greek but her mother is not. Her great-grandmother, Otis, drove a wagon alone from Barnstable on Cape Cod, Massachusetts, to Ohio. A quilt she left is dated 1833 and contrasts sharply with a blanket dated 1897, left by her father's mother who had woven it resentfully for her husband, who was on his way to make his fortune in the United States.[121] "The Monk Who Loved Little Girls," a chapter from her forthcoming novel *The Greek Garden*, has won her a National Endowment for the Arts Creative Writing Fellowship Grant and is being published in *Partisan Review.*

Thomas Doulis's *Paths for Our Valor* (1963) focuses on a Greek American paratrooper in World War II, his experiences with war and passion, and his return as a veteran whose spirit is broken.[122] *Hammer on the Sea* (1965), written by Theodore Vrettos, depicts the events of the occupation and resistance in the Greece of the 1940s.[123] Stephen Linakis's novel, *In the Spring the War Ended* (1965), deals with the character of Nick Leonidas and the nature of army justice in World War II.[124]

Elia Kazan gave us *America, America* (1962)[125] and *The Arrangement* (1967).[126] *Acts of Love* (1978) takes place in Tarpon Springs, Florida. The central character is an American girl, very rich and disturbed, who marries

Teddy Avaliotis—whose father bitterly objects to the marriage. She violates her marital vows but pretends to conform to the norms of Greek life. A series of circumstances leads to her father-in-law seducing her and then, out of loyalty to his son, killing her. He is tried and freed to walk about Tarpon Springs having recovered the honor of the Avaliotis family.[127]

In *The Bridge* (1972), H. L. Mountzoures relates the story of a Greek American family living in Connecticut. The hero represents another example of a youth growing up in a home beset with severe domestic problems, including the insanity of his mother.[128]

The internal struggle of growing up in America is also developed by Charles Jarvis in *Zeus Has Two Urns* (1976).[129] It is the story of a twelve-year-old boy in Lowell, Massachusetts, his ambivalence toward his ethnic background, and his search to find respite from a tension-filled home. Jarvis's novel *The Tyrants* (1977)[130] also takes place in Lowell, but here he focuses upon the "curse of the Hellenes"—the stubborn sense of personal pride that plagues both educated and uneducated Greeks. It reflects the schisms that split Greek American communities over the Royalist-Venizelist issue. Jarvis portrays the less positive aspects of the Greek rather than the immigrant's struggle for survival.

Athena G. Dallas-Damis does not write about the immigrant or the Greek American experience, but a strong ethnic identification led her to write *Island of the Winds*. The story is about the Turkish massacre on Chios that occurred in March of 1822.[131] The author writes, "I lived with the villagers of Chios, most of them descendants of the survivors of the great massacre of 1822." The historical events, however, are the background for the story of a woman whose twin sons are separated and one is raised as an Ottoman janissary. Its sequel, *Windswept* (1981),[132] continues the story from 1824 until 1829, the end of the Greek Revolution. The last book of the trilogy, *Follow the Winds* is forthcoming and will cover the period 1830 to 1860, taking the janissary-turned-Christian back to the island of Chios.

Nicholas Gage, a journalist for the *New York Times*, was born in Greece but came here as a boy. His novel, *The Bourlotas Fortune* (1976), depicts the struggle and competition in the shipping industry. The real-life rivalry between Onassis and Niarchos finds its parallel in the rivalry between Bourlotas and Malitas.[133] In his book *Eleni*, published by Random House in 1983, Nicholas Gage is involved in a personally compelling mission to learn of the events that led to his mother's death by a Communist firing squad in the Greek Civil War. Lia, the village in which he was born in 1939, was close to the Albanian border and the Greek communists took control of it in 1948. Curtailing the freedom of the villagers, the communists also proceeded to separate children from their parents. This policy was called pedomasoma meaning "the gathering of the children," who would then be sent to People's Democracies behind the Iron Curtain. Eleni Gatzoyiannis, Nicholas Gage's mother, was unwilling to part with her children and organized a group of villagers for an escape. As fate would have it she, and one of her daughters, were ordered to work at threshing fields quite a distance from their village. The others, not being able to wait, escaped. Among them were Nicholas Gage with three of his sisters. That some villagers escaped infuriated the communists; someone had to pay. That someone was Eleni. After being barbarically tortured for a confession, she was finally executed on August 28, 1948, at the age of 41.

The author's initial missions: to learn the circumstances surrounding the death of his mother, whom he last saw when he was nine years old, and then to seek revenge were partly fulfilled. The legacy of love and sacrifice personified in his mother's life triumphs; he walks away from the opportunity to take vengeance on the executioner.

Another writer, Stratis Haviaras, emigrated to the United States in 1967. He has had five volumes of poetry published; his first novel, *When the Tree Sings* (1979), is the story of a boy emerging into manhood in occupied Greece of the forties.[134]

A poet and writer, Demetrios A. Michalaros, edited *Athene* magazine (1940–67), which became a major source of information on the Greek experience in America. In 1930, he gave us *Sonnets of an Immigrant*.[135] Michalaros did not stress the negative aspects of the immigrant's adjustment but rather exalted the American dream and the immigrant's contribution to the building of America; his poem *I Am the Immigrant* exemplifies this.

Konstantinos Lardas has written both fiction and poetry. *The Devil Child* (1961) became an Atlantic First, a literary distinction shared by two other Greek Americans, Petrakis and Mountzoures.[136] A book of poetry by Lardas, *And in Him Too; In Us,* was nominated for a Pulitzer Prize in 1964.

Beginning with O (1977) is a volume of poetry by an American-born woman, Olga Broumas, which won her first place in the Yale Series of Younger Poets competition. Its foreword reads, "This is a book of letting go, of wild avowals, unabashed eroticism; at the same time it is a work of integral imagination, steeped in the light of Greek myth that is part of the poet's inheritance."[137]

Dino Siotis came to this country in 1971 to escape the oppression of the junta regime. He was twenty-seven years old and settled in San Francisco, determined not only to oppose the dictatorship of Greece but to develop his own creative efforts. He published the *Wire,* an antijunta journal in 1974. He founded both the *Wire Press* and the *Coffeehouse* magazine (1975), presenting contemporary Greek arts and letters in English translation. He is the former Greek editor of the *Hellenic Journal,* a biweekly Greek American newspaper. Four volumes of his poetry have been published: *Attempt* (1969), *So What* (in English) (1972), *We and the Rainmaker* (1973), and *Thirteen Electric Poems* (1978).

Also active in the bay area of California and connected with the *Wire Press* is Thanasis Maskaleris who, in addition to the publication of his own poetry, has compiled two books of translated poetry. Another contributing poet is Nanos Valaoritis, who is prominent in Europe as a playwright and has been widely published as a poet in English, French, and Greek.

A new name on the horizon is that of American-born, twenty-two-year-old Steve Georgiou. His newly published volume of poetry is entitled *Alexander, My Alexander* (1982);[138] it is a collection of verse on the life of Alexander. The young poet noted, "My parents are Greek, so I was always in a Greek environment. One day, when I was nine, I found a copy of the *Iliad,* and I was hooked. I wanted to be like Achilles. When I was playing with my friends, it wouldn't be cowboys and Indians, but the Achaeans fighting the Trojans." When he was a sophomore in high school, he had a poem published in a national anthology of poetry. And when he went to Greece, he said of the experience, "Everything I read came to life."[139]

The other arts.   There are, to be sure, individuals, both prominent and emerging, in other areas of the arts. In the field of music, for example, composer Nicholas Roussakis, Gregoria Karides, Dino Constantinides, Dino Anagnost, Loukas Skiptaris, George Tsontakis, Tatan Troyanos and the late Maria Callas come to mind. Stage, screen, and television conjure up the names of Elia Kazan, John Cassavetes, Telly Savalas, George Maharis, Alexander Scourby, Yannis Simonides, Michael Constantine, Nicholas Kepros, Douglas Andros, Milton Katselis, Lou Antonio, Mary Carver, Christine Andreas, and Ernie Anastos among others.

There are, to be sure, outstanding figures in other fields as well. For example. Dr. George Papanicolaou was responsible for the "Pap smear," a test designed to detect cervical cancer. Dr. George Kotzias was a neurologist who discovered L-dopa, a drug used to treat Parkinson's disease. However, a chronology of accomplishments is not intended and can make for very tedious reading.

In an effort to preserve ethnic continuity across another medium, Yannis Simonides conceived the idea of organizing the Greek Theatre Company in the United States. Simonides is a Yale University graduate and former chairman of the drama department of New York University; a position he gave up to devote himself to the Greek theater.

This professional bilingual company performs in a theater on 28th Street in New York City. Its artistic director has attempted to stage diverse plays that would capture the attention of various groups of Greeks, both assimilated and nonassimilated. However, the fiscal problems of the theater have been overwhelming. Reaching out to the Greek American community for assistance has proved a formidable task. Despite these obstacles, the theater is entering its fourth year with considerable success in its presentations. In 1981, a group called the Friends of the Greek Theatre organized a series of events to assist the theater socially, culturally, and financially.

In a relatively short period of time, the theater has mounted a broad range of productions, including the ancient classics, contemporary plays, English translations of Greek plays, and Greek translations of English plays, and has presented comedies, reviews, and dance. However, support from the Greek American community remains tenuous.

Chapter Five

The Family: Redefining Sex Roles and Relationships

Gender Roles and Family Transactions

A brief review of traditional family norms will help orient us to the contemporary constellation of the Greek family in the United States. In Greece, as in most traditional societies, the group, not the self, is the basic unit of society. In the New World, the immigrant's ideal of hierarchical ranking in the family became increasingly outmoded, contradictory, and often detrimental to newly acquired attitudes in the acculturation process. Although social conditions were drastically different in the United States, the immigrant's cultural values and ideals often remained unchanged or changed slowly, creating a cultural lag that rendered the individual's experience ambiguous and marginal. This was particularly true for the native-born, the second generation. Roles appropriate to a rural society became obsolete, and the once stable expectations grew less arbitrary, less inflexible.

One's identity, once bestowed at birth and taken for granted throughout one's life, emerged as a formidable problem for the immigrant's progeny. The difficulty in trying to live without agreed-upon roles resulted in conflict over one's total social heritage and affected one's self-confidence and self-esteem. A synopsis of the problem is contained in the following excerpt from an article entitled "The Forgotten Generation," written by a second-generation Greek woman in 1950:

To be born a woman and intelligent is definitely risky. But to be born a sensitive, intelligent woman and to be born Greek—that is little short of calamity. Because, to Greek Americans, the concept of the equality of the sexes is so completely demoralizing that the superior woman is beaten before she begins. I spent my childhood and adolescence in constant inner and often

121

outward rebellion at the deference accorded to the male members of my family, even when they were patently in the wrong. Again and again I was told, "You must give in. You are a girl." But no one ever took time to explain *why* the woman must always give in.[1]

The deference described is dictated by clearly delineated lineal relationships in the Greek family; the father and sons, according to age, determine the lines of authority. The father's decisions are unilaterally made. He has responsibility for the economic welfare of his family, and his decisions are not to be challenged; but he is also completely responsible for the behavior and reputation of his family members. The wife's role is to support the decisions of her husband and to protect the family from external criticism. To do this requires that outsiders know little, if anything, about the weaknesses and faults of family members.

The subordinate role of the Greek woman is characteristic of the traditional European small farm family. In most peasant societies, while the woman may work as hard as her husband, or harder, her status is regarded as inferior to his. She is dependent upon his authority and power. Her concerns are restricted to "women's domain" which include matters concerned with children, the home, church, and religious ritual. She has no say in the public domain, and when she does appear in public, she is expected to behave in an unobtrusive manner. Her value resides in her producing sons. From this point of view, it is her sexuality that is considered valuable, and it is this that must be guarded. As a consequence, her behavior and appearance in public become very important, because any action that might attract the attention of others threatens her husband's sexual exclusivity.

Earlier it was stated that the constraining norm of endropi, or shame, which enforces honorable behavior, is the norm that protects a woman's basic feminine sexuality. This weakness, believed to be inherent to her nature, adds to the moral responsibility of the family whose constant vigilance guards against a woman bringing dishonor to the family. Each member bears a responsibility for the other which reinforces dependency, a dependency free of any puritanical stigma. Children are regarded as an economic and social asset, and insurance against the adversities of old age. These values of familism were brought to this country unchanged and influenced the socialization of subsequent generations.

We have seen that while the church, Greek schools, Greek press, and local organizations served to preserve the immigrant's world view, it was inevitable that cultural conflicts should manifest themselves within the family unit. Each generation constructed its reality in two different ways, living in two not merely different but antagonistic cultures. This push and pull on the developing personality affected family transactions and transformed the structure of the Greek family.

One can view the family as passing through three stages in the acculturation process: (1) the initial contact stage, (2) the conflict stage, and (3) the accommodation stage. The first stage is represented by the first decades of the immigrant's life in America. The children, being young, are insulated from the influences of the larger culture, and the family is permitted to continue as a stable integrated unit. Gradually, influences from within and without begin to disturb the old way of living. Various reasons for this include the new economic role assumed by the father in an urban society, the new role delegated to the mother as the major socializing agent of the children, the element of time which dimmed the immigrant's memory of village life, and the exposure of their children to the American education process.[2]

At this time in the United States, a strong belief in western and northern European supremacy prevailed, and it was through the eyes of this ideological bias, transmitted by middle-class teachers, that members of the native-born Greek generation began to view their parents and their culture. Neither world had their complete allegiance. Forfeiting one for the other evoked guilt and ambivalence. And yet, unknowingly, a reverse socialization was taking place that cast them in a leadership role. As Oscar Handlin describes the situation, the immigrants, unfamiliar with the language and hence dependent on their children, viewed them as a threat to their traditional authority. He wrote:

It was this superiority that gave the second generation its role as mediator between the culture of the home and the culture of the wider society in the United States. Accepting that role, the immigrants, nevertheless, resented it. It reversed the order of things.[3]

But what was the nature of the "order of things"? We have seen that the value structure of Greek rural life was hierarchical. Indeed, that was found to be one of its most salient values. In studying the contrasts between Greek rural values and American middle-class value orientations, psychologist John Papajohn identified authoritarianism, individualism, and cooperation as forming, in that order, the most important guides to Greek familial and extrafamilial behavior. In the United States, however, precedence is given to cooperation, followed by individualism, and last by authority.[4] At times, these two orientations collided; at other times, they merged into the mainstream. Our review of Greek American communities demonstrated the different rates of acculturation that prevailed in the adjustment to the American scene.

Whereas Americans profess to give priority to egalitarianism and to abhor authoritarianism, the educational, political, economic, and religious systems tacitly support authoritarianism. This covert endorsement of authoritarianism enabled the Greek immigrant to adapt to the competitive rigors of economic life in the New World. It permitted the expression of self-importance and individual resourcefulness in pursuing "the psychological equivalent of his own plot of land."[5]

In Greece, people's lives based upon family and community ties, although stable and secure, were not equal. Lineality, plus the low value placed upon cooperation outside the family, provided the needed impetus, however, for developing achievement drives and entrepreneurial skills in this country. Even cooperation within the family involved its correlate, authority. In other words, one might work with others, but one did not treat them as equals. The pursuit of educational achievement and improvement of one's economic status was done with an eye toward gaining control over others, to having the upper hand, not as an individual, but as a representative of the family. The notion of equality did not fit into the values of authoritarianism and individuality. The individualistic drive so characteristic of the Greek is not to be confused with the individualism espoused in the United States, which has its roots in the Protestant ethic, an ethic that stresses the individual's responsibility for failure as well as for success. For Greeks, individualism was the second preference in their relational orientation.[6]

The jealousy of others was always a potential threat and precluded cooperation beyond the trusted family circle. This orientation could be a salutary one for Greeks entering the highly competitive economy of the United States. It served to buffer one against the inevitable failures in the process of achieving occupational success.[7] In addition to preserving one's personal worth in the light of failure, the theme of external conspiracy provided a paranoia that was functional in a competitive economy where "survival of the fittest" remained a potent ideological force.

What strains did these values of authoritarianism and individualism produce in the Greek family? While Greek children were being socialized to a relational pattern stressing authority, the public school was overtly transmitting a value profile of another type: the individual was primary, followed by cooperation, and last, by authoritarianism. Democratic values of egalitarianism and individualism were regarded as primary in a society that espoused unity and collaborative efforts in meeting communal and societal problems. And yet, an inconsistency surfaced. The children absorbed the values of democracy and equality and reassessed parental roles from this new perspective. The school itself functioned in compliance with the values of individualism, authority, and last, cooperation. In other words, the actual functioning of the school was much more in line with the hierarchical authority to which Greek children had initially been socialized. This, in turn, permitted the second-generation child to adjust smoothly to the school's demand for obedience, respect, and dependence. The authority of the teachers and administrators was taken for granted.[8] The absence of delinquency problems in the school system among that generation was testimony to the fit between the Greek value of authority and that of the educational system. Given the Greek child's respect for authority and his motivation for individual achievement, the intergenerational mobility we previously noted is made much more intelligible.

However, the values absorbed by the immigrant's children were the values *professed* in the educational system, that is, self-reliance, self-sufficiency, and independent decision making, all values that clashed with those taught in the Greek home. Independent thinking, when it conflicted with that of the parent, was regarded as rebellion. Adolescence and young adulthood exacerbated these differences in value orientations and increased tensions within the family.

The tension created by lineal authority was especially apparent in the mother-daughter relationship. From the parents' perspective, dating and sexual behavior were taboo. Greek girls were severely restricted in their dating and were simply not trusted to be alone with boys. One second-generation woman, now a college student, relates the following:

In the back of my mind I always knew that I wanted to go to college. However, my parents could not afford to send me and my two brothers. They went and I became very active in the Greek community.

I became engaged to a Greek young man who was in Dental School. I remember he invited me to his school for the weekend. They were having a fund-raising affair. The school was located in the South. My mother wouldn't dream of letting me go. My mother ruled.

Finally, with my brothers' support and telephone calls to my mother from my fiancé, I was permitted to go providing I stayed at a women's hotel. She gave in, but only after she talked about how something might happen to me or someone might steal me, or, or . . .

As a student in high school I was not allowed to sleep at a girlfriend's house unless she was Greek; I couldn't participate in sports because something might happen to me.

After raising my three children, I wanted to go to college, but I didn't have the confidence. I would not have taken that giant step were it not for my husband who gave me the necessary push.

I wanted desperately to go to college, but fear held me back. If my husband had said no, I would never have done it.

The experience illustrates the persistence of lineality into adult life within the framework of prescribed male/female roles. A constant vigilance was maintained to see to it that daughters did not bring shame upon the family. While boys, too, could get into trouble, the onus of responsibility rested with the girls' families. But boys, too, felt the normative strictures even though they were accorded more lenient treatment. A second-generation male explains:

My two brothers and I had mainly Greek friends, although we did have non-Greek friends at school and in the neighborhood. But we knew that the ones who really counted were the Greeks, that is, mattered mainly to our parents.

Every day I was forced to go to Greek school which was held in the same building as the American school; I felt imprisoned from 9:00 to 6:00. Winters were particularly difficult; we never had a chance to play. I felt that I was learning nothing. It is true, however, that I still remember some of the history of Greece and its mythology. But it was having no play time that was really irritating. The teachers were irritating too. Most of them were authoritarian; one in particular had a penchant for pinching ears and slapping faces—but pulling ears was her favorite. We retaliated by being mischievous; often she would cry out of exasperation. We were worlds apart. I remember one teacher whom I actually enjoyed. He was a young man, Mr. Iliopoulos, who formed a Greek organization called the Y Olympians, a camp for Greek kids. Looking back, I can see that he was a man with considerable foresight.

In matters of going out, I was not as restricted as my sister. I was free to go pretty much where I wanted to. I guess it was a matter of sowing one's oats, although, eventually, it was expected that I would settle down and marry a Greek girl. When I didn't, my mother became hysterical. There was no calming her down. She screamed, pulled her hair, lamented her fate. My father was disappointed and furious, but all attention was focused on my mother and her reaction. I didn't marry in the Greek church; my parents didn't come to the wedding and, all in all, despite the justification I made for getting married to the girl I wanted, they kept pointing to the large number of Greek girls who were available.

The truth is that I didn't want to hurt my mother. I had a very strong love for her. I remember her as always being good to me, always working in and outside the home, and never losing her sense of humor. She was inflexible only when it came to marrying a xeni [a non-Greek].

At any rate, as the grandchildren came my parents were happy, and since the children were both boys, they would carry on the family name—"xeni" not-withstanding. My sons never learned Greek, and now I'm sorry I didn't urge them to do so.

Another second-generation male narrates the following:

My six brothers and I grew up in a family where my father ruled. He always impressed us with the fact that we were not to do anything that would bring shame on the family.

His concern was that we marry Greeks, raise our children as Greeks, and become professionals. He stressed that we should not work for somebody else. God forbid any of his children should wind up in a restaurant!

My father struggled; he went hungry in this country. He worked as a busboy, waiter, and eventually owned his own restaurant which he and my mother operated twenty-four hours a day.

My father's law was final. You just knew he was boss. And he was very, very stubborn. You just couldn't negotiate with him. It was helpful, and it was very bad. A person should have a little flexibility. He didn't have it. And when he said something, that was law, it was written in stone; there was no way you were going to change it.

The theme of lineality and its consequences for second-generation Greek Americans finds expression, as we have seen, in a number of literary works of that generation. The stress resulting from cultural conflict is poignantly expressed by Tom Chamales whose novel, *Go Naked in the World,* is a moving account of the frustrations he encountered as a member of a traditional authoritarian family of the forties.

Elia Kazan's *The Arrangement* portrays a Greek American, again with an unyielding father, who is both feared and respected by a son intent upon charting his own life-style, free of traditional expectations.

In *Lion at My Heart,* Harry Mark Petrakis piercingly touches the painful conflict between the patriarchal father and his sons and the subsequent despair and disillusionment experienced by the father.

In a recent novel by Georgia Gianakos Buchanan, *Paved with Gold,* a son grieving his immigrant father's death says, "I often wondered how a father and son could become almost strangers. . . . He continued to live in his

world while I made my way in a different one. . . . He was a little afraid
and skeptical of my world . . . I know . . . but I knew his Greek ways,
and the understanding should have come from me."[9] It is here that one
feels the pulse of the Greek experience across generations, and more
important, one feels and understands this experience in terms of gender.

For the son to be in harmony with his Greek environment, it would be
necessary for him to be responsible for his parents, his sisters, and finally,
his own welfare. The disparity between Greek and American cultural
values was exacerbated by the long absence of the father from the home.
The long hours of work demanded of him intensified the son's problem of
identification with the father and made his authoritarianism more deeply
felt. The father's absence enabled the son to identify closely not with his
father's self-reliance and individuality but only with his authoritarianism.
In Greece, a submissive pattern could be sustained by the son since he, in
turn, was able to express his own individuality outside the family context
in a pattern dominated by lineality. In the United States, the son's
exposure to egalitarian models simply magnified the father's authoritarianism, but not his self-reliance, thus creating for him a conflict between
dependency and independence.[10]

Papajohn highlighted the dilemma of the second-generation experience
in a study of thirty-four first-generation Greek American families. The
total sample was 144 men and women of both generations. Half the
families studied were selected upon the basis of a diagnosed psychotic
reaction in a second-generation son or daughter. A significant conclusion
of the study was that first-generation parents without a patient child were
more acculturated to American values than those who had a child as
patient. This is not to suggest that families without patients escaped the
strains of culture conflict, but it does point to the fact that rigid adherence
to traditional Greek orientation was found to be related to disequilibrium
of a more pervasive nature. This disequilibrium expressed itself in role
conflict within the family and acute culture conflict leading to psychological disorder in individual family members. (Studies of deeply disturbed
families are instructive because they put in high relief what is going on in
so-called normal families.)

A case study treated in depth focused upon a second-generation Greek
woman, the youngest of six children, four girls and two boys, whose father
had trouble finding gainful employment. The mother, adding to her
traditional role as housewife and mother, assumed full responsibility for
the family's support. In the process, the children responded differently to
the mother's authoritarian role. Of interest to us is the patient Ann who,

being the youngest, was more protected by the mother and more indulged. The researcher suggested that perhaps the mother saw her own ambitions being fulfilled through this daughter and that, as the youngest, she was selected to care for the parents in their old age, a role often ascribed to the youngest member of the family. Ann's orientation to both the Greek value system of familism and lineality and the American ideal of individualism and equality remained latent until her marriage to a second-generation male who had absorbed values of both cultures.[11]

Tragically, Ann adopted the individual-cooperative-authoritarian pattern of American values but did not develop the requisite skills for implementing them in her own life. While she reacted negatively against the "good Greek girl" image, she was not able to handle higher education and the upward social mobility that would have actualized her image of self-independence. Her problem was temporarily solved by working at a job less demanding than her abilities called for.

Since the pattern of individuality was not the major orientation of her family, Ann was exposed to considerable strain by being pulled in opposite directions. The inhibiting effect of anxiety prevented her from learning new patterns and redirecting her energies.[12]

The stress of her situation surfaced when she married a second-generation Greek male whose orientation was toward Greek values but who had also adopted the values of individuality and upward-mobility striving. His relations to family members were lineal, which stood in sharp contrast to the image that Ann had of herself. He expected her to behave in an egalitarian manner outside the family context, but not within it. Ann's resolution to authoritarianism was again solved temporarily by ministering to her aging mother. It became a refuge against the conflicting demands she experienced. "Upon the death of her mother, she could no longer contain the anxiety that engulfed her."[13]

While her husband was able to compartmentalize the two value orientations by dividing them between work and home with considerable success, the contradictory stance was not easily resolved for his wife.

The structure of authority relations was a significant source of tension in Greek family life. Theano Papazoglou-Margaris portrays the problem of acculturation faced by the early immigrant woman in the story "Escape." The wife becomes so well assimilated that her husband, feeling threatened, is no longer able to function in his business. With confidence and assertiveness, the wife suggests how their grocery store business can be expanded. The more successful her ideas are, the more he withdraws, until finally he abandons the business to her.[14] Clearly, women whose personal resources enabled them to deviate from the cultural norm brought havoc to their domestic lives.

The persistence of the double standard is portrayed in the work of Harry Mark Petrakis. In *The Ballad of Daphne and Apollo,* Daphne is not permitted to enjoy happiness with the man she loves because of her prior sexual experiences. Apollo cannot reconcile her past with his love for her. In this case, tradition triumphs over romantic love. Finding no solution, Daphne finally commits suicide.[15] In *The Shearing of Samson,* another short story by Petrakis, Samson's friends pity him because his wife tries to remold him to her personality rather than adjusting to his.[16] These values reflect the normative ideal patterns of the Greek American community as individuals attempt to make a cultural shift in value orientations.

The overall image that emerges of the Greek woman as seen through the eye of the novelist, the therapist, the ethnographer, and the social scientist is that of a good wife, good mother, and good housekeeper whose needs are always subservient to those of her husband and children. This is vividly depicted in the work of Thalia Cheronis Selz. "The Death of Anna" presents us with a dying woman as she reflects upon her life for the last time. She is her own severest critic. She reprimands herself for not having been a good enough mother—for had she been, would her son and daughter have married xenoi? And would her daughter have been divorced? Had she been a good wife, her daughter would have been a better wife herself. She further castigates herself for not having provided enough support for her husband who might have become a more successful man. "I've been a bad woman, a bad wife, and a bad mother. God is punishing me."[17] The story reveals to us the values internalized by the traditional Greek woman.

We have seen as well that many women played roles that were not part of the traditional normative standards for a variety of reasons. To be sure, there were the manipulators, the schemers, the prodders, but there were also those who might have preferred not to assume economic responsibility for the family, but financial hardship or widowhood had cast them in new roles. Others had husbands who, because of personality problems or other reasons, forced them into roles they were not prepared for. The relinquishment of the passive role undoubtedly had a profound impact as a model for their second-generation daughters; particularly those first-generation women who felt a sense of pride and accomplishment in their work.

There were also those women who were energetic and resourceful but who accepted a subordinate role in the family where the husband demanded subservience. Often the ambitions of these mothers were actualized through their daughters, so that they became active role models in a different sense.

Gender and Generational Changes

That traditional role expectations continue to be the norm for the Greek male and female across generations is evidenced in the 1970 census data which showed that 82 percent of native-born males of Greek descent, twenty-five years and over, had completed four years of college or more, whereas only 20 percent of the females did. Less than half of the females who entered college completed it. The data also showed that 8.5 percent of Greek-born males completed college compared with 3.1 percent of Greek-born females.[18]

Given this differential in goal-directed behavior, one would expect that students, exposed to an egalitarian milieu over the past decades and with increased educational opportunities, would tend to reject traditional role expectations. To assess this, a sample of males and females was drawn from three generations of college students. The seventy-six students attended four colleges in the New York Metropolitan area (N = 31 males; N = 45 females). Attitudes toward the church, family, and ethnicity were elicited.

The findings disclosed that students of Greek descent showed some differences in conformity to traditional norms. Their views varied sometimes according to generation, sometimes according to sex, and at other times, both were irrelevant. For example, while the females of all generations indicated a favorable attitude toward the church, they overwhelmingly wanted the word *obey* removed from the marriage service. Thus, on the one hand, there was traditional adherence to the ethnic church, but on the other, a nontraditional rejection of female deference. The opposite result obtained with the males who were less favorable toward the church, but strongly opposed to removing *obey* from the marriage service. Along the generational continuum, first-generation men tended to be more conservative than either their second- or third-generation peers. Contrary to expectations, the relationship between attachment to the church and conservatism was not predictable.

The female's stronger ties to a traditional value orientation were exemplified in ethnic identification. Women tended to identify as "Greek Orthodox" or "Greek American," reaffirming their positive response to the church. They were also inclined to be less critical of the church, although some differences were discerned among generations. The second and third generations were less critical of the church than were the first generation of both sexes. This may have been due to different cultural perceptions regarding the appropriate role of the church. The native-born students were more apt to see it as the locus of identity in a pluralist society, whereas the first generation continued to identify nationalism with religion in a taken-for-granted manner.

Endogamy, one of the most important indices of assimilation, elicited quite different responses from males and females. Most of the males, irrespective of generation, were in favor of exogamy. The vast number of females, however, expressed a preference for marriage within the ethnic group. This sexual division regarding endogamy was not very different from the findings of earlier researchers on Greek communities, as we have already noted.

The male's weaker attachment to the church, and his ethnic identity and attitude toward exogamy suggest a more rapid assimilation to the success goals of American society. Men are inclined to deviate from those ethnic norms that tend to curtail fulfillment of their instrumental role as the provider, the ambitious, self-reliant, assertive male.

In open-ended interviews following the completion of the question-naire, several points emerged with considerable frequency. One concerned equality between the sexes. The females of all generations were generally sympathetic to the goals of the women's movement but did not subscribe to full equality between the sexes. Although they were all motivated to find employment after graduation, they also expected to marry, remain home during the child-rearing years, and eventually re-enter the work force. The idea of a dual-career family did not appear feasible to them. The men were divided in their attitudes toward the women's movement. The first-generation men were overwhelmingly opposed to the goals of the movement; the second- and third-generation men tended to be more liberal. At the same time, all three generations of males did not believe that premarital sex should stigmatize the female. Paradoxically, as noted earlier, they were averse to removing the word *obey* from the marriage service. One might conceivably view the aforementioned liberalism on premarital sex as self-serving, or view the contradictory stance as part of a "lagging emulation."[19]

The males perceived their role primarily to be breadwinners. It seems probable that the sex-role stereotyping in the Greek family encourages the male's upward mobility. Bernard Rosen's study confirmed that Greeks and Jews have attained middle-class status more rapidly than most of their fellow immigrants. "In this country," Rosen wrote, "the Greek is ex-pected to be a credit to his group."[20]

During the interviews referred to earlier, both sexes articulated strong attachments to their mothers which surfaced in expressions of not wanting to displease them. All generations articulated a gnawing sense of guilt over this issue. The sentiments expressed by the female respondents, irrespective of generation, were: "I know my mother does what's best for me, I don't want to hurt her." Or "I would like to live away from home, but my mother would really be crushed." Another added, "I don't think my mother means to do it, but she always makes me feel guilty." And "I find myself thinking about how something I do will make her feel before I do it."

Two first-generation males had already assumed economic responsibility for their widowed mothers, adding, "I still have to think of my sister in Greece and help with the dowry." The father was not consciously perceived as forming an integral part of the emotional matrix expressed by both males and females.

Mother/Daughter Relationships

The attachment of the daughter to the mother is a very interesting one. In the early seventies, a study of sixty first-generation recent immigrant women who were seriously maladjusted was undertaken. The research revealed that their pathology was directly related to the fact that their strongest loyalty was not to their husbands but to their mothers who had remained in Greece. Their need was for love and approval by their mothers rather than by their husbands. This "Persephone Syndrome" was one that the female respondents understood very well.[21]

Persephone, it will be remembered, was the daughter of Demeter, the earth mother goddess. Zeus, her brother, jealous of her power, devised a plan with the aid of their brother Hades, ruler of the underworld, to abduct Persephone and, thus, take part of life away from Demeter. Zeus places a narcissus of great beauty in a field of flowers to lure Persephone. When Persephone goes to the flower, the earth opens and Hades seizes her, taking her down into the depths of the earth. Demeter hears the cries of her daughter but does not see where she has been taken or by whom. She wanders for nine days and finally learns the truth from Helios, the sun. In her grief, she withholds her nurturant gifts from the earth, which withers up and becomes lifeless.

Zeus intercedes and sends Hermes to Hades to return Persephone to her mother. Meanwhile, Hades, who is not eager to let her go, offers her a pomegranate seed, knowing that if she eats of the fruit, she must return to him. Upon learning this, Demeter knows that she must lose her daughter for that period of the year that we know as winter. Demeter, the goddess of life, becomes the sorrowing mother who sees her daughter die each year, to be reborn in spring and summer.[22]

Although the females in the sample had been urged to leave, that is, to do well academically, they may also have been encouraged to develop a type of dominant-dependence personality that thwarts autonomy. The daughter may have been the recipient of two different messages: one to achieve, the other to submit. Cross-cultural studies of this phenomenon show that intensive interaction with the mother encourages seeking or dependent behavior.[23] While the individual may be taught to value self-reliance, the dependence bond remains. The Greek female, compared with the Greek male, seems particularly vulnerable to this "dependency hang-up."

It may be that the "fear of success" that operates to thwart the ascendancy drives in the Greek case stems from a fear of negative consequences that include emotional rejection as well as feelings of being unfeminine.[24] In meeting two equally imperative needs, self-reliance and affection, the daughter's success may engender both pride and apprehension in the mother. The fear of being abandoned, which forms the crux of the mother's apprehension, may result in a subtle form of rejection and ultimately in her withholding total approval. This solution to the mother's dilemma may very well function to preserve the dependency bond and limit the daughter's achievement orientation.

The mother/daughter relationship must be understood within the patriarchal framework of Greek life as well as in the larger American patriarchal value system. Whether the mother is idolized or blamed, it is always the mother who appears responsible for either overcoming or perpetuating the problem of female victimization. While she herself may be a victim—victimized by her own mother and so on and so on—the victimization *appears* to be produced and perpetuated by women. To be sure, the interaction between mothers and daughters may, and probably does, perpetuate a particular female personality structure from generation to generation. However, what is critical is that identification with the mother takes place within a patriarchal value system. The devaluation of women within that particular authority system perpetuates the dependency chain of mother/daughter relationships.

It is not only the daughter who identifies with the mother but also the mother who identifies with the daughter, far more than she does with the son. As a result, she does not allow her daughter to separate herself as much from her and achieve independence. In the experience of mothering, a double identification takes place. "A woman identifies with her own mother, and through identification with her child, she re-experiences herself as a cared for child."[25] In identifying with both her mother and her daughter, a woman will produce her own mother's caring for her as a child. Despite efforts to socialize daughters differently, this double identification allows for interaction patterns to be perpetuated from generation to generation.

Clearly, this relationship is linked to gender learning. By remaining close to the daughter and not encouraging the independence she gives a son, the mother keeps her daughter's ego confounded with her own. As a result, the daughter does not develop a clear sense of who she is. This ego-boundary weakness compels the daughter to define herself in terms of others, a pattern in keeping with the relational system that has characterized Greek family life. This very dependence results in a responsibility for the welfare of others. If something goes wrong, the mother feels responsible, even though the event may not have been caused by her. She is caught in an "inescapable embeddedness in relationships to others."[26] The subculture of Greek life and American culture reinforce these gender-related patterns, so that the dependent daughter becomes the dependent wife and then becomes the dependent mother. What has to be made clear is that the psychological component is itself embedded in a male-defined milieu that perpetuates the context in which mother and daughter relate. The double standard generates both responsibility and powerlessness on the part of the female. With limited options, the need of the mother to remain close to her daughter is exacerbated and thereby creates and reinforces the contradiction between submission and refusal, between patriarchal domination and female autonomy.[27]

In order to shed more light on the relations between gender-role expectations and achievement drives among Greek female immigrants attending college, we administered the *Bem Sex Role Inventory* to eleven first-generation students who were part of our larger sample of seventy-six. This was followed by in-depth interviews. The majority of the fathers were blue collar; three were designated as white collar. The mothers' occupations were divided equally between blue-collar workers and homemakers.

The *Bem Sex Role Inventory* consists of sixty masculine traits (ambitious, self-reliant, assertive); twenty traditionally feminine traits (affectionate, gentle, understanding, sensitive to the needs of others); and twenty neutral traits (truthful, friendly, likable). An individual receives a masculinity score, a femininity score, and an androgynous score.[28]

Traditional concepts of masculinity and femininity tend to restrict a person's behavior in important ways. In a modern complex society like ours, an adult has to be assertive, independent, and self-reliant, but traditional femininity makes many women unable to behave in these ways. An androgynous sex role presumably frees individuals from rigid sex-role identification and gender stereotyping.

The masculinity and femininity scores of ten students were approximately equal, indicating that they had internalized an androgynous sex role. The eleventh student had a high femininity score. Whether the students who perceived themselves as androgynous actually behave androgynously was explored. In probing this question, the students were asked to respond to a variety of issues. One question explored their attitude toward the women's liberation movement. Although none was an active member, all were sympathetic to most of its goals. In response to the statement, "Women can be too bright for their own good," only one student was undecided. All agreed that the media degrade women by portraying them as sex objects. In response to the statement, "Raising a child provides many rewards, but as a full-time job, it cannot keep most women satisfied," all students agreed.

When asked to respond to the statement, "Men and women are born with the same human nature; it's the way they are brought up that makes them different," all agreed. And to the statement, "When both husband and wife work, household chores should be shared equally," they again concurred. "Women should be as free as men to take the initiative in sex relations"—all agreed with this.

However, when asked to consider the following, "It is only right that women be allowed to become priests in the Greek Orthodox church," only one student agreed; eight were undecided and two disagreed. Up to this point, the responses elicited were consistent with the androgyny scores on the *Bem Sex Role Inventory*. However, this response and further probing disclosed some inconsistencies in their ideological stance.

For example, eleven students favored endogamous marriages for themselves, even though they agreed that Greek men tend to feel superior to women and would refuse to share equally in household chores if both spouses were employed. As one young woman put it, "No matter how you cut the cake, you will always be subservient to a Greek male. Maybe not the way our mothers were, but we would be submitting unconsciously." They described the Greek male as "domineering, jealous, antagonistic, prejudiced, one who tends to relegate women to subordinate jobs." On the other hand, he is also regarded as "gregarious, generous, hardworking, family oriented, and affectionate." They explained that it was important for Greek men to be in control; their masculinity depended upon a superordinate/subordinate relationship, a norm in conflict with the responses they gave on the Bem Scale and with the newer mode of intellectual companionship between the sexes.

The students agreed that even though their parents support their educational achievements, they are expected to play a deferential role at home. Examples given were serving their fathers and brothers before anyone else and being generally attentive to their needs. One of the girls remarked, "We just hope that the Greek men we marry will be different or that they will change after marriage."

In discussing alternate life-styles such as singlehood and premarital cohabitation, the students agreed that living with someone outside of marriage was not acceptable. They might, they reasoned, do so if they lived away from family and the Greek community; but clearly, the constraints of group norms prevented them from considering it as an alternative life-style or as a precursor to marriage. There was general agreement that their own socialization stressed "femininity" which they defined as not taking risks. At this point, the relationship of mother to daughter again surfaced as a very close one. Taking any action that their mothers opposed caused such extreme guilt that the consensus was, "It's just not worth it."

Since risk taking is an integral part of the motive to achieve and since the students expected to utilize the skills they were developing in college, they were asked if they would seek educational or occupational advancement in another state. Their response was that they regarded the present ethnic community as central to their identity and would not wish to leave it. One student said, "I feel safe and secure when I'm with the family; I feel nothing can happen to me." One young woman stated it for all of them when she said, "My friends and I tend to be conservative regarding marriage and family life and have put our priorities in marriage." They were all mindful of the fact that not being married by the age of twenty-five could prove embarrassing to their families.

And, yet, the students regarded themselves as very liberated when compared with their peers in Greece, where a girl is stigmatized if she isn't married by the age of twenty-one and where she is still burdened with the tradition of the dowry, a practice our sample found reprehensible. While the law pertaining to dowry no longer obtains, they admitted that many Greek men still expect it, even in the United States. Their reaction to the dowry was, "No dowry, the only thing he's going to get is me." Another added, "If he would ask for a dowry, I would never marry him." And, again, "Absolutely no, not here, not in Greece." One young woman said, "My parents are very traditional, and they insist on providing me with a dowry even though I'm opposed to it." One girl was absolutely vociferous: "Dowry? My father says he's sending me to college, I can build my own house." The students pointed out that they were receiving an education and that the degree was a form of dowry.

While it is true that the traditional view of boys as an economic asset and girls as a dowry problem is slowly diminishing, centuries-old male supremacy is still evident. In an effort to ascertain if the traditional preference for a male child persisted, the students were asked what their own preference would be. One respondent volunteered, "I would prefer to have a boy. I am more certain of what traits a male should have. If it's a boy, he can make many of his own decisions. I'm afraid that I'll bring a girl up to be like a boy." Another added, "I would like a girl in order to socialize her to an alternative she can have, alternatives I don't think I have." Again, "I know what a male is, but not a female. It would bother me if I had a passive little girl."

Clearly, the responses reflected the type of role conflicts the students themselves were experiencing. The identification with an androgynous perspective along with their close ties to the primary group were not, at this point, easily reconcilable for them. While the traditional male role continues to be reinforced by Greek norms, the emerging egalitarian woman does not find the necessary family and communal support to sustain her. Obviously, cultural attitudes of such long standing are not easily eradicated.

Although first-generation Greek females in this study perceived themselves androgynously, they had not integrated these values into the world of career and marriage. Obviously, identification with androgyny was not following an easy straightforward pattern. The students seemed to have a very positive self-image and expressed both instrumental and expressive traits. They were keenly aware that the first-generation Greek men they were interacting with had a long way to go in achieving an egalitarian relationship, but they were prepared to make the necessary adaptations at this point in their lives.

Their ambivalent commitment to culturally defined sex-typed roles was articulated by one of the students in the following way: "If I am not married by the age of thirty, I would have a child anyway—just to prove that I'm a woman."

Research suggests that gender-role stereotyping within the Greek American family persists as a viable force in the lives of students as they try to reconcile traditional norms with egalitarian ones. Its structure of sex-segregated role expectancies may be short-circuiting the achievement orientation of Greek women in the larger pattern of American life.

Eclipse of Authority

Minority-group family behavior in the United States can be scaled on a continuum between the poles of rebellion and withdrawal, which indicates that alienation is not a monopoly of any one social class. Somewhere toward the middle of the continuum would be family behavior and ideology reflecting the American dream, namely, aspiring to emulate or to identify with the norms of the dominant middle class. During periods of rapid social change, family behavior, in the same groups, tends to have higher incidence of polarization. At one extreme are those in rebellion against the dominant group norms who pursue a goal of changing from a double standard to a single standard, thus accelerating the trend from patriarchal to egalitarian patterns. At the opposite end are those who have accepted withdrawal or retreatism as a consequence of alienation or disenchantment.

What mode of adaptation do academics of Greek descent reflect? In order to assess this, we surveyed the attitudes of Greek American academics toward a variety of issues relating to traditional sex roles.[29] The group as a whole did not conform to rigid sex typing; however, the female academics tended to be more liberal on issues identified as "feminist" issues. For example, in response to the statement, "It is a reflection on a husband's manhood if his wife works," 85 percent of the females and 64 percent of the males disagreed with it. In replying to, "It is best that mothers with small children stay at home," 69 percent of the males agreed with the statement, whereas only 30 percent of the females did.

With regard to discrimination toward women, the following statement was included: "Women are exploited in this country as much as minority groups are." Fifty-six percent of the females agreed, compared with 32 percent of the males. When asked to respond to the statement, "A woman has the right to put her own self-fulfillment ahead of her obligations to her husband and children," 75 percent of the females and 44 percent of the males agreed. There was divergence with regard to the statement that "The unmarried mother is morally a greater failure than the unmarried father." Ninety-four percent of the females and 77 percent of the males disagreed. Although both demonstrated an open attitude, the women were inclined to be more liberal.

The response to a question concerning the ordination of women in the Greek Orthodox church proved very interesting. Forty-five percent of the female academics approved, 21 percent disapproved, and 33 percent were undecided. Thirty-four percent of the males approved, 42 percent disapproved, and 24 percent were undecided. The response elicited from the women was not as effusive as expected, given their liberal stance on other feminist issues. It is interesting to note that in the survey conducted by the Gallup organization, it was found that, by a wide margin (57 percent to 23 percent), males and females expressed opposition to the ordination of women as priests. Among church members, the ratio was three to one (64 percent to 19 percent).[30] In comparing our sample with the findings of the Gallup poll in which a total population of both males and females opposed the ordination of women, the academic sample proved the more liberal of the two. This does not, however, alter the fact that our sample was more conservative on this issue than on others.

The relatively conservative stance of the academic woman with regard to ordination can perhaps be explained by the compartmentalization of authority itself. That is to say, while authoritarianism is eschewed in interpersonal relations and in the sphere of work, it may not be viewed as dysfunctional in the religious sphere. The church, which is empowered by men along with other major institutions of our society, remains, unlike the others, a remote institution, one that does not necessarily directly affect the lives of women in their secular pursuits. The church may play an invaluable role on the primary level, but it remains separated from the secular orientation that governs the professional expectations of these women. Like men, their key status may be the occupational one, so that the persistence of the double standard in the church may be viewed as irrelevant to what is regarded as their primary concern. Another explanation may be that there is a "lagging emulation" in operation. The nonactivism of Greek American women in the feminist movement suggests that some traditional views may still be reinforcing sex-appropriate roles of the past.

The position of the Orthodox church regarding ordination of women is clear. In an unprecedented visit to the United States, his Beatitude Elias IV, patriarch of Antioch and all the East, joined other Greek Orthodox leaders who are opposed to the ordination of women.[31] In a position paper, "The Ordination of Women," presented at the Ladies Philoptochos Convention in Detroit, Michigan, it was maintained that

. . . for Orthodox women to seek and/or attain ordination to the priesthood would constitute a violation of the orthodox tradition of faith. Consequently,

Greek Orthodox women categorically and unequivocally reject any such innovation in the Christian Orthodox Church.[32]

At the invitation of the World Council of Churches: Sub-Unit on Women in Church and Society held in Agapia, Rumania, women from Orthodox churches met to discuss "The Role of Orthodox Women in the Church and in Society." The keynote speaker, Elizabeth Behr-Sigel of France, stated that the ideology of the women's movement has its origins in the gospel, in which Christ broke down all barriers that separated human beings and affirmed the dignity of men and women.

For in Christ Jesus you are all sons of God through faith. For as many of you as were baptized into Christ have put on Christ. There is neither Jew nor Greek, there is neither slave nor free, *there is neither male nor female* [italics mine] for you are all one in Christ Jesus [Galatians 3:26–28].[33]

On the issue of ordination of women to a sacramental priesthood, Behr-Sigel noted that up till at least the tenth century, particularly in Byzantium, women were ordained as deaconesses to a specific ministry that was liturgical, pastoral, and charitable.[34] She added, "The diaconate of women which has fallen into abeyance could be restored if circumstances required it."[35] She was cautious, however, in asserting that ordination is, in fact, a true and right way for the church because the priest, in his liturgical office, represents Christ. It is the iconic character of the figure of the priest in Orthodox worship, which, in her opinion, offers the strongest argument against the ordination of women.[36] At this time, it cannot be said that the issue of ordination has attracted any significant attention in Orthodox circles. However, very recently a publication by St. Vladimir's Seminary Press, *Women and the Priesthood,* provides the theology that underlies and sustains the position of the Orthodox Chruch on this subject.

The New Immigrants

Returning our focus to the family and its implications for male and female roles, we see that the new immigrants represent a prototype within that framework. Spurred by a desire for economic betterment and opportunities for their children, they have repeated in large measure the experience of those who preceded them. The American economy since the mid-1960s was less expansive, inflation was becoming a permanent feature of the economic landscape, and job opportunities have dwindled

for the newcomer. Their situation has been exacerbated by the fact that
their expectations exceeded the realities of economic life. The built-in
possibility of failure involved a loss of face, a sense of failure, of humiliation
within the family and the community.

Not all the stories, however, are grim. There are Christos and Joanna
Kapolonis, for example, who arrived in New York in 1968 with all their
belongings in valises and boxes. They now make their home in Astoria,
Queens. Theirs is a tale of the success that countless other immigrants have
sought over the decades. Helene, their daughter, is graduating from high
school and plans to study science at New York University. "Can you
imagine us on the plane?" she asks. "My father saw the silver buckle of the
seat belt and thought, for sure, he had just found a cigarette lighter."[37]

They were fortunate in that they were helped by Mrs. Kapolonis's
brother who had arrived in the United States seven years earlier and who
assured them that New York was a place for the future. Mrs. Kapolonis
explained their decision to emigrate: "There was no future in Athens. My
daughters would not have gone to school. They would have worked. They
would have a dowry and they would have gotten married. I wanted them
to have an education—a full education."[38]

Mr. Kapolonis, who is manager of a fruit store, said, "At their age, I had
nothing. No eat; no bread; nothing. I am here for my children." He
added, "I want them to remember my country, remember the traditions
and customs and never forget them. As for Astoria," he said, "it's like a
little bit of Athens in New York."[39]

It is estimated that New York City has a Greek population of approximately 400,000 to 500,000, with sixty to eighty thousand concentrated
in Astoria, followed by the second largest Greek Town in Chicago with a
population of twenty to thirty thousand.

The new arrivals, regardless of when they emigrated, become old
arrivals, and with the passage of time, attitudes pertaining to familial roles
become modified to meet new social and economic conditions. An interesting example of the diversity that exists in Astoria is exemplified by
the parishioners of two churches. St. Demetrios, comprised largely of
middle-class parishioners, is affiliated with the Greek archdiocese of
North and South America. St. Markela, attended by blue-collar workers,
remains unaffiliated with the archdiocese and is referred to as a "rebel
church." The latter views St. Demetrios Church as being deleterious to
ethnic survival because of its assimilationist position. St. Markela rejects
bilingualism in the church and what it regards as encroaching secu-
larism.[40]

In a study based on sixty-five in-depth interviews with members of St. Demetrios Church and thirty interviews with members of St. Markela Church, it was found that each church reflects two conflicting points of view as to what constitutes Greek ethnicity. Of interest to us is the differential perception each has of male and female roles. Among the adherents of St. Markela's, it was found that hierarchical ranking prevails with rights and duties associated with sex and age. In general, the male holds a superordinate position by virtue of his place in the world of work. Woman's role as homemaker is not considered as important because it falls into the personal domain and is devalued as a consequence. One informant commented,

The woman has some power, subtle power. The man has the major power. The woman may think she has. Americans can't understand when you say that I have the power in this house. . . . It comes out of the fact that we have a lot of "maleness." . . . How can you really be free with an open spirit if you know that the wife holds the power in the home? She, of course, let's face it, is there with the children. She has a lot to say, but once the father comes in she agrees to whatever he decides. She'll fight him, and even win one when he gets very old. She usually steps on him at that point. All women seem to like to do it. But when he is young, he is the power in that house. He brings home the money. He makes the decisions. He dictates what goes on in the house.[41]

The study confirmed that women do, indeed, defer to their husbands but not without complaining about their selfless devotion to both husband and children. The spouses agreed that their worlds are separate and that the woman is exclusively identified with the domestic role. On the whole, they subscribed to the idea that employment outside the home poses a danger to the wife's physical and sexual safety.[42] The church seemed to be the only safe place for women. As a result, Sundays and Saints' Days are extremely important events in both religious and secular terms for the women.

Whereas the wife's social life revolves around the church, the male finds his social outlets with other men by either playing cards or drinking. The men tend to become active in the church when the need to raise funds emerges. Their view is that neither women nor priests are sufficiently competent to handle money matters. The experiences of the male in the economic sphere confirm superior status upon him and reinforce the validity of the double standard.

Among the parishioners at St. Markela Church, the parishioners consider male children more important than females, despite the fact that

girls no longer present dowry problems. Male children are given preferen-
tial treatment. At the same time, it is the parents and not the children who
are the focus of familial concern. A dilemma surfaces. On the one hand,
the parents expect their children to defer to their decisions regarding
education and marriage; on the other hand, they want their children to be
occupationally upwardly mobile.[43] The fear of losing control over their
children is of paramount importance and, in many instances, takes precedence over their concern for upward mobility. A situation of such stress
places the growing child in a position of unresolved marginality.

The strains produced in the family during the process of cultural
dislocation among the new immigrants (or migrant workers, as many
perceive themselves) has to be seen within the context of differential
expectations when compared with the old immigrants. Unlike the older
immigrant experience, the new group is more sexually balanced with
almost as many women coming over as men.[44]

While the old immigrants were confronted with seemingly insur-
mountable obstacles, they were buoyed by the expansion of the American
economy up to the Great Depression and again during and following the
Second World War. While many new migrants follow the older path of the
restaurant business, the majority work for someone else. Indeed, many
have moved into new areas of business such as construction, painting, and
maintenance work. In many instances, both husband and wife enter the
labor force as blue-collar workers. While all immigrant women of sixty
years ago were admonished to stay in the house, except under dire
circumstances, outside employment for the recent arrival becomes an
economic necessity. Some of the men who worked at skilled jobs in Greece
find that they are not employed in a job commensurate with their abilities
and, therefore, experience downward mobility. The resultant stress has
negative consequences for the family.

The old immigrants started together on the same rung of the ladder;
they were economically destitute, they found no church, no support
system, and they were their own reference group. Whatever they earned
was regarded as an improvement over the economic situation they left
behind in the Old World. Further, with the passage of time, the new
immigrant continues to identify with Greece because of modern air travel,
improved communications, and the constant flow of friends and relatives
to and from Greece. This sustains their nostalgia for and loyalty to their
native country, and the idea of returning is always potentially a reality.

Their situation is also characterized by rising expectations. They have
seen the accomplishments of other Greeks and want to achieve or surpass

them. Failure to succeed is, as we noted, humiliating. Avoidance of failure is crucial to their sense of pride and engulfs the family in an attempt to protect itself against the alienating aspects of Americanization. The pressures create anxiety and stress for both male and female.

The hierarchical relations between children and parents is steadily reinforced by trying to keep the socialization of the children within the confines of the ethnic enclave—church, Greek school, day nursery schools located in the church, and social gatherings in church and home.

Among the families at St. Markela Church, a child's education is secondary to family interests, whereas the parents at St. Demetrios Church tend to place their children's achievements before other considerations. In the former case, boys of high school age will discontinue their education to work as busboys and dishwashers in order to help the family financially. The child's personal interests, although affirmed to be important, are not as important as the welfare of the collective family unit. The traditional belief that aging parents belong with their adult children and will receive, in turn, the care and sacrifices they made for their children has been accentuated over generations.[45] It is part of a reciprocal relationship, and not without its concomitant ambivalence. There is, on the one hand, the expectation that children will care for them and, on the other, the perceived reality that this may not be so.

Another way in which control is exercised by immigrant parents is their attempt to arrange the marriages of their children. The fear that interaction with other teenagers might have a deleterious effect upon their children prompts parents to increase their surveillance. At the same time, as might be expected, it ignites guilt and hostility within young people who are seeking to test their own autonomy.

The nature of this conflict has been highlighted in a study conducted by the staff of the Hellenic American Neighborhood Action Committee (HANAC), an agency serving the immigrant community since 1972 in New York City. HANAC's Child and Family Counseling Service, established in 1977, serves approximately one hundred families annually. It reports that family dysfunctions caused by immigration result in various antisocial behavior, ranging from wife and child abuse, learning disabilities, teenage pregnancies, drug abuse, and dropping out of school.[46]

Families seeking psychological counseling are mainly unskilled workers with a gross income of $3,300 with both mother and father working full or part time in most of the cases. They tend not to be affiliated with a local church nor do they belong to any fraternal organization. The majority of parents have not completed elementary school.[47] The acute anomie experienced by family members results in a desire to return to their country of origin where every individual is seen as linked by social bonds to others. To be sure, the life they left behind is greatly idealized; they express a desire to return but are reluctant to do so without having succeeded economically in this country. Their insecurity with the English language and their consequent frustration is compounded by the rejection they feel from other Greeks who have made it. Adjustment to their new country is a difficult one. As we previously saw, there is a direct correlation between acculturation and emotional health; feeling disadvantageously located, some members of the new immigrant population are finding the period of psychosocial adjustment particularly stressful as they shift from an extended-family structure to that of the nuclear family, from bonded systems to anomie.

In general, Greeks tend to mistrust the mental health field and are reluctant to seek help outside the family. They tend to view emotional problems as nervous problems having an organic base. As reality attests, no one gets through the acculturation process unscathed, even in the so-called healthy families. In all cases, it is taboo to be critical of one's parents, even when they are hurting you. It is easier to express angry feelings toward one's parents through others. The others become the focus, the scapegoat, for unexpressed hostility stemming from the family nexus.

When the child has a learning problem, the parents' position in the relational family circle and the community is threatened. The child, being an extension of the parent, has the power to discredit and to devalue parental worth. Further, the child who has a learning disability cannot be the superior person he has been told he is. The discrepancy between reality and wish fulfillment is painful for the whole family. The child is confused: he is trying to deal with parents who tell him that nothing is wrong with him, that the problems are external to him, but his feelings and performance tell him otherwise. Even when the child adjusts to school, the emotional problem may be hidden because the child has merely learned to conform to authoritarian norms.

The Greek male seems more reluctant to accept therapy than females. Apparently he has greater difficulty in dealing with himself as a failure. Such an admission stands in sharp contrast to his perceived self as a successful man. The externalized self takes on a reality of its own. To protect this "objective" existence, the male is compelled to devalue the therapeutic process and, particularly, the male therapist who personifies the very success he aspires to. Dealing with female therapists becomes more acceptable since she does not pose a threat to the Greek male's manhood and, hence, reduces appreciably his level of anxiety.

The tendency is not to seek outside help and hope that the problem will be taken care of within the family unit. When they do reach out for help, an interpreter is frequently needed which further demeans and embarrasses the Greek patient. The reluctance to seek help is rooted in this cultural component and in the impersonal therapeutic relationship, which is abhorrent to the Greek who functions more successfully in a one-to-one personalized relationship. Thus, help is sought only when the problem is perceived to be unmanageable, caused by an outside source beyond their control. In some instances, exorcism is sought as the ultimate solution.

Another study concentrating primarily upon the Greeks who migrated to Detroit reported that parents were experiencing acute stress with regard to their children who were emulating the young people in this country. The parents complained about the lack of respect for parents and for authority figures in general. Problems they cited as affecting the Greek family were drug addiction, street crimes, and liberal dating customs. In one family interviewed, the father would not allow his son to bring his friends home because there was a daughter in the family and he feared that if he were too liberal, all the misfortunes of American society would befall him.[48]

Intermarriage

The fear of intermarriage has been for all immigrant parents a most formidable one. It threatens the very fabric of family life. It is difficult to ascertain how pervasive intermarriage is in the United States, but judging from available data, the rate is high. The Greek archdiocese reports that from January 1 to December 31, 1978, there were a total of 4,740 weddings in the church. Of these, 2,295 were Greek Orthodox and 2,445 were mixed marriages.[49] The latter included only those mixed marriages performed in the church.

It should be remembered that most publicized rates of mixed marriages are based upon the total number of a group's marriages. Sometimes they are interpreted as if they are based upon the number of individuals who marry. A marriage rate refers to the percentage of marriages involving individuals in a specific category. A marriage rate of individuals refers to the percentage of married individuals in a specific category who enter a mixed marriage.[50]

For example, if we have six homogamous Greek Orthodox marriages and four mixed Greek Orthodox marriages, we can speak of either a 40 percent or a 25 percent mixed-marriage rate. Four of the ten marriages, or 40 percent of the marriages involving Greek Orthodox are mixed, but four Greek Orthodox out of 16, or 25 percent, are in mixed marriages.[51]

The mixed marriage rate for marriages is always greater than the mixed marriage rate for individuals. Thus, if you wanted to prove that mixed marriages are occurring in greater frequency, you could use the mixed marriage rate for marriages. If you wished to prove that the incidence of mixed marriage is not very great, you could use the mixed marriage rate for individuals. Statistically, both figures would be accurate.[52]

The second point about intermarriage concerns the size of the group. The smaller the group relative to the total population, the faster its rate goes up with each intermarriage.[53] In the case of the Greeks, religious homogamy means ethnic homogamy. The triple melting pot concept, which hypothesizes that ethnic lines are being crossed repeatedly in the United States while people continue to marry within their own religious group, does not apply to the Greeks. The ethnic factor defines homogamy and restricts the field of eligibles to *Greek* Orthodox, not to Orthodox per se.

In terms of the archdiocese's figures, the number of mixed marriages performed within the church increased from slightly more than 28 percent of the total in 1963 to almost 50 percent in 1976 and probably more than 50 percent in 1978.[54]

This does not mean that most individuals marry non-Greeks. Approximately two-thirds of all Greeks who marry now are marrying other Greeks even though their marriages constitute about 50 percent of all marriages performed in recent years. It would take an exogamous rate of about 60 percent of all marriages performed for 50 percent of all Greek American individuals to be out-marrying.[55]

In a large church community of approximately 1,400 families in Nassau County on Long Island, New York, the out-marriage rate was reported to be 65 percent. Marriages among Greeks in Nassau County (Town of Hempstead) tend to be exogamous. The parish averages about seventy-five marriages a year, and of these, 75 percent are mixed. An influx of new immigrants has recently caused the percentage to decline to 65 percent. There seems to be few Orthodox-Orthodox marriages outside the ethnic group. The Reverend Patrinacos observes that because of national emnities of long standing among the Balkan peoples, the Greek Orthodox church still is very hesitant about having open relations with other Orthodox churches. Many priests, he adds, would prefer to see the young marry outside the church rather than marry an Orthodox of non-Greek extraction.[56] This attitude, however, seems to be undergoing change with the younger clergy giving greater weight to religion than ethnicity.[57]

Marrying another Orthodox, however, has not yet emerged as a viable alternative for the Greek Orthodox. What matters is that the marriage take place within the Greek Orthodox church. In this way, a link is preserved to the Greek community. Undoubtedly, in the future, Americanization will facilitate the acceptance of Orthodoxy as a preference in mate selection rather than ethnicity.

As one goes further east on Long Island, New York, the out-marriage rate increases to about 80 percent.[58] Class and generation seem to be operative variables here. While first- and even many second-generation Greek Americans in urban ghettos are, in effect, "urban villagers," the second and third generations (middle class, upwardly mobile, suburban or urban) are familistic only to the degree that others in their class, regardless of ethnicity, may also be familistic.

In Orange, New Jersey, a community with five hundred Greek families, it is reported that 52 percent of fourteen yearly marriages are mixed.[59] The rate of intermarriages would be higher were it not for the presence of a growing population of new immigrants.

In Newark, New Jersey, six hundred Greek families are actively involved in the parish life of the community. Its exogamous rate is about 75 percent; approximately 45 percent of the mixed marriages end in conversion regardless of the sex of the non-Greek spouse, and almost all the children are raised as Orthodox. The Greek church in Clifton, New Jersey, is also strongly ethnically oriented. About one-third of its parish is not proficient in English; nevertheless, in 1974, its exogamy rate was 50 percent, and by 1978, it was 75 percent.[60]

In Bay Ridge, Brooklyn, New York, a Syrian and Greek community has existed for many years. Their ethnic commitments have discouraged inter-Orthodox contact and marriage between these two groups. Their churches are only two blocks away from each other but social mixing is at a minimum. In the Greek church, twenty out of sixty marriages a year are mixed marriages and none are with the Syrians. The growth of a large immigrant population of Greeks has undoubtedly reinforced the ethnic component in mate selection.[61] It is probably correct to state that rapid de-ethnicization might actually alienate the religion's most committed followers.

Studies generally indicate that the rate of mixed marriages is on the increase; these increases result from a combination of factors: decline in immigration, the vertical and horizontal mobility that characterizes our society, and the increased number of contacts facilitated by ease of communication and transportation. Even where ethnic feelings run high, it is difficult to sustain ethnic loyalty in the realm of marital choice in the United States where love is considered to be a matter of individual choice and personal happiness.

Religious institutions, in general, including the Greek Orthodox church, are opposed to mixed marriages because they fear communal dissolution. The Greek case is compounded by the limited field of eligibles that its ethnic boundaries impose, a fact that does not apply to Irish, Italian, or Polish Catholic populations. For them, marrying outside their ethnic group does not alienate them from group loyalty. A broader view encompassing an American Orthodoxy would increase interethnic marriages and would sustain, at the same time, a monolithic religious group. This, in turn, would open the door to approved marriages between Greeks, Syrians, Russians, and so forth. A minimal understanding of Orthodoxy tends, of course, to highlight the importance of ethnicity and circumscribe mate selection.

Studies tend to reveal that Greeks most likely to intermarry are unfamiliar with the Greek language, customs, ethnic celebrations, and holy days, and lack contact with relatives or friends in Greece. However, this does not necessarily imply that a pattern of social isolation with regard to Greek friends after marriage persists, regardless of which spouse is Greek. Whether it is the male or female who marries out (but has an Orthodox wedding ceremony), the children are likely to be baptized in the Greek Orthodox church and to be raised according to Greek traditions, depending on how the individual spouse defines *tradition*.

Data from the Greek archdiocese of North and South America, covering the period from 1970 through 1981, also indicate that mixed marriages are increasing. In 1970, 2,663 Greek Orthodox marriages were performed in the church as compared with 2,473 mixed marriages from a total of 5,136 marriages. There is no way of knowing how many mixed marriages occur outside the church. In 1981, the number of Greek Orthodox marriages was 1,781, and mixed marriages numbered 3,104, indicating that a 20 percent increase in mixed marriages had taken place. In 1970, approximately 48 percent of the marriages that took place in the church were mixed; in 1981 this rose to 67 percent.[62]

With regard to divorce statistics in 1970, 261 Greek Orthodox marriages were dissolved as compared with 100 mixed marriages. In 1981, 405 Greek Orthodox divorces took place, while 339 mixed marriages ended in divorce out of a total of 744. Between 1970 and 1981, a 70 percent increase in divorces took place among mixed marriages as compared with less than 50 percent in the Greek Orthodox category.[63] Proportionately speaking, there were more mixed marriages that ended in divorce since 1970; percentagewise, there were more Greek Orthodox divorces in 1970 than in 1980. The statistics do not tell us what the duration of these marriages were before they were dissolved.

Whether or not the individual who marries out of the religion sustains contact with the Greek community depends upon a number of variables that include support or nonsupport of parents regarding the marriage, personalities of the spouses, length of marriage, education of spouses, their ages, and the extent of communication between them. Other variables include attitudes toward religion, knowledge of Orthodoxy, the extent and quality of ethnic internalization, and the cohesiveness of family ties.

The continual redefinition of ethnicity and the role of the Greek Orthodox church within the larger framework of Orthodoxy will continue to be dominant factors in determining the social boundaries within which marital bonds between Greek Americans and non-Greeks are to be found in the future.

Chapter Six
Epilogue

The Greeks in America have never been nor are they now a homogeneous ethnic group. Historical, economic, demographic, and ecological conditions conspired to shape the destiny of each influx of immigrants variously located within the social structure of the United States.

There was no singular American experience in which all Greeks participated collectively. The challenge of the cities, the coal mines, the tanneries, the textile mills, and the vagaries of small businesses produced varying degrees of assimilation and ethnic antagonism. And yet, to be sure, they shared a common ground, bound as they were by religious and traditional values that were transposed to the New World to produce the prototype of the Greek American. But one must tread cautiously lest the prototype blur the ever-present diversity that makes up the American experience of any ethnic group.

Generally, ethnic studies, and specifically those relating to the Greeks in America, have tended to follow the assimilationist model.[1] This approach has inevitably resulted in a scenario that has polarized the native- and foreign-born into a we/they dichotomy. Psychological propensities notwithstanding, it has been suggested that exclusive focus on majority versus minority relations cannot adequately explain interethnic relations. Ethnic minorities are not only acted upon, they themselves initiate responses (often unconsciously), which generate ethnic antagonism. One explanation offered when discussing ethnic antagonism is that of the split labor market; the theory seems more value free than the assimilationist or melting-pot variety, and allows for the fact that conflict is mutual between groups, that is, it is a product of interaction.[2]

Central to this perspective is that ethnic antagonism is generated by a labor market where ethnic groups are willing to work for less than are the indigenous workers of a particular area. Obviously, the ethnics, lacking skills, will sell their labor relatively cheap, partly because of their ignorance of the labor market, their exploitation by their own compatriots, their absence of options, and their perception of themselves as sojourners in a new country. Sojourner status encourages short-range planning and comes into conflict with native workers who tend to perceive their work role in long-range terms. For example, the violence in South Omaha occurred after the arrival of large numbers of Greeks seeking employment during the winter months when work on the railroads was at a low ebb. Meanwhile, in the greater Omaha area, the Greek population had increased to 3,000 during a period of labor unrest in the meat-packing industry. The native workers struck for higher wages, while the Greeks were willing to work for lower wages. This aroused great resentment toward the Greeks, to say the least.[3]

A split labor market, which represents one source of ethnic antagonism, need not develop among ethnic groups, providing they share similar goals or are equal in resources in the same economic system.[4] Tarpon Springs, Florida, is a case in point. Not only were the Greeks accepted as an economic asset, but racial antagonisms between Greeks and blacks were absent. Not only did the two groups work cooperatively, but the blacks learned to speak the Greek language, acquiring, in the process, the unique dialect of the particular Greek they worked for.

If the labor market is split ethnically or racially, class antagonism takes the form of ethnic antagonism, although, in reality, it is class and not ethnic antagonism that is being expressed.[5] When one ethnic group provides decidedly cheaper labor, the higher paid worker fears not only the loss of his job but that the standard of earning in all jobs will be substantially undermined. This fear leads toward exclusion—discrimination in hiring, in education, and in residential segregation—thus preserving a nonsplit labor market. Thus, Spartanburg, South Carolina, reflected an ethnic equanimity not found in Salt Lake City, Utah. Unlike the Marxist view, the conflict is not between capital and labor, but between high-priced and cheap labor. The basic interests being served are not those of the capitalist class which is being deprived of cheap labor, but those of the high-priced working class.

A split labor force tends, therefore, toward exclusion. The sojourner status of the Greeks made it possible to use them as strikebreakers, thus exacerbating the labor market split in Salt Lake City, Utah. However, it is interesting to note that the Greeks who mined coal in southeastern Colorado in 1913–14 were hemmed in by the mountains to the west and the almost uninhabited prairies to the east which isolated the miners from the normal industrial, social, and civil life of the state. This enabled mine operators to exercise more control over resources of the region as well as over the miners and their families who depended on them for survival. The land and houses were company owned and neglected, and the streets, which were the only means of entry and exit, were also company owned. Wages were paid in company script redeemable only in company stores. These conditions led to a strike against the Colorado Fuel and Iron Company. In this instance, the Greeks were prominent in the strike. If the Greeks in South Omaha, Nebraska, served as antiunionists and strike-breakers, the Greeks in the mines of southeastern Colorado strongly supported efforts to unionize workers. Their earlier arrival in the country and their changing self-perception as sojourners made the Greeks of Colorado more receptive to organized action. Their collective action became clear soon after the strikers moved their families out of the company-owned homes to those established by the United Mine Workers of America.[6]

However, in most situations, a split labor force prevailed, which functioned to insulate the Greeks through discriminatory measures. The Immigration Law of 1924 represented the concrete step taken to reduce, not ethnic antagonism, but economic or class antagonism, of which ethnicity was made the culprit.

One unintended consequence of a split labor market is that it pushes the foreign-born into their own ethnic enclave and into their own economic enterprises. The Greek's newly achieved economic role in the twenties as a "middleman minority" placed a large segment of the group into an intermediate rather than a low-status position. It has been observed that certain ethnic groups tend to occupy particular economic positions within the social structure, that is, the Jews in Europe, the Chinese in Southeast Asia, the Asians in East Africa, the Armenians in Turkey, the Syrians in West Africa, the Japanese and Greeks in the United States.[7] The consensus regarding the causes for this among ethnic groups is not unanimous; however, a dominant theme seems to be that it is a reaction to discrimination resulting in a significant reinforcement of ethnic cohesiveness. An opposing view is that middleman minorities emerge as a reaction to sojourner status, including a tendency toward thrift and a concentration in certain occupations. Middleman minorities generally demonstrate a resistance to exogamy; the tie of blood provides a basis for trust and is reinforced by formal and informal ethnic institutions.[8] Whether host hostility is experienced depends, of course, upon the ethnic's competitive conflict with business groups that predate the middlemen's migration. Anderson, Indiana, and Spartanburg, South Carolina, are but two examples previously cited where intergroup hosility was held in abeyance despite the fact that the Greek's role as middleman was dominant.

The role of middleman is inclined to set in motion the need for intraethnic dependence and inadvertently encourages segregation itself. A case in point is Astoria in New York City, which was heading toward economic decay until the wave of Greek immigrants following the Second World War assumed middleman roles and transformed the economic and residential ambiance into a thriving part of the metropolis. The dynamics of small-business activity galvanizes forces that tighten and revitalize intracommunity organizations and religious institutions. This ensures the probability of a minority's continued concentration in middle-rank economic roles.

The role of middleman minority, while regarded as hardworking, shrewd, and clannish, is also regarded as an economic asset to the community. As early as 1909, Grace Abbott wrote an article for the *American Journal of Sociology* in which she paid the Greeks an underhanded compliment.

During the short time he has been in Chicago, the Greek has established his reputation as a shrewd businessman. On Halsted St. they are already saying, "It takes a Greek to beat a Jew."[9]

And a proponent of the split labor market writes:

In all our examples, middleman groups are charged with being clannish, alien, and unassimilable. They are seen as holding themselves aloof, believing they are superior to those around them, and insisting on remaining different.[10]

But how is one to explain the Greek's role as middleman given his premigratory rural status? According to the sociological thesis developed by Stephen Steinberg in *The Ethnic Myth: Race, Ethnicity, and Class,* one's cultural baggage "has little to do with a group's economic mobility or educational achievement." What matters is economic circumstances, time of arrival, and educational opportunities that follow. In the case of the Jews, attitudes and values pale beside the materialistic considerations of their premigratory economic experience. They came from urban sectors of the world and had developed skills that were congenial to the industrial needs of America. Steinberg suggests that in the process of adapting to America, the Jews gave up their cultural baggage, which is documented in

the increasing rates of interfaith marriages.[11] But is this so? Is ethnicity or
ethnic identity discarded in *all* exogamous marriages? It is an unanswered
question. Steinberg does not deal with the nature of ethnicity per se. There
is no way of knowing what is being "discarded" in the process of acculturation and assimilation. Is it a folk culture, a religion, a language, or a sense
of collective identity that gives way? Steinberg's materialistic interpreta-
tion is difficult to apply to the Greek case. They were not an urban people.
Their premigratory status of peasant farmer would not seem to lend itself
to developing skills receptive to a burgeoning industrial society.

Historian William McNeill points out two aspects of Greek rural life
that seem relevant to this issue. He notes that traditional peasant life was
and remains market oriented. This provided the villager with an orientation that augured well for urban living. Also, as we have seen, Greek
family life was centered upon viewing outsiders as "them" rather than
"us." Given this family focus, the group was able to function as a buffer
against the impersonality of competitive individualism. What cannot be
stressed enough is the importance of buying and selling in traditional
Greek life. "This was the really critical activity, even when it occupied
only a few days of the year. . . . Prestige and repute in village opinion
depended on how skillfully the head of the household made his deals."[12]

Cultural explanations, such as close family ties and mutual help,
undoubtedly explain to some extent the upward mobility strivings of the
Greeks. Unlike the Jews, the Greeks emigrated largely from rural areas
and started off at the bottom rung of the economic ladder, filling jobs
others did not want to do. The accumulation of some capital enabled them
to demonstrate their skills for middleman roles. Their tendency to go into
the restaurant business again reflects the peasant background and the
traditional skills they brought with them.[13]

McNeill maintains that the recent diaspora continues to reflect the
values and attitudes of village life despite the migrants' general claim to
urban origins. Structural and cultural factors seem mutually reinforcing,
although Steinberg tends to see them as exclusive. Many of the values
inculcated in Greek family life became readily transferable to centers
offering new economic opportunities, and they have been able to respond
with less disruption than other groups because both structural and cultural
factors have simultaneously reinforced each other.[14] Even with the dramatic changes that have taken place in Greece since 1960, these cultural
values continue to play an integral part in the migratory experience of the
Greeks.

The Greeks, unlike other ethnic groups, have continued to emigrate to the United States since the Second World War and have continued to define the boundaries of Greek ethnicity, ranging from folk culture to the idiom of the educated. In general, along with the native-born of Greek descent, they have concerned themselves with a broad range of social problems, some directly related to Greece and others to the general Greek American experience in America. Various organizational networks such as the Modern Greek Studies Association, Krikos, a professional resources organization for Greece, the Modern Greek and Byzantine programs founded on United States campuses, of which Queens College of the City of New York is the largest with a Greek student body of 1,500, the recently established Greek Theatre of New York, and other innovative ethnic enterprises, reflect a serious and scholarly concern with the transmission of Greek tradition.

Whether this behavior can be labeled "symbolic ethnicity," as sociologist Herbert J. Gans does in distinguishing the instrumental component of ethnicity from its expressive one, is difficult to say. In essence, symbolic ethnicity provides a sociopsychological identity that requires none of the constraining organizational networks of the past. Although Gans perceives this fundamentally as a product of the third and fourth generations, he nevertheless acknowledges its incipient presence among the second generation of ethnics as well. It is, at best, difficult to draw generational boundaries when dealing with ethnicity as a sociopsychological phenomenon.

Gans's position is that the current ethnic role in America is a voluntary rather than ascriptive role, one that people assume along with the myriad other roles demanded by our society. The masking and unmasking allows the individual to play his ethnic role in terms of his own perception of ethnicity. Believing that there is little stigma attached to being ethnic, Gans writes as follows:

Today ethnics are admitted everywhere, provided they meet economic and status requirements, *except at the very highest levels of the economic, political and structural cultural hierarchies.* . . . Moreover, since World War II, the ethnics have been able to shoulder blacks and other racial minorities with the deviant and scapegoat functions they performed in an earlier America, *so that ethnic prejudice and "institutional ethnism" are no longer significant, except again at the very top of the society hierarchies.*[15] (Italics mine.)

One wonders: is this exclusionary imposed policy an attribute of class, ethnicity, or both? Does it apply only to the descendants of white Europeans or to Chicanos, blacks, and American Indians as well? Is symbolic ethnicity as viable a component in their identity as is claimed for their white counterparts? It is highly improbable that any proposition stated in general terms could possibly fit the experience of all immigrant groups in the United States; nevertheless, the notion that ethnicity is voluntary and not imposed would be an interesting one to test intergenerationally.

In line with his sociological analysis, Andrew Greeley describes the plight of the Irish by saying that now that it is respectable to be Irish, the Irish have forgotten how it is to act Irish. The ethnic boundaries having become blurred in the thrust for respectability and assimilation has left them with only the parades on St. Patrick's Day, which are monuments to lost possibilities of which few people in the parade are aware.[16]

Basically, what *is* being reflected in symbolic ethnicity? Is it the irrelevant tradition of generations past? the cultural baggage that is discarded en route to inescapable assimilation? What is the nature of tradition itself, and what role does it play as it is transmitted from generation to generation? Social scientists have been inclined to view tradition as an obstacle to progress and an impediment to individual freedom. Because of this implicit ideological bias, they have tended to skirt the substantive aspect of tradition in the sociological analysis of ethnic groups.

In a recent book entitled *Tradition,* Edward Shils explores not a particular tradition but tradition itself, and its role in shaping human experience and perception over time. Arguing against the conservative stigma attached to tradition, Shils postulates that tradition does not remain the same as it is transmitted from generation to generation; it is its very centrality that enables people to build upon, and chart their lives with, the past. Progressivists have been inclined to view tradition as reactionary, as antithetical to progress, novelty, and innovation, but even those who pride themselves on the imperious nature of reason must themselves rely upon tradition to do so. Since traditionalism has come to mean backwardness in contemporary society, it is serious business to infringe upon the imperative of change, a word consonant with improvement.[17]

In exploring the role of tradition per se in human life, Shils expresses its continuous flux and its stability, both being essential to the avoiding of social disorder and demoralization. He writes:

The loss of contact with the accomplishments of ancestors is injurious because it deprives subsequent generations of the guiding chart which all human beings, even geniuses and prophets, need. . . . Without this experience one is left without a sense of being members of a collectivity which transcends themselves and transcends their contemporaries. . . . It is not that emancipation is to be eschewed or innovation ignored, the mistake lies in regarding them as the *only* goals to be pursued. An individual cannot chart the world himself. This is one of the limits to the ideal of total emancipation and total self-regulation.[18]

Over thirty years ago, theologian Reinhold Niebuhr observed the rapid pace of modern history and the urgent need to preserve communal unity. He wrote:

Democratic institutions are the cause, as well as the consequence, of cultural variety and social pluralism. Once freedom is established, economic interests, cultural convictions, and ethnic amalgams proliferate in ever greater degree of variety. Traditional communities were ethnically homogeneous. . . . Modern nations are no longer ethnically homogeneous though most of them do have a core of ethnic unity. Furthermore, they all must contend with dynamic class forces. . . . Yet the complexities of a technical civilization make it impossible to bring them back into the narrow confines of coerced unity. Democracy must find a way of allowing them to express themselves without destroying the unity and life of the community.[19]

The solution requires a high form of commitment, preserving a humble recognition of the fact that any social phenomenon is subject to historical contingency and relativity. Humility is, after all, in perfect accord with the presuppositions of a democratic society.[20]

Notes and References

Preface

1. "The Interview with Czeslaw Milosz," *Novak Report on the New Ethnicity* 3 (February 1981):4–5.

Chapter One

1. Deno J. Geanakoplos, *Byzantine East and Latin West: Two Worlds of Christendom in Middle Ages and Renaissance* (Oxford, 1966), pp. 40–54.
2. C. M. Woodhouse, *A Short History of Modern Greece* (New York, 1968), p. 101.
3. Ibid., pp. 102–5.
4. Timothy Ware, *The Orthodox Church* (Baltimore, Md., 1964), pp. 97–98.
5. Kenneth Young, *The Greek Passion* (London, 1969), pp. 146–53.
6. T. A. Couloumbis, J. A. Petropulos, and H. J. Psomiades, *Foreign Interference in Greek Politics* (New York, 1976), p. 22.
7. Jane Perry, Clark Carey, and Andrew Galbraith Carey, *The Web of Modern Greek Politics* (New York: Columbia University Press, 1968), pp. 52–53.
8. Couloumbis, Petropulos, and Psomiades, *Foreign Interference in Greek Politics,* p. 78.
9. Perry, Carey, and Carey, *The Web of Modern Greek Politics,* pp. 59–68.
10. Woodhouse, *A Short History of Modern Greece,* p. 12.
11. Eliot G. Mears, *Greece Today* (Berkeley, Calif., 1929), p. 63.
12. Ware, *The Orthodox Church,* p. 9.
13. Sir James Rennell Rodd, *The Customs and Lore of Modern Greece* (London, 1892), pp. 48–49; F. A. Smothers, W. H. McNeill, and E. D. McNeill, *Report on the Greeks* (New York: 20th Century Fund, 1948), p. 53.
14. Theodore Saloutos, *The Greeks in the United States* (Cambridge, Mass., 1964), p. 29.
15. Couloumbis, Petropulos, and Psomiades, *Foreign Interference in Greek Politics,* pp. 78–79.
16. Ibid., p. 79.
17. Perry, Carey, and Carey, *The Web of Modern Greek Politics,* pp. 131–32.

18. Kenneth R. Legg, *Politics in Modern Greece* (Berkeley, Calif., 1969), p. 58.

19. Aphrodite Mavroede, "Makronisos Journal," *Journal of the Hellenic Diaspora* 5, no. 3 (Fall 1978):116.

20. Ibid., p. 119.

21. Ibid., p. 128.

22. Woodhouse, *A Short History of Modern Greece*, p. 265.

23. Ibid., p. 292.

24. "Greece," in *The New Encyclopaedia Britannica* (1974), 8:318.

25. Constantine Mitsotakis, "Inflation: An International and Greek Problem," *Greek World*, April–May 1978, p. 24.

26. "Greece," in *The New Encyclopaedia Britannica*, 8:318.

27. Saloutos, *The Greeks in the United States*, p. 8.

28. John Campbell and Philip Sherrard, *Modern Greece* (New York, 1969), pp. 359–61; William H. McNeill, "The Texture of Life in Greek Cities," in *The Metamorphosis of Greece since World War II* (Chicago, 1978), pp. 206–46.

29. "More Greeks Return than Emigrate Now," *New York Times*, July 6, 1980, p. 11, col. 1.

30. Rodd, *The Customs and Lore of Modern Greece*, pp. 47–48.

31. Perry, Carey, and Carey, *The Web of Modern Greek Politics*, p. 33.

32. Dorothy Demetracopoulou Lee, "Greece," in *Cultural Patterns and Technical Change*, ed. Margaret Mead (New York, 1955), p. 74.

33. Campbell and Sherrard, *Modern Greece*, pp. 359–60.

34. Ernestine Friedl, "Hospital Care in Provincial Greece," *Human Organization* 16 (Winter 1958):31.

35. "Crimes of Honor: Still the Pattern in Rural Greece," *New York Times*, February 10, 1980, p. 11, col. 1.

36. Ibid.

37. Ibid.

38. Constantina Safilios-Rothschild, ed., "Honor Crimes in Contemporary Greece," in *Toward a Sociology of Women* (New York: John Wiley & Sons, 1972), pp. 89–90.

39. "Traffic Deaths in Greece Are Highest in Western Europe," *Hellenic Times* (New York), March 24, 1980, pp. 1–4.

40. Jane Lambiri-Dimaki, "Dowry in Modern Greece: An Institution at the Crossroads between Persistence and Decline," in *Toward a Sociology of Women*, ed. Safilios-Rothschild, p. 26.

41. Irwin T. Sanders, *Rainbow in the Rock* (Cambridge, Mass., 1962), p. 165.

42. Scott G. McNall, *The Greek Peasant* (Washington, 1974); (Source cited: *Statistical Yearbook of Greece*, 1968, p. 79.)

43. Lambiri-Dimaki, "Dowry in Modern Greece," p. 78.

44. Edward C. Banfield, *The Moral Basis of a Backward Society* (New York: Fredd Press, 1967), p. 87.

45. Rodd, *The Customs and Lore of Modern Greece,* p. 27.

46. Duckett A. Ferriman, *Home Life in Hellas* (London, 1910), p. 239.

47. Juliet du Boulay, *Portrait of a Greek Mountain Village* (Oxford, 1974), p. 27.

48. Ibid., p. 28.

49. Friedl, "Hospital Care in Provincial Greece," p. 77.

50. du Boulay, *Portrait of a Greek Mountain Village,* p. 66.

51. Campbell and Sherrard, *Modern Greece,* p. 362.

52. Adamantia Pollis, "Political Implications of the Modern Greek Concept of Self," *British Journal of Sociology* 16 (1965):30.

53. Ibid., p. 41.

54. Lee, "Greece," p. 42.

55. Ibid., p. 68.

56. Legg, *Politics in Modern Greece,* pp. 32–34.

57. Campbell and Sherrard, *Modern Greece,* p. 349.

58. J. Mayone Stycos, "Patterns of Communication in a Rural Greek Village," *Public Opinion Quarterly* 16 (Spring 1952):66.

59. Ibid., pp. 59–70.

60. David Riesman, *The Lonely Crowd* (New York: Doubleday Anchor Books, 1953), pp. 24–42.

61. McNall, *The Greek Peasant,* p. 25.

62. du Boulay, *Portrait of a Greek Mountain Village,* p. 108.

63. Ibid., p. 133.

64. Ibid., p. 109.

65. Campbell and Sherrard, *Modern Greece,* p. 341.

66. du Boulay, *Portrait of a Greek Mountain Village,* p. 124.

67. Ibid., p. 185.

68. Ernestine Friedl, *Vasilika: A Village in Modern Greece* (New York: Holt Rinehart & Winston, 1964), p. 80.

69. du Boulay, *Portrait of a Greek Mountain Village,* p. 193.

70. Friedl, *Vasilika,* p. 80.

71. du Boulay, *Portrait of a Greek Mountain Village.*

72. Ibid., p. 76.

73. Friedl, *Vasilika,* p. 80.

74. McNall, *The Greek Peasant,* p. 25.

75. Harry C. Triandis, cited in George Flouris and Theophilos Mantzanas, "A Study on Self-Concept of Elementary Students in Greece," *Epistemoniko Vema* (Scientific Tribune), January-March 1978, pp. 14–15.

76. Kiki Vlachouli Roe, "A Study in Young Greek and U.S. Children," *Journal of Cross-Cultural Psychology* 8 (1977):493–502.

77. Jane Schneider, "Of Vigilance and Virgins: Honor, Shame and Access to Resources in Mediterranean Societies," *Ethnology* 10, no. 1 (January 24, 1971): 1–3.

78. "Fight for Equality: Greek Women versus Church and State," *Miami Herald,* February 13, 1981, p. 3c, col. 1.

Chapter Two

1. Thomas Burgess, *Greeks in America* (Boston, 1913), p. 16.
2. Ibid., pp. 190–225.
3. Ibid.
4. Louis Adamis, "Greek Immigration in U.S.," *Commonweal Magazine,* January 31, 1941, p. 366.
5. E. P. Panagopoulos, "The Greeks in America during the Eighteenth Century," unpublished paper.
6. E. P. Panagopoulos, *New Smyrna: An Eighteenth Century Greek Odyssey* (Gainesville, 1966; reprint ed., Brookline, Mass., 1978).
7. Theodore Saloutos, *The Greeks in the United States,* p. 24.
8. Ibid., p. 29.
9. Ibid., pp. 44–45.
10. Ibid., p. 39.
11. Ibid., pp. 42–43.
12. Henry P. Fairchild, *Greek Immigration to the United States* (New Haven, Conn., 1911), p. 39.
13. Saloutos, *The Greeks in the United States,* p. 42.
14. Ibid.
15. Theodore Saloutos, *The Greeks in America: Student's Guide to Localized History* (New York: Teachers College Press, Columbia University, 1967), p. 6.
16. Burgess, *Greeks in America,* pp. 21–22.
17. Saloutos, *The Greeks in the United States,* p. 43.
18. Burgess, *Greeks in America,* p. 48.
19. Charles C. Moskos, *Greek Americans: Struggle and Success* (Englewood Cliffs, N.J., 1980), pp. 13, 26.
20. Helen H. Balk, "Economic Contributions of the Greeks to the United States," *Economic Geography* 19 (1943):273.
21. This and subsequent quotations were obtained by the author mainly through interviews and conversations with the respondents.
22. Balk, p. 271.
23. Helen Zeese Papanikolas, *Toil and Rage in a New Land: The Greek Immigrants in Utah* (Salt Lake City: Utah Historical Society, 1974), pp. 141–42.
24. Theodore Saloutos, "Cultural Persistence and Change: Greeks in the Great Plains and Rocky Mountain West, 1890–1970," *Pacific Historical Review* 49, no. 1 (February 1980):77–78.

25. Ibid., p. 24.

26. Ibid., p. 25.

27. Ibid., p. 84.

28. Burgess, *Greeks in America,* pp. 163–64.

29. Saloutos, "Cultural Persistence and Change," pp. 85–86.

30. John G. Bitzes, "The Anti-Greek Riots of 1909," *South Omaha Nebraska History* 51 (1970):201–3.

31. Papanikolas, *Toil and Rage in a New Land,* p. 112.

32. Ibid.

33. Ibid., p. 114.

34. Helen Zeese Papanikolas, ed., "The Exiled Greeks," in *The Peoples of Utah* (Salt Lake City: Utah State Historical Society, 1976), p. 413.

35. Ibid., p. 416.

36. Ibid., p. 412.

37. Papanikolas, *Toil and Rage in a New Land,* 127.

38. Ibid., p. 168.

39. Ibid., p. 110.

40. Ibid., pp. 141–42.

41. Ibid., p. 143.

42. Ibid., p. 145.

43. Bruce L. Campbell and Eugene E. Campbell, "The Mormon Family," in *Ethnic Families in America: Patterns and Variations,* ed. Charles H. Mindel and Robert W. Habenstein (New York: Elsevier, 1976), p. 385.

44. LaVon B. Carroll, "On Being a Woman in Utah," unpublished paper, p. 11.

45. Papanikolas, *Toil and Rage in a New Land,* p. 18.

46. "Patriarchate Gives Directive on Marriage with Mormons," *Orthodox Observer* (New York), April 12, 1978, p. 1.

47. Theodore Saloutos, "The Greeks of Milwaukee," *Wisconsin Magazine of History* 53, no. 3 (Spring 1970):176.

48. Ibid., p. 177.

49. Ibid., p. 178.

50. Ibid., pp. 178–79.

51. Ibid., p. 184.

52. Ibid., p. 187.

53. Ibid., p. 191.

54. Ibid.

55. Ibid., p. 187.

56. Theodore Saloutos, "Growing Up in the Greek Community of Milwaukee," *Historical Messenger of the Milwaukee County Historical Society* 29, no. 2 (Summer 1973):52.

57. Saloutos, *The Greeks in the United States,* p. 47.

58. Burgess, *Greeks in America,* p. 231.

59. Ibid., pp. 135–36.
60. Andrew T. Kopan, "Greek Survival in Chicago: The Role of Ethnic Education, 1890–1980," in *Ethnic Chicago*, ed. Peter d'A. Jones and Melvin G. Holli (Grand Rapids, Mich., 1981), p. 86.
61. Moskos, *Greek Americans*, p. 21.
62. Kopan, "Greek Survival in Chicago," pp. 87–88.
63. Ibid., pp. 111–13.
64. Ibid., p. 99.
65. Saloutos, *The Greeks in the United States*, p. 126.
66. Fairchild, *Greek Immigration to the United States*, p. 150.
67. Saloutos, *The Greeks in the United States*, pp. 259–60.
68. Ibid., pp. 261–62.
69. Kopan, "Greek Survival in Chicago," p. 104.
70. Saloutos, *The Greeks in the United States*, p. 265.
71. Ibid., pp. 206–7.
72. Ibid., p. 269.
73. Ibid., p. 271.
74. Philip S. Foner, *The Policies and History of the Labor Movement in the United States, 1900–1909*, vol. 3 (New York: International Publishers, 1973), pp. 266–67.
75. Kopan, "Greek Survival in Chicago," p. 122.
76. Ibid., p. 125.
77. Moskos, *Greek Americans*, pp. 56, 65.
78. Burgess, *Greeks in America*, pp. 60–61.
79. Stella Coumantaros, "The Greek Orthodox Ladies Philoptochos Society," in *The Greek American Community in Transition*, ed. Harry J. Psomiades and Alice Scourby (New York, 1982), pp. 191–96.
80. Spartanburg was named for the "Spartan" regiment of Revolutionary troops who were recruited in that area.
81. Rosamonde R. Boyd, *The Social Adjustment of the Greeks in Spartanburg, South Carolina* (Spartanburg, S.C., 1948), p. 12.
82. Ibid., p. 54.
83. Ibid., p. 55.
84. Ibid., p. 60.
85. Ibid., p. 47.
86. Ibid., p. 15.
87. Ibid., p. 57.
88. Ibid., p. 35.
89. Ibid.
90. Ibid., p. 15.
91. Ibid., pp. 49–50.
92. Ibid., p. 66.
93. Ibid., p. 59.

94. Ibid., p. 50.

95. Edwin C. Buxbaum, *The Greek American Group of Tarpon Springs, Florida* (New York, 1980), pp. 31–37.

96. Ibid., pp. 46–47.

97. Ibid., p. 50.

98. Ibid., p. 54.

99. Dan Georgakas, "The Story of a Greek American Community: Tarpon Springs," *Greek Accent,* January 1981, p. 20.

100. Buxbaum, *The Greek American Group of Tarpon Srpings, Florida,* p. 47.

101. Ibid., p. 54.

102. Ibid., p. 226.

103. Georgakas, "The Story of a Greek American Community," p. 19.

104. Ibid., p. 20.

105. Ibid., p. 19.

106. Ibid., p. 21.

107. Burgess, *Greeks in America,* p. 141.

108. Ibid., pp. 139–41.

109. Ibid., p. 154.

110. Ibid., p. 144.

111. Ibid.

112. Ibid., pp. 146–47.

113. Mary B. Treudley, "Formal Organization and the Americanization Process with Special Reference to the Greeks of Boston," *American Sociological Review* 14, no. 1 (February 1949):44–53.

114. Ibid., p. 51.

115. U.S., Department of Commerce, Bureau of Census, *Census of Population: 1970; Subject Reports: Final Report PC (2)-1A, National Origin and Language* (Washington: Government Printing Office, 1973), Table 14, p. 150.

116. Ibid., Table 13, p. 140.

117. Ibid.

Chapter Three

1. Theodore Saloutos, *Courses and Patterns of Greek Emigration to the United States* (Cambridge, Mass.: Harvard University Press, 1974), p. 426. (Offprint from *Perspectives in American History,* vol. 7).

2. Ibid., p. 427.

3. Ibid., pp. 430–31.

4. Ibid., p. 431.

5. George Coutsoumaris, "Greece," in *The Brain Drain,* ed. Walter Adams (New York: Macmillan Co., 1968), p. 169.

6. Evangelos C. Vlachos, "Historical Trends in Greek Migration to the United States," unpublished paper.

7. Saloutos, *Courses and Patterns of Greek Emigration to the United States*, p. 434.

8. U.S., Department of Justice, *Immigration and Naturalization Service* (Washington, D.C.: Government Printing Office [INSI] 1977), p. 47.

9. Saloutos, *The Greeks in the United States*, p. 407.

10. George A. Kourvetaris, "Patterns of Subculture and Intermarriage of the Greeks in the United States," *International Journal of Sociology and the Family*, May 1971, pp. 34–48.

11. J. Mayone Stycos, "The Spartan Greeks of Bridgetown: Community of Cohesion," *Common Ground* 8 (Spring 1948):24–34.

12. Will Herberg, *Protestant, Catholic, Jew* (New York: Anchor Book, 1950).

13. Alice Scourby, *Third Generation Greek Americans: A Study of Religious Attitudes* (New York: Arno Press, 1980).

14. Alice Scourby, "Three Generations of Greek Americans: A Study in Ethnicity," *International Migration Review* 14, no. 1 (Spring 1980):43–52.

15. Israel Zangwill, *The Melting Pot: Drama in Four Acts* (New York: Macmillan Co., 1921), p. 33.

16. Milton M. Gordon, *Assimilation in American Life* (New York, 1964), pp. 60–83.

17. Evangelos C. Vlachos, *The Assimilation of Greeks in the United States* (Athens, Greece, 1968).

18. Ibid., p. 46.

19. Ibid., p. 132.

20. Marcus L. Hansen, *The Problem of the Third Generation Immigrant* (Rock Island, Ill.: Augustana Historical Society, 1938), p. 7.

21. Vlachos, *The Assimilation of Greeks in the United States*, pp. 138–39.

22. Herberg, *Protestant, Catholic, Jew*, p. 30.

23. Vlachos, *The Assimilation of Greeks in the United States*, p. 143.

24. Ibid., p. 145.

25. Ibid., pp. 148–49.

26. Ibid., p. 132.

27. Ibid., p. 152.

28. Ibid., p. 153.

29. Ibid., p. 185.

30. Donna M. Collins, "Ethnic Identification: The Greek Americans of Houston, Texas" (Ph.D. diss., Rice University, 1976).

31. Fredrik Barth, ed., Introduction to *Ethnic Groups and Boundaries* (Boston: Little, Brown & Co., 1969), pp. 9–38.

32. Collins, "Ethnic Identification," pp. 34–39.

33. Ibid., pp. 351–56.

34. Ibid., pp. 316–20.

35. Ibid., p. 361.

36. Robert Donus, "Greek Americans in a Pan-Orthodox Parish: A Sociologist's View," *St. Vladimir's Theological Quarterly* 18, no. 1 (1974):44–52.

Chapter Four

1. Saloutos, *The Greeks in the United States,* p. 122.
2. Charles C. Moskos, *Greek Americans,* p. 34.
3. Saloutos, *The Greeks in the United States,* p. 286.
4. Theodore Saloutos, "The Greek Orthodox Church in the United States and Assimilation," *International Migration Review* 7, no. 4 (Winter 1973): 395–407.
5. Ware, *The Orthodox Church,* p. 15.
6. Saloutos, *The Greeks in the United States,* p. 120.
7. Peter T. Kourides, *The Evolution of the Greek Orthodox Church in America and Its Present Problems* (New York: Cosmos Greek-American Printing, 1959), p. 8.
8. Ibid., pp. 10–11.
9. George Papaioannou, *From Mars Hill to Manhattan* (Minneapolis, Minn., 1976); *Yearbook of the Greek Orthodox Archdiocese of North and South America* (New York: Cosmos Greek American Printing, 1966), pp. 13–20.
10. "Greek Archdiocese Forms Communications Commission," *Hellenic Times* (New York), February 19, 1981, p. 2., col. 2.
11. "U.S.A. Honors Greek Orthodoxy: White House Tribute to Archbishop Iakovos," *Orthodox Observer* (New York), October 10, 1979, p. 9.
12. Nicon D. Patrinacos, "The Role of the Church in the Evolving Greek-American Community," in *The Greek American Community in Transition,* ed. Psomiades and Scourby, p. 130.
13. Lee, "Greece," p. 84.
14. Peter L. Berger, *The Heretical Imperative* (New York, 1979), pp. 26–27.
15. Gallup Organization, Inc., "Study of the Greek Orthodox Population in the U.S." (New York: Byzantine Fellowship Printing Office, coordinated through the Princeton Religious Center, January 1980), p. 133.
16. Ibid., p. 136.
17. Ibid., pp. 23–26.
18. Cited in Ware, *The Orthodox Church,* p. 310.
19. Talcott Parsons, *The Structure of Social Action* (Glencoe, Ill.: Free Press, 1949), p. 54.
20. Ware, *The Orthodox Church,* p. 207.
21. Ibid.
22. Ibid., p. 271.
23. Ibid., p. 189.
24. Stanley Harakas, "Greek Orthodox Archipelago," in *Greek Orthodox*

Congress XXII (New York: Greek Orthodox Archdiocese of North and South America, 1974), p. 60.

25. Private interview, California, May 1980.

26. Ibid.

27. "Study of the Greek Orthodox Population in the U.S.," p. 24.

28. Ibid., p. 101.

29. Ibid., pp. 84–87.

30. George Vescey, "Iakovos to Mark 20th Year as Primate," *New York Times,* March 31, 1979, p. 24, col. 3.

31. Harry J. Stathos, "An Interview with Archbishop Iakovos," *Hellenic Times* (New York), March 29, 1979, pp. 1–8.

32. "Letter to the Editor," *Orthodox Observer* (New York), May 7, 1980, p. 20.

33. "Letter to the Editor," *Orthodox Observer* (New York), May 21, 1980, p. 16.

34. "Letter to the Editor," *Orthodox Observer* (New York), May 21, 1980, p. 17.

35. Alice Scourby, *Third Generation Greek Americans,* p. 54.

36. Ibid., p. 56.

37. Ibid., p. 54.

38. John E. Hofman, "Mother Tongue Retentiveness in Ethnic Parishes," in *Language Loyalty in the United States,* ed. Joshua A. Fishman (The Hague, 1966), p. 133.

39. Fishman, ed., *Language Loyalty in the United States,* p. 31.

40. Nathan Glazer, "Process and Problems of Language Maintenance," in *Language Loyalty in the United States,* ed. Fishman, p. 367.

41. Joshua A. Fishman and Vladimir C. Nahirny, "Organizational Interest in Language Maintenance," in *Language Loyalty in the United States,* ed. Fishman, pp. 182–84.

42. Emmanuel Hatziemmanuel, "Hellenic Orthodox Education in America," in *The Greek American Community in Transition,* ed. Psomiades and Scourby, p. 184.

43. *Yearbook, 1983,* Greek Orthodox Archdiocese of North and South America (New York, 1983) p. 98.

44. "Unwarranted Attack Made against Archbishop Iakovos and Faithful in America," *Orthodox Observer* (New York), November 26, 1975, pp. 1, 3.

45. Harry J. Psomiades, "Contemporary Hellenism in the English-Speaking World: Problems and Prospects" (Paper delivered at the Conference on the Teaching of Modern Greek in the Universities of the English-Speaking World, Athens, Greece, December 1980).

46. M. Byron Raizis, " 'Romiosyne' in Modern Greek Literature," *Greek World,* August–September 1978, p. 31.

47. Barth, ed., *Ethnic Groups and Boundaries,* p. 119.

48. Panos D. Bardis, *The Future of the Greek Language in the United States* (San Francisco, 1976), pp. 31–35.

49. Alice Scourby and Gus Grammas, "A Study of Equalitarian Sex Roles among Greek American Academics," unpublished study.

50. Robert Ricklefs, "Voices of the Past: Newspapers Published in Foreign Languages Struggle to Survive—Assimilation of Immigrants in U.S. Slashes Readership, Forces Hundreds to Fold," *Wall Street Journal,* February 17, 1972, pp. 1, 13, col. 3.

51. Robert E. Park, *The Immigrant Press and Its Control* (New York: Harper & Bros., 1922; reprint ed., Montclair, N.J.: Patterson Smiter, 1971), pp. 86–88.

52. Ibid., p. 468.

53. S. Victor Papacosma, "The Greek Press in America," *Journal of the Hellenic Diaspora* 5 (Winter 1979):61.

54. Ibid., p. 46.

55. Saloutos, *The Greeks in the United States,* p. 93.

56. Papacosma, "The Greek Press in America," p. 51.

57. Saloutos, *The Greeks in the United States,* pp. 92–93.

58. Robert A. Dahl, "The Ex-pletes," in *Who Governs?* (New Haven: Yale University Press, 1961), pp. 32–51; Dahl, "The New Man," in *Who Governs?* pp. 52–62.

59. Papacosma, "The Greek Press in America," p. 60.

60. Ibid., p. 58.

61. Ibid., pp. 58–59.

62. Moskos, *Greek Americans,* p. 79.

63. Park, *The Immigrant Press and Its Control,* pp. 67–88, 359, 468.

64. Peter N. Marudas, "Greek American Involvement in Contemporary Politics," in *The Greek American Community in Transition,* ed. Psomiades and Scourby, pp. 96–101.

65. Ibid.

66. Ibid.

67. Ibid.

68. Ibid.

69. Ibid.

70. Craig R. Humphrey and Helen Brock Louis, "Assimilation and Voting Behavior," *International Migration Review* 7, no. 1 (1973):40–41.

71. Ibid., p. 44.

72. Marudas, "Greek American Involvement in Contemporary Politics," p. 102.

73. Ibid.

74. Ibid.

75. Ibid.

76. Ibid., p. 98.

77. Scourby, *Third Generation Greek Americans,* pp. 72–73.

78. Nathan Glazer and Daniel P. Moynihan, *Ethnicity: Theory and Experience* (Cambridge, Mass., 1975), p. 24.

79. Sallie M. Hicks and Theodore A. Couloumbis, "The Greek Lobby: Illusion or Reality?" in *Ethnicity and U.S. Foreign Policy,* ed. Abdul Said (New York: Praeger Co., 1981), pp. 92–98.

80. Morton Kondracke, "The Greek Lobby," *New Republic,* April 29, 1978, pp. 14, 16.

81. Hicks and Couloumbis, "The Greek Lobby," pp. 83–116.

82. Ibid., p. 86.

83. "What Should be the Role of Ethnic Groups in U.S. Foreign Policy?" (AEI Forum sponsored by the American Enterprise Institute for Public Policy Research, Washington, D.C., October 15, 1979), p. 7.

84. Ibid., p. 6.

85. Hicks and Couloumbis, "The Greek Lobby," p. 110.

86. Israel Rubin, "Ethnicity and Cultural Pluralism," *Phylon* 36, no. 2 (June 1975):141–42.

87. Harold Isaacs, "The One and the Many: What Are the Social and Political Implications of the New Ethnic Revival?" *American Educator* 2, no. 1 (Spring 1978):9–10.

88. Hicks and Couloumbis, "The Greek Lobby," p. 92.

89. Peter L. Berger, "In Praise of Particularity: The Concept of Mediating Structures," *Review of Politics* 3 (July 1976):399–410.

90. "The Greek Lobby: Washington Political Force in Tradition," *Novak Report on the New Ethnicity* 18 (November–December 1980):1, 6–7.

91. Theodore G. Stylianopoulos, "The Orthodox Church in America," *Annals of the American Academy,* January 1970, pp. 41–48.

92. Savvas Agourides, "The Social Character of Orthodoxy," *Greek Orthodox Theological Review* 8 (1962–63):7–20; Demetrios Constantelos, "Social Consciousness of One Greek Church," *GOTR* 12 (1967):306–39.

93. Stylianopoulos, "The Orthodox Church in America," pp. 46–47.

94. Hicks and Couloumbis, "The Greek Lobby," p. 92.

95. This discussion is drawn from an unpublished paper by Thalia Cheronis Selz, "Greek-Americans in the Visual Arts," unless notes indicate otherwise. The list of artists is not intended to be all inclusive.

96. "Theo Hios to Exhibit His Paintings at New School," *Hellenic Times* (New York), March 29, 1979, p. 5, col. 1.

97. Margot Granitsa, "Nassos Daphnis," *Pilgrimage,* December 1975, pp. 20–22.

98. Penelope Karageorge, "Beyond the Blue Door: Theodoros Stamos," *Hellenic Times* (New York), May 12, 1977, p. 5.

99. Ibid.

100. "Lucas Samaras," in Penelope Prattas, curator, *Noemata: Contemporary Greek American Artists* (New York: Hellenic American Neighborhood Action Committee, Brooklyn Museum, Museum of Modern Art, 1977).

101. "Tom Boutis," in Prattas, curator, *Noemata: Contemporary Greek American Artists.*

102. Margot Granitsa, "Donald Odysseus Mavros," *Pilgrimage,* November 1975, pp. 15–18.

103. Ibid.

104. Personal interview, Louis Trakas, New York City, November 1982.

105. Prattas, curator, *Noemata: Contemporary Greek American Artists.*

106. "Text of the Nobel Lecture of Isaac Bashevis Singer," *New York Times,* December 9, 1978, p. 4.

107. Richard Burgin, "Isaac Bashevis Singer Talks . . . About Everything," *New York Times Magazine,* November 26, 1978, p. 42.

108. Alexander Karanikas, *Hellenes and Hellions: Modern Greek Characters in American Literature, 1825–1975* (Urbana, 1981), p. 507.

109. Mary Vardoulakis, *Gold in the Streets* (New York: Dodd, Mead, 1945).

110. Ariadne Pasmezoglu Thompson, *The Octagonal Heart* (Indianapolis, Ind.: Bobbs-Merrill, 1956).

111. Harry Mark Petrakis, *Lion at My Heart* (Boston: Little, Brown & Co., 1959).

112. Harry Mark Petrakis, *A Dream of Kings* (New York: David McKay, 1966).

113. Harry Mark Petrakis, *The Odyssey of Kostas Volakis* (New York: David McKay, 1963).

114. Harry Mark Petrakis, *Stelmark: A Family Recollection* (New York: David McKay, 1970).

115. Harry Mark Petrakis, *Nick the Greek* (Garden City, N.Y.: Doubleday, 1979).

116. Harry Mark Petrakis, *A Petrakis Reader* (Garden City, N.Y.: Doubleday, 1978).

117. Harry Mark Petrakis, *The Hour of the Bell* (New York: Doubleday, 1976).

118. Tom T. Chamales, *Never So Few* (New York: Charles Scribner's Sons, 1957).

119. Tom T. Chamales, *Go Naked in the World* (New York: Charles Scribner's Sons, 1959).

120. George Christy, *All I Could See from Where I Stood* (Indianapolis, Ind.: Bobbs-Merrill, 1963).

121. Thalia Cheronis Selz, "The Education of a Queen," *Partisan Review* 28 (1961), pp. 553–687.

122. Thomas Doulis, *Paths for Our Valor* (New York: Simon & Schuster, 1963).

123. Theodore Vrettos, *Hammer on the Sea* (Boston: Little, Brown & Co., 1965).

124. Stephen Linakis, *In the Spring the War Ended* (New York: G. P. Putnam's Sons, 1965).

125. Elia Kazan, *America, America* (New York: Stein & Day, 1962).

126. Elia Kazan, *The Arrangement* (New York: Stein & Day, 1967).

127. Elia Kazan, *Acts of Love* (New York: Alfred A. Knopf, 1978).

128. H. L. Mountzoures, *The Bridge* (New York: Charles Scribner's Sons, 1972).

129. Charles E. Jarvis, *Zeus Has Two Urns* (Lowell, Mass.: Apollo Books, 1976).

130. Charles E. Jarvis, *The Tyrants* (Lowell, Mass.: Ithaca Press, 1977).

131. Athena Dallas-Damis, *Island of the Winds* (New Rochelle, N.Y.: Caratzas Brothers, 1976).

132. Athena Dallas-Damis, *Windswept* (New York: NAL/Signet, 1981).

133. Nicholas Gage, *The Bourlotas Fortune* (New York: Bantam Books, 1976).

134. Stratis Haviaras, *When the Tree Sings* (New York: Simon & Schuster, 1979).

135. Demetrios A. Michalaros, *Sonnets of an Immigrant* (Chicago: American Hellenic Publishing Co., 1930).

136. Konstantinos Lardas, "The Devil Child," *Atlantic Monthly* 108 (July 1961):55–56.

137. Olga Broumas, *Beginning with O* (New Haven: Yale University Press, 1977).

138. Steve Georgiou, *Alexander, My Alexander* (Burlingame, Calif.: Advance Publishing Division, 1982).

139. Christine Eliopoulos, "Young Poet Pays Homage to Alexander the Great," *Hellenic Times* (New York), October 28, 1982, p. 11.

Chapter Five

1. Anonymous, "The Forgotten Generation," *Athene* 10, no. 4 (Winter 1950):22.

2. Alice Scourby, *Third Generation Greek Americans*, pp. 22–26.

3. Oscar Handlin, *The Uprooted* (New York, 1951), p. 254.

4. John Papajohn and John Spiegel, *Transactions in Families* (San Francisco, 1975), p. 180.

5. Ibid., p. 185.

6. Ibid., p. 183.

7. Ibid., p. 203.

8. Ibid., p. 188.

9. Georgia Gianakos Buchanan, *Paved with Gold* (New York: Vantage Press, 1979), p. 216.

10. Papajohn and Spiegel, *Transactions in Families*, p. 193.

11. Ibid., p. 259.

12. Ibid., p. 260.

13. Ibid.

14. Theano Papazoglou-Margaris, "Escape," in *A Tear for Uncle Jimmy* (Athens: Thipros, 1958).

15. Petrakis, *A Petrakis Reader,* pp. 262–77.

16. Ibid., pp. 291–305.

17. Thalia Cheronis Selz, "The Death of Anna," in *Virginia Quarterly Review* 33, no. 2 (Spring 1957):262–69.

18. U.S., Department of Commerce, Social and Economic Statistics Administration, Bureau of Census, *1970 Census of Population Subject Reports: National Origin and Language* (Washington: Government Printing Office, 1971), p. 114.

19. Ernestine Friedl, "Lagging Emulation in Post-Peasant Society," *American Anthropologist* 66, no. 3 (June 1964):569–86.

20. Bernard C. Rosen, "Race, Ethnicity, and the Achievement Syndrome," in *Achievement in American Society,* ed. B. C. Rosen, H. J. Crockett, and C. Z. Nunn (Cambridge, Mass.: Schenkman Publishing Co., 1969), p. 137.

21. Nicholas Dunkas and Arthur G. Nikelly, "The Persephone Syndrome," *Social Psychiatry* 7 (1978):211–16.

22. Rhode Island Feminist Theatre Group, "Persephones Return," *Frontiers: A Journal of Women's Studies* 3, no. 2 (Summer 1978):60–74.

23. Beatrice B. Whiting, "The Dependency Hang-Up and Alternative Life Styles" (Paper delivered at the Meetings of the American Sociological Association, Chicago, Illinois, September 1977).

24. Matina Souretis Horner, "Toward an Understanding of Achievement-Related Conflicts in Women," *Journal of Social Issues* 28 (1972):157–75.

25. Nancy Chodorow, "Family Structure and Feminine Personality," in *Woman, Culture and Society,* ed. Michelle Zimbalist Rosaldo and Louise Lamphere (Berkeley, Calif., 1974), pp. 43–66.

26. Ibid., p. 58.

27. Adrienne Rich, *Of Woman Born: Motherhood as Experience and Institution* (New York, 1976), p. 195.

28. Sandra L. Bem, "The Measurement of Psychological Androgyny," *Journal of Consulting and Clinical Psychology* 42, no. 2 (1974):155–62.

29. Scourby and Grammas, "A Study of Equalitarian Sex Roles among Greek American Academics."

30. Gallup Organization, Inc., "Study of the Greek Orthodox Population in the U.S.," p. 125.

31. Harry J. Stathos, "Patriarch Elias IV of Antioch Firmly against Women Priests," *Hellenic Times* (New York), January 2, 1977, p. 4.

32. Alice Nicas, "The Ordination of Women" (Paper delivered at the Philoptochos Convention, Detroit, Michigan, July 1–8, 1978), p. 2.

33. Elizabeth Behr-Sigel, "The Meaning of the Participation of Women in the Life of the Church" (Paper delivered at the World Council of Churches: Sub-Unit on Women in Church and Society, Agapia, Rumania, September 11–17, 1976), p. 20.

34. Ibid., p. 20.

35. Ibid., p. 26.

36. Ibid., p. 27.

37. Dena Kleiman, "Graduation Day a Milestone for an Immigrant Family," *New York Times,* June 23, 1979, pp. L23–24.

38. Ibid.

39. Ibid.

40. Andrea Simon, "The Sacred Sect and the Secular Church: Symbols of Ethnicity in Astoria's Greek Community" (Ph.D. diss., City University of New York, 1977), pp. 3–4.

41. Ibid., p. 171.

42. Ibid., p. 173.

43. Ibid., pp. 173–74.

44. Charles C. Moskos, *Greek Americans,* p. 54.

45. Chrysie M. Costantakos, *The American-Greek Subculture: Processes of Continuity* (New York: Arno Press, 1980), p. 251.

46. Theoni Velli-Spyropoulos, "Mental Health Services to the Greek American Community," in *The Greek American Community in Transition,* ed. Psomiades and Scourby, pp. 204–5.

47. Ibid.

48. Marios Stephanides, *The Greeks in Detroit: A Critical Analysis of Greek Culture, Personality, Attitudes, and Behavior* (San Francisco: R. & E. Research Associates, 1975), p. 141.

49. *Yearbook of the Greek Orthodox Archdiocese of North and South America* (New York: Cosmos Greek American Printing, 1981), p. 54.

50. Ross Eshleman, *The Family: An Introduction* (Boston: Allyn & Bacon, 1978), p. 301.

51. Hyman Rodman, "Technical Note on Two Rates of Mixed Marriage," *American Sociological Review* 30 (October 1965):776–78. (Greek Orthodox was substituted for Catholic.)

52. Eshleman, *The Family,* pp. 301–2.

53. Ibid.

54. Philip M. Kayal, "Eastern Orthodox Exogamy and 'Triple' Melting Pot Theory: Herberg Revisited" (Paper delivered at the Meetings of the American Sociological Association, Boston, August 1979), p. 15.

55. Ibid.

56. Patrinacos, "The Role of the Church in the Evolving Greek-American Community," in *The Greek American Community in Transition,* ed. Psomiades and Scourby, p. 129.

57. Ibid.

58. Kayal, "Eastern Orthodox Exogamy and 'Triple' Melting Pot Theory," p. 24.

59. Ibid., p. 12.

60. Ibid., pp. 12–13.

61. Ibid., p. 20.
62. *Vital Statistics: Decade 1970–1981* (New York: Greek Orthodox Archdiocese of North and South America, 1982).
63. Ibid.

Chapter Six

1. Eva E. Sandis, "The Greek Population of New York City," in *The Greek American Community in Transition,* ed. Psomiades and Scourby, p. 92.
2. Edna Bonacich, "A Theory of Ethnic Antagonism: The Split Labor Market," in *Majority and Minority: The Dynamics of Race and Ethnicity in American Life,* ed. Norman R. Yetman with C. Hoy Steele (Boston: Allyn & Bacon, 1982), p. 374.
3. Theodore Saloutos, "Cultural Persistence and Change," p. 85.
4. Bonacich, "A Theory of Ethnic Antagonism," p. 317.
5. Ibid., p. 378.
6. Saloutos, "Cultural Persistence and Change," pp. 93–94.
7. Jonathan H. Turner and Edna Bonacich, "Toward a Composite Theory of Middleman Minorities," *Ethnicity* 7 (1980):144.
8. Ibid., pp. 145–49.
9. Grace Abbott, "A Study of the Greeks in Chicago," *American Journal of Sociology* 15, no. 3 (November 1909):386.
10. Turner and Bonacich, "Toward a Composite Theory of Middleman Minorities," p. 146.
11. Stephen Steinberg, *The Ethnic Myth: Race, Ethnicity and Class* (New York, 1981).
12. William H. McNeill, *The Metamorphosis of Greece since World War II,* p. 17.
13. Ibid., p. 55.
14. Ibid., pp. 210–11.
15. Herbert J. Gans, "Symbolic Ethnicity: The Future of Ethnic Groups and Cultures in America," *Ethnic and Racial Studies* 2, no. 1 (January 1979):15.
16. Andrew Greeley, *The Most Distressful Nation* (Chicago, 1972), pp. 262–70.
17. Edward Shils, *Tradition* (Chicago, 1981), pp. 4–25.
18. Ibid., pp. 326–28.
19. Reinhold Niebuhr, *The Children of Light and Darkness* (New York: Charles Scribner's Sons, 1944), pp. 122–23.
20. Ibid., p. 135.

Selected Bibliography

Bardis, Panos D. *The Future of the Greek Language in the United States.* San Francisco: R and E Research Associates, 1976.

Berger, Peter L. *The Heretical Imperative.* New York: Doubleday, 1979.

Boyd, Rosamonde R. *The Social Adjustment of the Greeks in Spartanburg, South Carolina.* Spartanburg, S.C.: William Printing Co., 1948.

Burgess, Thomas. *Greeks in America.* Boston: Sherman, French & Co., 1913.

Buxbaum, Edwin C. *The Greek-American Group of Tarpon Springs, Florida.* New York: Arno Press, 1980.

Campbell, John and Sherrard, Philip. *Modern Greece.* New York: Frederick A. Praeger, 1969.

Collins, Donna M. "Ethnic Identification: The Greek Americans of Houston, Texas." Ph.D. dissertation, Rice University, 1976.

Couloumbis, T. A.; Petropulos, J. A.; and Psomiades, H. J. *Foreign Interference in Greek Politics.* New York: Pella Publishing Co., 1976.

d'A. Jones, Peter, and Holli, Melvin G. *Ethnic Chicago.* Grand Rapids, Mich.: William B. Eerdman's Publishing Co., 1981.

du Boulay, Juliet. *Portrait of a Greek Mountain Village.* Oxford: Clarendon Press, 1974.

Fairchild, Henry P. *Greek Immigration to the United States.* New Haven, Conn.: Yale University Press, 1911.

Ferriman, Duckett A. *Home Life in Hellas.* London: Mills & Boon, 1910.

Fishman, Joshua A., ed. *Language Loyalty in the United States.* The Hague: Mouton & Co., 1966.

Friedl, Ernestine. *Vasilika: A Village in Modern Greece.* New York: Holt, Rinehart & Winston, 1964.

Geanakoplos, Deno J. *Byzantine East and Latin West: Two Worlds of Christendom in Middle Ages and Renaissance.* Oxford: Basil Blackwell, 1966.

Glazer, Nathan, and Moynihan, Daniel P. *Ethnicity: Theory and Experience.* Cambridge, Mass.: Harvard University Press, 1975.

Gordon, Milton M. *Assimilation in American Life.* New York: Oxford University Press, 1964.

Greeley, Andrew. *The Most Distressful Nation.* Chicago: Quadrangle, 1972.

Handlin, Oscar. *The Uprooted.* New York: Grosset & Dunlap, 1951.

Karanikas, Alexander. *Hellenes and Hellions: Modern Greek Characters in American Literature, 1825–1975.* Urbana: University of Illinois Press, 1981.

Legg, Kenneth R. *Politics in Modern Greece.* Berkeley, Calif.: Stanford University Press, 1969.

McNall, Scott G. *The Greek Peasant.* Washington: American Sociological Association, Ross Series, 1974.

McNeill, William H. *The Metamorphosis of Greece since World War II.* Chicago: University of Chicago Press, 1978.

Mead, Margaret, ed. *Cultural Patterns and Technical Change.* New York: New American Library, 1955.

Mears, Eliot G. *Greece Today.* Berkeley, Calif.: Stanford University Press, 1929.

Moskos, Charles C. *Greek Americans: Struggle and Success.* Englewood Cliffs, N.J.: Prentice-Hall, 1980.

Novak, Michael. *The Unmeltable Ethnics.* New York: Macmillan, 1971.

Panagopoulos, E. P. *New Smyrna: An Eighteenth Century Greek Odyssey.* Gainesville: University of Florida Press, 1966. Reprint. Brookline, Mass.: Holy Cross Orthodox Press, 1978.

Papaioannou, George. *From Mars Hill to Manhattan.* Minneapolis, Minn.: Light & Life Publishing, 1976.

Papajohn, John and Spiegel, John. *Transactions in Families.* San Francisco: Jossey-Bass, 1975.

Papanikolas, Helen Zeese. *Toil and Rage in a New Land: The Greek Immigrants in Utah.* Salt Lake City: Utah Historical Society, 1974.

Psomiades, Harry J., and Scourby, Alice, eds. *The Greek American Community in Transition.* New York: Pella Publishing Co., 1982.

Rich, Adrienne. *Of Woman Born: Motherhood as Experience and Institution.* New York: W. W. Norton, 1976.

Rodd, Sir James Rennell. *The Customs and Lore of Modern Greece.* London: David Scott, 1892.

Rosaldo, Michelle Z., and Lamphere, Louise, eds. *Woman, Culture and Society.* Berkeley, Calif.: Stanford University Press, 1974.

Saloutos, Theodore. *The Greeks in the United States.* Cambridge, Mass.: Harvard University Press, 1964.

————. *They Remember America: The Story of the Repatriated Greek Americans.* Berkeley: University of California Press, 1956.

Sanders, Irwin T. *Rainbow in the Rock.* Cambridge, Mass.: Harvard University Press, 1962.

Scourby, Alice. *Third Generation Greek Americans: A Study of Religious Attitudes.* New York: Arno Press, 1980.

Shils, Edward. *Tradition.* Chicago: University of Chicago Press, 1981.

Simon, Andrea. "The Sacred Sect and the Secular Church: Symbols of Ethnicity in Astoria's Greek Community." Ph.D. dissertation, City University of New York, 1977.

Steinberg, Stephen. *The Ethnic Myth: Race, Ethnicity and Class.* New York: Atheneum, 1981.

Vlachos, Evangelos C. *The Assimilation of Greeks in the United States.* Athens: National Center of Social Research, 1968.

Ware, Timothy. *The Orthodox Church.* Baltimore, Md.: Penguin Books, 1964.

Woodhouse, C. M. *A Short History of Modern Greece.* New York: Frederick A. Praeger, 1968.

Young, Kenneth. *The Greek Passion.* London: J. M. Dent & Sons, 1969.

Index

Addams, Jane, 44–45
Agnew, Spiro, 102
Alfange, Dean, 101
Allen, Peter S., 9
American Hellenic Educational
  Progressive Association
  (AHEPA), 41–42, 49, 71
Anagnos, Michael, 23
Antonakos, Stephen, 112
Artists, Greek: musicians, 119;
  painters, theater, 119–20; writ-
  ers, 114–19
Assimilation. *See* Change
Athenagoras, Archbishop, 83–84
Atlantis, 46, 48, 98, 99

Baziotes, William, 110
Berger, Peter L., 87
Boosalis, Helen C., 102
Boutis, Tom, 112
Brademas, John, 101
Broumas, Olga, 118
Buchanan, Georgia Gianakos, 127–
  28

Carter, Jimmy, 86
Cavacos, Emmanuel A., 108
Center Union party, 6
Chamales, Tom, 116
Change: in the church, 80–90;
  among generations, 63–79; in
  immigrant families, 121–47; in
  language used, 90–97
Cheyney, John K., 53
Chicago, immigrants in, 43–51

Chicago Pnyx, 99
Children, rearing of, in Greece, 18,
  19, 20–21
Christopher, George, 101
Christy, George, 116
Chryssa, 112
Church. *See* Greek Orthodox church
Cocoris, John M., 53
Collins, Bill, 101
Colvocoresses, George M., 23
Constant, George, 108, 109, 111
Constantine II, king of Greece, 6–
  7, 37, 41, 81

Dallas-Damis, Athena G., 117
Damaskinos, Metropolitan, 83
Daphnis, Nassos, 109, 111
Democrat, 99
Divorce, in Greece, 11–12, 22
Doulis, Thomas, 116
Dowry system, 11, 12–13, 21, 33

Education: in Chicago, New York
  City, 48–49; and family change,
  124–26; and generational
  change, 64, 65, 66; in Greece,
  16–17; in Milwaukee, 42; use of
  language in schools, 94–97
Eleutheria, 99
Embros, 99
Emigration, from Greece, 4, 8–9,
  26–27, 61–63
Endropi ("shame"), 18, 122
"Evil eye," 14–15

Fairchild, Henry P., 26
Family: authority change in, 139–
40; changes in Greece in, 21–22;
and choice of marriage partners in
Greece, 13–14; and generational
change, 63–79, 121–33, 141–
47; importance of, in Greece,
10–12, 16; mother/daughter relationships in, 133–39; roles in,
in Greece, 18–20. *See also*
Marriage
Florovsky, Georges, 88
Friedl, Ernestine, 11, 15, 19
Fuca, Juan de, 24

Gage, Nicholas, 117–18
Galbraith, John Kenneth, 7
Gans, Herbert J., 157
Gatzoyiannis, Eleni, 118
Generational change. *See* Change
Geocaris, Angelo, 101
Georgiou, Steve, 119
Germanos, Patriarch, 83
Giannopoulos, John, 24
Gompers, Samuel, 48
Gordon, Milton, 70
Greece: cultural patterns in, 9–22,
121–24; economic crisis and em-
igration, 26; history of, 1–8, 10;
political issues in, 81–82, 103–8
Greek American Progressive Asso-
ciation, 42
Greek American Tribune, 47–48
Greek Orthodox church: in Chi-
cago, New York City, 45; and
clash with Mormons, 38–39; es-
tablishment of in U.S., 37; evo-
lutionary change in, 80–90; as
indicator of generational change,
64–65, 67–68, 69, 73, 78; in
Greek cultural patterns, 15; in
Greek history, 2, 10; in Milwaukee, 41, 42–43; ordination of

women in, 140–41; schism in,
37; social consciousness in, 107–
8; in Spartanburg, S.C., 52; in
Tarpon Springs, Fla., 54–55; use
of Greek language in, 66, 90–97
Greek Peoples' Liberation Army, 5
Greek Republican National League,
5
Greeley, Andrew, 158
Griego, John, 24

Hadzi, Dimitri, 112
Haviaras, Stratis, 118
Heleno-Amerikaniko Vema, 99
Helis, William, 101
Hellenic American Neighborhood
Action Committee, 49–50
Hellenic Chronicle, 99
Hellenic Foundation of Chicago, 50
Hellenic Journal, 99
Hellenic Times, 99
Hios, Theo, 109
Howe, Samuel Gridley, 23

Iakovos, Archbishop, 85–86, 91,
106
Immigrants: in Anderson, Ind.,
70–76; in Bergenfield, N.J., 78–
79; characteristics of, after 1945,
63–70; in Chicago, New York
City, 43–51; earliest, 23–24; experiences of, 27–29; female, 29–
33; and generational change, 63–
79, 121–33, 141–47; in Houston, 76–78; in Lowell, Mass.,
58–59; in Milwaukee, 40–43;
number of, in 19th, 20th centuries, 26–28; number of, after
1945, 61–63; in Salt Lake City,
33–40; in Spartanburg, S.C.,
51–53; in Tarpon Springs, Fla.,
53–58
Intermarriage, 39, 56, 67, 74, 78,
147–51

Jarvis, Charles, 117
Johnson Act (1951), 35

Karamanlis, Constantine, 7
Karanikas, Alexander, 114
Kazan, Elia, 116–17, 127
King, Martin Luther, Jr., 86
Kontogeorge, Christopher, 84
Kotzias, George, 119

Language: and the Greek press, 97–
  98, 99, 100; use of Greek vs.
  English, 66, 90–97
Lardas, Konstantinos, 118
Lee, Dorothy D., 16
Lekakis, Michael, 109, 110, 111
Leventis, John, 36
Linakis, Stephen, 116
Linakis, Yorka C., 102
Literacy, in Greece, 13, 16–17
Lowell, Mass., immigrants in, 58–
  59

McNall, Scott G., 18
McNeill, William H., 156
Maliotis, Charles, 101
Manatos, Michael, 102
Marriage: in Greece, 13–14; inter-
  marriage, 39, 56, 67, 74, 78,
  147–51. *See also* Family
Marros, Basil, 108
Maskaleris, Thanasis, 119
Mavroede, Aphrodite, 5
Mavros, Donald Odysseus, 113
Megali Idea, 3, 4
Men: attitude toward, in Greece,
  18–19, 20, 21; and dowry sys-
  tem, 12–13; and family honor,
  11–12; and gender-role changes,
  121–33, 139–47; number of im-
  migrants, 29
Metaxakis, Metropolitan, 82–83
Metaxas, General, 4
Michael, Archbishop, 85

Michalaros, Demetrios, 118
Miller, Jonathan, 23
Milwaukee, immigrants in, 40–43
Mormon church, 38–39
Mountzoures, H. L., 117
Musicians, Greek, 119

Nassikas, John, 102
National Herald, 46, 98, 99, 100
National Philoptochos Society, 50–
  51, 84
New Democratic party, 7
New World, 98
New York City, immigrants in, 43–
  51
Nicolaides, Kimon, 108
Niebuhr, Reinhold, 159

Occupations of Greeks in U.S., 27–
  28, 33, 34, 35, 40–41, 43–44,
  46–47, 51, 53–54, 56, 58, 59,
  60, 154–55
Orthodox Observer, 92
Orthodoxy. *See* Greek Orthodox
  church

Padrone system, 35, 43–44
Painters, Greek, 108–14
Panhellenic Socialist Movement, 7
Papajohn, John, 123, 128
Papandreou, Andreas, 6, 7
Papandreou, George, 6, 7
Papanicolaou, Dr. George, 119
Papanikolas, Helen Z., 38
Papazoglou-Margaris, Theano, 129
Pappas, Tom, 101
Park, Robert E., 97
Patrinacos, Nicon D., 87
Persephone syndrome, 133–34
Peterson, Peter, 102
Petrakis, Harry Mark, 115, 127,
  130
Philotimo ("honor"), 10–12, 17, 19
Phocas, Ioannis, 24

Politics, Greeks in, 100–108
Population rates, in Greece, 2, 3, 8
Pougialis, Constantine, 110
Prejudice, anti-Greek, 33–36, 47, 58, 152–55
Press, Greek, 97–100
Proini, 100
Psomiades, Harry J., 95

Rallis, George, 7
Religion. *See* Greek Orthodox church
Riesman, David, 17–18
Rodd, Sir Rennell, 4, 14
Rodostolou, Archbishop Alexander, 83
Rossides, Eugene R., 102, 104–5
Rousseas, Stephen, 7

St. Augustine, immigrants in, 24
Saloutos, Theodore, 4
Salt Lake City, immigrants in, 33–40
Samaras, Lucas, 111–12
Sanders, Irwin, 13
Sarbanes, Paul, 102
Schlesinger, Arthur, 7
Selz, Thalia Cheronis, 116, 130
Shils, Edward, 158–59
Simonides, Yannis, 119–20
Singer, Isaac Bashevis, 114
Siotis, Dino, 118–19
Skliris, Leonides G., 35, 36
Snowe, Olympia Bouchles, 102
Spartanburg, S.C., immigrants in, 51–53
Stamos, Theodore, 110–11
Superstition, in Greece, 14–15

Tarpon Springs, Fla., immigrants in, 53–58
Teodoro, Don, 24
Theater, Greek, 119–20

Thompson, Ariadne Pasmezoglu, 115
Trakas, Louis, 113
Trakas, Nicholas, 51
Triandis, Harry C., 20
Truman, Harry, 5
Tsakonas, Christos, 24–26
Tsavalas, Theodore, 108
Turnbull, Andrew, 24

Vagis, Polygnotos, 108, 109, 110
Vardoulakis, Mary, 114–15
Vasilios, Archbishop, 83
Vassos, John, 108, 109
Venizelos, Eleutherios, 3, 4, 37, 41, 81–82
Vlastos, Solon, 98
Voulkos, Peter, 112–13
Vournas, George, 101
Vrettos, Theodore, 116

Ware, Timothy, 89
Women: changes in role of, in Greece, 21–22; and dowry system, 12–13; employment among, in Greece, 13; and gender-role change, 121–33, 139–47; in Greek resistance movement, 5–6; and Greek societies, 50–51; as immigrants, 29–33, 36, 37, 39; literacy rates of, in Greece, 13; mother/daughter relationships, 133–39; as mothers in Greece, 18–19, 20; ordination of, 140–41
Woodhouse, C. M., 3, 7
Writers, Greek, 114–19

Xceron, Jean, 110

Young, Brigham, 38

Zachos, Ioannis Celivergos, 23
Zangwill, Israel, 69